# DEFENDING PORNOGRAPHY

# DEFENDING PORNOGRAPHY

*Free Speech, Sex, and the Fight
for Women's Rights*

## NADINE STROSSEN

ANCHOR BOOKS
DOUBLEDAY
NEW YORK   LONDON   TORONTO   SYDNEY   AUCKLAND

AN ANCHOR BOOK
PUBLISHED BY DOUBLEDAY
a division of Bantam Doubleday Dell Publishing Group, Inc.
1540 Broadway, New York, New York 10036

ANCHOR BOOKS, DOUBLEDAY, and the portrayal of an anchor are trademarks of
Doubleday, a division of Bantam Doubleday Dell Publishing Group, Inc.

*Defending Pornography* was originally published in hardcover by Scribner in 1995. The
Anchor Books Edition is published by arrangement with Scribner.

Library of Congress Cataloging-in-Publication Data
Strossen, Nadine.
Defending pornography : free speech, sex, and the fight for
women's rights / Nadine Strossen.
p.   cm.
Includes bibliographical references and index.
1. Pornography—Social aspects—United States.   2. Feminism–
–United States.   3. Feminist criticism—United States.   I. Title.
HQ472.U6S87   1996
363.4′7′0973—dc20        95-25157
CIP

1   3   5   7   9   10   8   6   4   2

# Contents

# Acknowledgments

This book builds upon the words and work of many other people too numerous to name individually. Therefore, I express my deep gratitude, collectively, to the many women and men who have spoken, written, organized, and acted to defend liberty *and* equality, free speech *and* feminism, words *and* women, including all those who are quoted or cited in these pages and all those who have supported the American Civil Liberties Union, Feminists Against Censorship, the Feminist Anti-Censorship Taskforce, Feminists for Free Expression, and the National Coalition Against Censorship's Working Group on Women, Censorship and "Pornography." Among the many people in this category, I'd like to single out for special, individualized thanks four women with whom I have had the privilege of working especially closely: Marjorie Heins, executive director of the ACLU's Arts Censorship Project; Leanne Katz, executive director of the National Coalition Against Censorship; Carlin Meyer, professor of law, New York Law School; and Marcia Pally, president of Feminists for Free Expression. I'd also like to extend a special thanks to the other women whose writings have been especially influential upon my own thinking: Varda Burstyn, Lisa Duggan, Nan Hunter, Wendy Kaminer, Sylvia Law, Thelma McCormack, Katha Pollitt, Ann Snitow, and Carole Vance.

Many other individuals made important contributions to my work on this book. The dean and associate dean of New York Law School, Harry Wellington and Ellen Ryerson, have consistently provided intellectual, moral, financial, and logistical support for my research and writing. Harry Wellington's leadership, inspiration, and support for scholarly activity at New York Law

7

School have been particularly stimulating to my work. Cardozo Law School professor Michel Rosenfeld, by teaching one of my classes, made it possible for me to write this book in a timely fashion. The indefatigable staff of the New York Law School Library, including William Mills, Joelle Lemmons, and Joyce Saltalamachia, helped me to locate even the most arcane, elusive sources. In particular, Joseph Molinari, the library's head of public services, provided invaluable assistance with both the text and the images. Other NYLS staff members to whom I am especially grateful are our resident computer whiz, Dorothea Perry-Coleman, Claire (Knows Everything) Voulgarelis, and Carmen Frazier.

Thomas Hilbink, my outstanding assistant, himself provided skilled and thorough research assistance, oversaw the work of all other researchers, including finalizing the endnotes—herculean tasks—and held the fort in my hectic office. Tom's conscientious attention to all other areas of my work allowed me to devote the time required to write this book. The lionesses' share of the wide-ranging legal and factual research underlying the book was carried out by Karen Shelton and Carolyn Richmond, with principal support from Stephen Hendricks, Carmen Tausik, and Dolly Voorhees. Additional, valued research assistance was provided by Martin Adler, Nina Carpiniello, I-Jung Chiang, Gabriel Falcon, Tyler Kandel, Debra Klinek, Ronak Kordestani, Stephanie Landess, Nancy Meyers, Vinit Parmar, Tara Phelan, Tony Ross, Helen Ullrich, and Donna Wasserman.

Many people have provided information, documents, and other materials to me and my research assistants. Although we have tried to keep detailed records of all these individuals, for the purpose of acknowledging them here, I fear that—given the scope of the project and the number of people involved—some omissions are probably inevitable. If you did help and are not listed here, please accept our apologies for the omission and, more important, our sincere gratitude. Thanks, then, to the following individuals and organizations: Nancy Abraham, Floyd Abrams, Michelle Adams, Shoshanna Addley, Alternative Tentacles Records (especially Jello Biafra and Greg Werckman), the American Association of University Professors, Art Resource (including Paul Evans and Ita Gross), Peter Awn, *Bad Attitude* magazine (especially Jasmine Sterling), Leslie Barany, Marianna Beck, Floyd Beckford, Kevin Beigel, Zoravia Bettiol, Toni Blake, Boston Women's Health Book Collective (especially Judy Norsigian), Anne Boudreau, Bradley Smith Productions, Susie Bright, Mimi Brown, Ken Burrows, Karen Busby, Jamie Cameron, the Canadian Civil Liberties Association (especially Alan Borovoy and Danielle McLaughlin), Dennis Cauchon, Rebecca Chalker, M. Chemiakin, Roberta Cohen, David Cole, Columbia University's "Draw the Line" Project (including Alex Davis, Molly Eagan, James Stoterau, and John Vagelatos), Carol Connolly, Sandra Corti, A. J. Cortman, Cathy Crosson, Marsha Cummings, Nicole Cummings, Dorit Cypis, Josh Dare, Edward de Grazia, Harriette and Norman Dorsen, Carol Downer, Claudia Dreifus, Mark Duran, Susan Fall, *Feminist Bookstore News* (especially Jean Tust), Femme Productions (especially Candida Royalle), Patricia Flynn, Allison Foster, Lisa Frank, Jessica Fredericks, Jill Frisch, Andrew Frothingham, Gemini Smith, Inc., Michael Greve, Barry Gross, Gerald Gunther, Shona Gupta, Randy Hecht, Jack Hafferkamp, Nat Hentoff, Paul Hoffman, Peter Holtberg, Jenny Holzer, Penn Jillette, Burt Joseph, Fred Kallister, Leslie Kantor, Steve Kass, Sam Kerson, Paula Klaw, Michael Krauss, Robert Kreiser, Bill Kuntz, Gara LaMarche, Judith Levine, Doris Linneman, Lacey Logan, Bill Love, Jennifer Maguire, Adál Maldonado, Sally Mann, Mary Ellen Mark, Kimberly McCollum, Wendy McElroy, *Michigan Journal of Law & Gender* (especially Elise Bruhl), Frank Miller, Julia Molinder, John Morris, David Moshman, Liza Mundy, the National Association of Scholars, National Campaign for Free Expression (including Steve Johnson and David Mendoza), National Coalition Against Censorship (including Max Cartagena, Jamie Katz, Jennifer Lopes, Stephen McCammon, Joanna Samuels, and Roz Udow), David Ogden, *On Our Backs* magazine (especially Melissa Murphy), Chris Penner, Miko Pfund, Naomi Pritchard, Debra Raskin, Nicole Rice, Roger Rosenblatt, Jo-anne Savio, Liana Scalettar, Mark Schapiro, David Schoenbrod, Maimon Schwarzschild, Ntozake Shange, Josh Shenk, Judith Singer, Elliott Sparkman, Christine Sperber, Lawrence Stanley, Jeff Stephenson, Laura Strauss, Hudson Talbott, Douglas Tausik, Marcia Teronas, John Thompson, William Tourtillote, Suzanna Turman, Michelle Urry, Veronica Vera, Sam Walker, Liz Weisberg, Joel Peter Witkin, and Roger Worsham.

Many staff members of the ACLU and its state affiliates have been very helpful; in particular, I'd like to thank Steve Bates, Robyn Blumner, Jean Bond, Harv Dean, Lynn Decker, Dorothy Ehrlich, Arthur Eisenberg, John Fahs, Ira Glasser, Edward Gomez, Florence Green, Phil Gutis, Douglas Honig, Deborah Leavy, Kenia Olivera, Kevin O'Neill, Kathy Parrent, Robert Peck, Bill Saks, Steve Shapiro, Loren Siegel, Barry Steinhardt, Vic Walczak, Diane Weiss, and Jane Whicher. I also wish to acknowledge my debt to the ACLU in general, which has given me the opportunity to develop many of the ideas in this book. However, this book is a personal statement, not an organizational one, for which I alone bear responsibility.

Vital to the development of this book were my literary agent, Carol Mann, and her assistant, Deborah Clifford. Essential encouragement and superb editorial assistance were also provided by my editor, Bill Goldstein; Billy was the first person who asked me to think seriously about writing a book, several years ago, and I'm delighted that he was also the first to propose a subject that compelled me to carve out the time to write my first book. Copy editors Carole McCurdy and Kristine Larson Vesley combined meticulous technical skills with gifted facilities with words and ideas; the title "copy editor" doesn't do justice to their contribution. For helpful comments on my manuscript, I thank Cathy Crosson, Marjorie Heins, Gara LaMarche, Joan Mahoney, Eli Noam, and Marcia Pally.

For their constant companionship throughout my work on this book, pets go to my purring paperweights, Winnie and Squeaky 2.1. Finally, my deepest thanks go to my beloved husband, Eli M. Noam, whose manifold contributions would take another book—a love story—to describe.

# Introduction

Pornography, in the feminist view, is a form of forced sex, . . . an institution of gender inequality. . . . [P]ornography, with the rape and prostitution in which it participates, institutionalizes the sexuality of male supremacy.

CATHARINE MACKINNON[1]

Feminist women are especially keen to the harms of censorship. . . . Historically, information about sex, sexual orientation, reproduction and birth control has been banned under the guise of . . . the "protection" of women. Such restrictions have never reduced violence. Instead, they have led to the jailing of birth control advocate Margaret Sanger, and the suppression of important works, from *Our Bodies, Ourselves* to . . . the feminist plays of Karen Finley and Holly Hughes. Women do not require "protection" from explicit sexual materials. . . . Women are as varied as any citizens of a democracy; there is no agreement or feminist code as to what images are distasteful or even sexist. It is the right and responsibility of each woman to read, view or produce the sexual material she chooses without the intervention of the state "for her own good." . . . This is the great benefit of being feminists in a free society.

FEMINISTS FOR FREE EXPRESSION[2]

> The strain of anti-pornologism is hardly what's dis-
> tinctive about feminism; whereas anti-anti-pornology—
> the critique of the anti-porn movement on grounds
> other than constitutional formalism or First Amend-
> ment pietism—is a distinctive feminist contribution.
>
> HENRY LOUIS GATES
> W. E. B. Du Bois Professor
> Harvard University[3]

In the past decade, some feminists have dramatically altered the long-standing debate in this country about sex and sexually oriented expression. Liberals—including those who advocated women's rights—had long sought increased individual freedom, and decreased government control, in the realm of sexuality. Accordingly, liberals had urged the repeal both of laws restricting consensual private sexual conduct between adults, and laws restricting the production of or access to sexually oriented materials, including books, photographs, and films.

Conversely, conservatives—including those who opposed women's rights causes—had consistently advocated strict government controls over both sexual conduct and sexual expression. With the 1980 election of Ronald Reagan and the growing mobilization of the so-called Religious Right, what had become a conservative clamor gained enormous political clout. It led to the 1986 Report of the Meese Pornography Commission,[4] which in turn led to sweeping new law enforcement crackdowns on all manner of sexual materials, including popular, constitutionally protected works such as *The Joy of Sex*[5] and *Playboy* magazine.

The startling new development is that, since the late 1970s, the traditional conservative and fundamentalist advocates of tighter legal restrictions on sexual expression have been joined by an increasingly vocal and influential segment of the feminist movement. Both groups target the sexual material they would like to curb with the pejorative label "pornography." Led by

University of Michigan law professor Catharine MacKinnon and writer Andrea Dworkin, this faction of feminists—which I call "MacDworkinites"[6]—argues that pornography should be suppressed because it leads to discrimination and violence against women. Indeed, MacKinnon and Dworkin have maintained that somehow pornography itself *is* discrimination and violence against women; that its mere existence hurts women, even if it cannot be shown to cause some tangible harm.[7]

I share the fears, frustration, and fury about the ongoing problems of violence and discrimination against women, which no doubt have driven many to embrace the "quick fix" that censoring pornography is claimed to offer. Who wouldn't welcome an end to the threat of violence that so many women feel every time they venture out alone in the dark? But censoring pornography would not reduce misogynistic violence or discrimination; worse yet, as this book shows, it would likely aggravate those grave problems. In the words of feminist attorney Cathy Crosson, while the procensorship strategy may be superficially appealing, at bottom it reflects "the defeated, defeatist politics of those who have given up on really altering the basic institutions of women's oppression and instead have decided to slay the messenger."[8]

The pornophobic feminists have forged frighteningly effective alliances with traditional political and religious conservatives who staunchly oppose women's rights, but who also seek to suppress pornography. As noted by feminist anthropologist Carole Vance, "Every right-winger agrees that porn leads to women's inequality—an inequality that doesn't bother him in any other way."[9]

Under their joint antipornography banner, the allies in this feminist-fundamentalist axis have mounted increasing—and increasingly successful—campaigns against a wide range of sexually oriented expression, including not only art and literature, but also materials concerning such pressing public issues as AIDS and other sexually transmitted diseases, abortion, contraception, sexism, and sexual orientation.

So influential have the MacDworkinites become that all too

many citizens and government officials believe that the suppression of sexually oriented materials is a high priority for all feminists, or even for all women. But nothing could be further from the truth.

An increasingly vocal cadre of feminist women who are dedicated to securing equal rights for women and to combating women's continuing second-class citizenship in our society strongly opposes any effort to censor sexual expression. We are as committed as any other feminists to eradicating violence and discrimination against women; indeed, many of us work directly for these goals every day of our lives. But we believe that suppressing sexual words and images will not advance these crucial causes. To the contrary, we are convinced that censoring sexual expression actually would do more harm than good to women's rights and safety. We adamantly oppose any effort to restrict sexual speech not only because it would violate our cherished First Amendment freedoms—our freedoms to read, think, speak, sing, write, paint, dance, dream, photograph, film, and fantasize as we wish—but also because it would undermine our equality, our status, our dignity, and our autonomy.

Women should not have to choose between freedom and safety, between speech and equality, between dignity and sexuality. Women can be sexual beings without forsaking other aspects of our identities. We are entitled to enjoy the thrills of sex and sexual expression without giving up our personal security. We can exercise our free speech and our equal rights to denounce any sexist expressions of any sort—including sexist expressions that are also sexual—rather than seek to suppress anyone else's rights.

Women's rights are far more endangered by censoring sexual images than they are by the sexual images themselves. Women do not need the government's protection from words and pictures. We *do* need, rather, to protect ourselves from any governmental infringement upon our freedom and autonomy, even—indeed, especially—when it is allegedly "for our own good." As former Supreme Court Justice Louis Brandeis cautioned: "Experience should teach us to be most on our guard to protect liberty when the government's purposes are beneficent. . . . The greatest dangers to liberty lurk in insidious encroachment by men of zeal, well-meaning but without understanding."[10] Or *women* of zeal.

The feminist procensorship movement* is a far greater threat to women's rights than is the sexual expression it condemns with the epithet "pornography." For women who cherish liberty and equality, Big Sister is as unwelcome in our lives as Big Brother. Defending the sexual expression that some feminists condemn with the dread *P* word is thus a critical element in our support of free speech, sexual and reproductive autonomy, and women's equality.

Traditional explanations of why pornography must be defended from would-be censors have concentrated on censorship's adverse impacts on free speech and sexual autonomy. This book supports the anticensorship position from an important different perspective, which is not as widely understood. In light of the increasingly influential women's rights–centered rationale for *censoring* pornography, this book focuses on the women's rights–centered rationale for *defending* pornography. It explains why the procensorship faction of feminism poses a serious threat not only to human rights in general but also to women's rights in particular.

---

*Dworkin, MacKinnon, and others have protested that their proposals for suppressing pornography should not be labeled "censorship." To borrow the title of MacKinnon's latest book, such a protest is "only words." The reasons why the MacDworkinites' antipornography scheme is fairly considered censorship, no matter what euphemism they might prefer, are discussed in chapter 3.

# DEFENDING
# PORNOGRAPHY

## CHAPTER 1

# The Sex Panic
# and the Feminist Split

The American feminist movement's battle over censorship—those who favor legal limits on pornography versus those who oppose them—has escalated dramatically in the past year [1993]. . . . Anti-porn feminists have won significant courtroom, campus, and public-relations victories in the past year. . . . Anticensorship feminists—who've long maintained that it is people, not books or pictures, that harm women, and that women have historically been targets of censure when censorship is condoned—find their ideological opponents' growing influence alarming.

MAUREEN DEZELL, journalist[1]

### "Pornography" Is a Dirty Word

The term "pronography" is ordinarily reserved for sexually explicit words and images whose sole purpose is sexual arousal. However, literature, art, sex education and information about women's sexuality are often attacked—and suppressed—as "pornography." Recently, "pornography" has been employed by certain feminists as though sexually explicit expression is inherently "subordinating" or "degrading" to women (and as though these terms are themselves not subject to disagreement).

LEANNE KATZ, Executive Director
National Coalition Against Censorship[2]

People have very different definitions of the term "pornography," but it has become a convenient weapon, just as
"communism" was during the McCarthy era, to brand
any person or work with whose ideas the censor disagrees.

MARJORIE HEINS, Director
American Civil Liberties Union
Arts Censorship Project[3]

"Pornography" is a vague term, which *Webster's International
Dictionary* defines as "a depiction (as in writing or painting) . . .
of erotic behavior designed to cause sexual excitement."[4] In
short, it is sexual expression that is meant to, or does, provoke
sexual arousal or desire.

The term has no legal definition or significance. The category of sexually oriented expression that the Supreme Court
has held to be subject to restriction is labeled "obscenity." In
recent times, the word "pornography" has assumed such negative connotations that it tends to be used as an epithet to describe—and condemn—whatever sexually oriented expression
the person using it dislikes. As one wit put it, "What turns *me*
on is 'erotica,' but what turns *you* on is 'pornography' "! Likewise, Walter Kendrick's comprehensive 1987 study of the subject, *The Secret Museum: Pornography in Modern Culture,* makes
clear that the term "pornography" consistently has been applied
to whatever sexual representations a particular dominant class
or group does not want in the hands of another, less dominant
class or group.[5]

Indeed, the dread *P* word has been used still more loosely
and pejoratively, to tar *any* disfavored idea or expression. A striking—and ironic—example of this phenomenon is contained on
the jacket of Catharine MacKinnon's 1993 book *Only Words*.
Reinforcing fears about the vague, expansive bounds of the
"pornography" that MacKinnon and her allies seek to suppress,
the book jacket blurb by law professor Patricia Williams castigates
criticism of MacKinnon's ideas as "intellectual pornography."

Even the so-called Meese Pornography Commission, which issued its controversial report in 1986, did not attempt to define the term. In contrast, the procensorship feminists use this stigmatized word to underscore that they seek to suppress a category of sexual expression that is, in theory, distinguishable from the category banned under traditional "obscenity" laws. Essentially, "obscene" speech is sexual speech that the community deems "immoral," whereas in model legislation drafted by MacKinnon and Dworkin, "pornography" is defined as the "sexually explicit subordination of women through pictures and/or words."[6]

Although various supporters of the feminist procensorship faction have proposed slight variations on the MacKinnon-Dworkin definition of pornography, the core concept is always the same—sexual expression that allegedly demeans women. In 1992, for example, the Canadian Supreme Court issued a decision that Catharine MacKinnon hailed as a victory for women (it apparently was influenced by a brief she had coauthored). In that case, entitled *Butler v. the Queen*,[7] Canada's high court interpreted the Canadian obscenity laws as embodying the Mac-Dworkin concept of pornography and hence outlawed materials that are "degrading" or "dehumanizing" to women.

Throughout this book, I use the term "pornography" to refer to the sexually oriented expression that MacKinnon, Dworkin, and their supporters have targeted for suppression. As I show, though, this definition is so amorphous that it can well encompass any and all sexual speech.

### "Sex" Is Also a Dirty Word

This culture always treats sex with suspicion. . . . Sex is presumed guilty until proven innocent.

GAYLE RUBIN, anthropologist[8]

Although the strange bedfellows in the current campaign against sexual speech—Meese, MacKinnon, and their respective allies—employ some differing rhetoric in their unified call for censoring sexually oriented expression, they sound many common chords, notably that sex and materials that depict or describe it inevitably degrade and endanger women. In short, the war on sexual expression is, at bottom, a war on sex itself, at least as far as women are concerned. Because the philosophy of leading antipornography, procensorship feminists reflects a deep distrust of sex for women, such feminists are, in my view and in the view of others, aptly labeled "antisex" (see chapter 5).

Taken together, the traditional and feminist antipornography, antisex crusaders appeal to a broad gamut of the ideological spectrum in both the government and the public. They pose an unprecedented danger to sexual expression, which has always been uniquely vulnerable in the United States, as well as to the concept that the First Amendment protects such expression. Moreover, their attacks have been alarmingly successful.

We are in the midst of a full-fledged "sex panic," in which seemingly all descriptions and depictions of human sexuality are becoming embattled. Right-wing senators have attacked National Endowment for the Arts grants for art whose sexual themes—such as homoeroticism or feminism—are allegedly inconsistent with "traditional family values." At the opposite end of the political spectrum, students and faculty have attacked myriad words and images on campus as purportedly constituting sexual harassment. Any expression about sex is now seen as especially dangerous, and hence is especially endangered. The pornophobic feminists have played a very significant role in fomenting this sex panic, especially among liberals and on campuses across the country.

The fear of sexual expression has become so high-pitched lately that it even has deterred an AIDS clinic from giving out information about combating the deadly spread of the virus. In Oklahoma City, the American Civil Liberties Union (ACLU) represented a doctor who was prosecuted for displaying a safe-sex poster on the windows of his AIDS clinic, which was located in an area frequented by gay men. Yet public health experts maintain that the allegedly illegal and offensive image in the poster—a man wearing a condom—is an important instrument in the life-or-death campaign to halt the spread of HIV. Although the charges were dismissed, the city has threatened further prosecutions, thus deterring the clinic from mounting similarly explicit educational displays in the future.[9]

Society's wariness toward sex is highlighted by contrasting it with the greater societal tolerance toward violence. This dichotomy is especially vivid in the media and mass culture, where violent depictions are far more accepted than sexual ones. The contrast was aptly capsulized by Martin Shafer, a top executive at a film production company, when he noted, "If a man touches a woman's breast in a movie, it's an R rating, but if he cuts off a limb with a chain saw, it's a PG-13."[10]

Because the domain of sexual expression, always a difficult terrain, has lately been laced with land mines placed by diverse enemies, it has become more treacherous than ever. Not surprisingly, artists, academics, and others are increasingly deterred from entering and exploring this potentially explosive—but also rich, wonderful, and important—territory.

All over the country, artists say that they dare not pursue sexual themes for fear that their work will be perceived as too controversial to be funded or displayed. Indeed, outraged officials and citizens alike have indignantly demanded the defunding and deposing from display of art with a wide range of sexual themes; lately it seems that even a mere sexual connotation, no matter how subtle, is vulnerable.

In our current epidemic of erotophobia, even images of nude or seminude bodies in wholly nonsexual contexts have been attacked. For example, in 1993, Vermont officials hung bedsheets over a mural that artist Sam Kerson had painted in a state building's conference room. One press account described the mural, which was commissioned to mark the five-hundredth anniversary of Christopher Columbus's voyage, as "a politically correct rendition of Columbus and his men arriving in the New World, battle-axes and crucifix raised, ready to oppress the natives."[11] But the painting was not politically correct enough for a number of female employees, who complained that its depictions of bare-breasted native women constituted sexual harassment. Because the mural could not be removed without destroying it, the state resorted to the bedsheet "solution."

In 1992, a painting of the classical seminude statue the Venus de Milo was removed from a store in a Springfield, Missouri, shopping mall because mall managers considered the topless masterpiece "too shocking."[12] The painting of the ancient Greek sculpture, which was carved about 150 B.C., and which stands in a place of honor in Paris's Louvre museum, was replaced by a painting of a woman wearing a long, frilly dress.

Another example of a famous artistic masterpiece that has been suppressed in the current sex panic is *The Nude Maja,* or *Maja Desnuda,* by the celebrated Spanish painter Francisco de Goya. In 1992, Pennsylvania State University officials removed a reproduction of this acclaimed work from the front wall of a classroom following a complaint by English professor Nancy Stumhofer that it embarrassed her and made her female students "uncomfortable."[13]

No matter that the reproduction hung, along with reproductions of other masterpieces, in a room used for art history classes. No matter that university officials offered to move the painting to a less prominent position in the classroom, such as the back wall. No matter that they also offered to remove the Goya from the classroom altogether whenever Professor Stumhofer taught there, or even to relocate her classes to another classroom. No. Apparently, nothing short of extirpating the work from all campus classrooms would purge its taint, from her perspective.[14] And the university capitulated. As writer Nat Hentoff commented, at that Penn State campus the administration defines sexual harassment as "anything that makes people uncomfortable about sexual issues."[15]

Moving even beyond nudity or partial nudity, the sex panic has engulfed certain forms of clothing that some observers might deem provocative. In a 1994 *Ms.* magazine discussion on pornography, writer Ntozake Shange described one such situation that she said was "very heavy on my heart":

I was on the cover of *Poets & Writers* and I wore a pretty lace top. In the next two issues, there were letters asking if *Poets & Writers* is now a flesh magazine—why was I appearing in my underwear? Bare shoulders are exploitation now?[16]

In response, Andrea Dworkin, another participant in the *Ms.* discussion, confirmed that she would indeed see Shange's photograph as exploitation: "It's very hard to look at a picture of a woman's body and not see it with the perception that her body is being exploited."

Whether the stigmatizing epithet of choice for particular protesters happens to be "pornography" or "sexual harassment," the result is the same: the conclusory label intimidates campus officials and others who should defend artistic expression, so they instead suppress it. Objecting to another such suppressive incident, which occurred at Vanderbilt University in 1993 (and is described in the next section of this chapter), Vanderbilt art professor Marilyn Murphy said: "Human sexuality has been a recurring theme in art since antiquity. Visual arts is the most misunderstood discipline on this campus and on college campuses everywhere."[17]

Liza Mundy, a writer who has chronicled campus attacks on art with sexual themes, has concluded that "MacKinnonite ideas underlie many" such attacks, noting the irony that many of these battles "pit feminist students against feminist artists." At the University of Arizona in Tucson, students physically attacked a group of photographic self-portraits by graduate student Laurie Blakeslee, which were displayed in the student union. The alleged offense? Blakeslee had photographed herself in her underwear. In Mundy's words, "Young women and men influenced by crusading law professor Catharine Mac-Kinnon—and these are in the ascendance on many campuses—believe that . . . sexually explicit imagery create[s] an atmosphere in which rape is tolerated and even encouraged."[18]

An essential aspect of women's right to equal opportunity in employment and education is the right to be free from sexual

harassment. What is troubling, though, is the spreading sense—
perpetuated by the feminist antipornography movement—that
*any* sexual expression about a woman, or in her presence, *necessarily* constitutes such harassment. This presumption is stated
expressly as the basis for the sweeping sexual harassment codes
that are becoming increasingly common on campuses.

Syracuse University, for example, adopted a sexual harassment code in 1993 that prohibits not only "requests for sexual
relations combined with threats of adverse consequences" if
refused, and assaultive acts such as "pinching or fondling," but
also nonassaultive, vaguely described acts such as "leering,
ogling and physical gestures conveying a sexual meaning," and
loosely described expressions including "sexual innuendoes,
suggestive remarks, [and] sexually derogatory jokes." What all
of these seemingly disparate behaviors have in common, the
code informs us, "is that they focus on men and women's sexuality, rather than on their contributions as students or
employees in the University."[19]

But this should not be an either-or choice, should it? Are
women not—along with men—sexual beings, as well as students or employees? Is women's sexuality really incompatible
with their professional roles? Is it really increasing women's
autonomy, options, and full-fledged societal participation to posit
such an incompatibility? Have we not learned from history, and
from other cultures, that the suppression of women's sexuality
tends to coincide with the suppression of women's equality?
And that when women's sexuality has been banished from the
public sphere, women themselves are also banished from key
roles in that sphere?

Far from advancing women's equality, this growing tendency to equate any sexual expression with gender discrimination undermines women's equality. Women are, in effect, told
that we have to choose between sexuality and equality, between
sexual liberation and other aspects of "women's liberation,"
between sexual freedom and economic, social, and political
freedom. This dangerous equation of sexual expression with
gender discrimination, which is at the heart of the feminist

antipornography movement, is a central reason that movement is so threatening to the women's rights cause.

The misguided zeal to strip all sexual expression from workplaces and campuses, in an alleged effort to strip those places of gender-based discrimination, now has reached even to subtle interpersonal expressions, prone to subjective perceptions and interpretations, such as looks and glances. A growing number of campus policies, including the one at Syracuse University already quoted, extend the concept of harassment to "sexually suggestive looks." Likewise, a survey about the sexual harassment of female doctors by their patients, published in the prestigious *New England Journal of Medicine* in December 1993, included "suggestive looks" among the "offenses" reported.[20] In fact, though newspaper headlines trumpeted the dramatic conclusion that 75 percent of the female doctors surveyed said that they had been sexually harassed by patients, further reading revealed that "most of the offenses involved suggestive looks and sexual remarks."[21]

Are women doctors, faculty, and students to be relegated to a figurative equivalent of the purdah of traditional Hindus and Muslims, or the clothing and segregation requirements of orthodox Jews—designed to prevent men from looking at women, and to "protect" women from men's looks? While these traditional religious practices shield women from the eyes of anyone outside their domestic circles, they also imprison women within those domestic circles. The outside world cannot see women, and women cannot see the outside world.

To be sure, "sexual looks," as well as the other nonassaultive conduct proscribed in the Syracuse code, could constitute sexual harassment if they were sufficiently severe or pervasive— for example, if a professor repeatedly subjected a young student to such behavior. In contrast, isolated incidents where the behavior is not targeted at someone who has less authority or status should not be deemed harassment.

## No Classroom Talk about Sex Is Safe—
## Not Even Talk about Safe Sex

The sex panic that antiporn feminists have helped to spark and to spread has had another adverse effect that should be of particular concern to those who are committed to women's rights: on college and university campuses around the United States, students and faculty have been penalized for seemingly any sexually related expression, even in class discussion and other academic settings in which freedom of speech should be especially cherished and safe. The list of such incidents is long and rapidly expanding. Let me describe just a few of them here.

- At Vanderbilt University in 1993, associate fine arts professor Don Evans, a recognized photographer, was charged with sexual harassment and subjected to restrictions on his future teaching following the university's secretive, individual questioning of each of his students, without informing him. This furtive inquiry was launched by one female student's complaint about the display and discussion of nude and sexually oriented photographs in Evans's course on photography and design. The offended student complained that the sexually explicit photographs, which included some by Robert Mapplethorpe and some by Evans himself, "degraded women."[22]

  In response, the university ordered Evans to warn future students in advance about the "potential nature and content of material shown" in his courses.[23] As Evans noted, the same "logic" that would force him to warn students about what they might see in a photography class would also require English literature professors to warn students that they might be offended by some writings of Chaucer. (Indeed, Chaucer's writings have repeatedly provoked objections; to cite one incident of particular relevance here, in 1987, the Columbia County, Florida, school board barred students from reading a widely used humanities textbook because it contained Chaucer's "The Miller's Tale," which community members denounced as "pornography and women's lib.")[24] "I find it sad a professor has to warn adult students their sensibilities might be offended by course material," Evans said. "I guess we'll have to put a sign over the entrance of the university that says, 'Danger: some of the information you receive here might offend you.'"[25] Sadly, Evans's prediction proved prophetic. Several months later, Vanderbilt student leaders, at the request of other students, asked every faculty member to announce at the beginning of any course whether or not it would include any sexually explicit material.

- In 1993, the Iowa Board of Regents ordered all faculty members to warn students before presenting any materials that include "explicit representations of human sexual acts that could reasonably be expected to be offensive to some students."[26] Students had to be excused from those classes without penalty and allowed to complete an alternative assignment or to drop the course. Even beyond the paternalistic attitude toward students that this policy reflects—and its enormous chilling effect on faculty and student speech—it deprives students of information and ideas that are vitally important to themselves and others. Under the Iowa rules, for example, medical students could be exempted from learning about sexually transmitted diseases.

- In 1993, the University of New Hampshire suspended English professor J. Donald Silva from teaching for at least one year (without pay), and required him to undergo counseling at his own expense with a counselor selected by the university, after students complained that some of his in-class statements created a sexually intimidating atmosphere. His offenses? During a writing class covering rhetorical devices, Silva (who is also the longtime pastor at the Great Island, New Hampshire, Congregational Church) had given an example of a simile that came from an old record his wife had about belly dancing: "Belly dancing is like Jell-O on a plate, with a vibrator under the plate." In addition, in trying to explain the concept of focus in a way that would grab the students' attention, he said:

> Focus is like sex. You seek a target. You zero in on your subject. You move from side to side. You close in on the subject. You bracket the subject and center on it. Focus connects experience and language. You and the subject become one.[27]

(Silva sued the university for violating his constitutional rights to free speech and due process of law, and in September 1994 a federal judge issued a preliminary ruling in his favor.)

- In 1994, Chicago Theological Seminary professor Graydon Snyder, an ordained minister, was severely disciplined merely for reciting a lesson from the Talmud, the compendium of Jewish law, during a religion class. The lesson centers around a story about a man who falls off a roof, lands on a woman, and accidentally has intercourse with her; the Talmud comments that the man is innocent, because the act was unintentional. For thirty years, Snyder had used this lesson as a springboard for discussing Jewish and Christian concepts of responsibility, guilt, and sin. But when he did so in 1994, a female student filed a sexual harassment charge against him. In response, the seminary issued a formal reprimand and put notices in the mailboxes of every student and teacher at the school, telling them that Dr. Snyder had engaged in sexual harassment. Although Snyder was allowed to continue teaching, he has had to endure the further indignity of being visibly monitored by a school official, who sits near him in the classroom with a tape recorder—"a kind of word cop," according to *The New York Times*.[28]

- At the University of Nebraska-Lincoln in 1993, a male student accused female graduate instructor Toni Blake of sexual harassment because of her actions and statements in teaching a class about contraception and sexually transmitted diseases. In instructing her students about the appropriate use of condoms, she demonstrated how to put them on by using a banana. Moreover, to make a point about the timing of putting on condoms, she quoted to her class the old joke that men, like basketball players, "dribble before they shoot." Blake was trying to to give her students a memorable lesson on the crucially important subjects of contraception and safer sex. According to the male student who filed the complaint against her, though, she had "objectified" the penis and thereby created a hostile academic environment for men.

Toni Blake's experience demonstrates the long-range adverse effects of complaints by sex police in deterring students and faculty from any discussion of sexuality or, indeed, of any topic with any sexual connotations. In response to the complaint against her, Blake concluded that it would be prudent to delete material on human sexuality from her future courses to avoid further problems, and her department chair also advised her to do this. In short, there is no safe expression about safe sex.

Given statistics indicating that at least 80 percent of young people in the United States are sexually active by age twenty,[29] the alleged "protectionism" of shielding students from sexually oriented information and ideas is surely exactly the opposite. Our colleges and universities do not (and should not) protect the students from sex itself, with its attendant physical risks and emotional and psychological complications, but they do "protect" the students from learning about sex, including about safer-sex practices.

It is essential to derail the traditionalist–feminist antisex juggernaut before its impact on public perceptions and public policy becomes even more devastating. This juggernaut poses a great danger to free speech about sex, which is central to a range of urgent current concerns—abortion, contraception, other aspects of reproduction, gender roles, sexism, sexual orientation (and the legal status of homosexual or bisexual people), and sexually transmitted diseases. In addition, the conservative–feminist drive to suppress sexual expression threatens the movement for women's equality, since that movement depends on robust free expression, particularly in the realm of sexuality, which historically has been a focal point in defining—and limiting—women's societal and legal status.

## Women Having It All: Free Speech *and* Equality

From a feminist perspective, there is no choice between equality and freedom of expression; they are two sides of the same coin, and cannot be played off against each other any more than we can separate mind and body.

THELMA MCCORMACK, Director
York University Centre for Feminist Studies[30]

Since free expression about sexual issues is critically important to the women's rights cause, it is ironic that those feminists who advocate curbing such expression say they do so out of concern for women's rights. They define as pornography, and seek to suppress, sexually explicit expression that "subordinates" or "degrades" women, on the theory that this expression causes discrimination and violence against women. They argue that free speech protection for pornography is antithetical to women's rights, and therefore that we have to compromise the constitutional free speech guarantee to advance the constitutional equality guarantee. This was the major theme, for example, of Catharine MacKinnon's 1993 book *Only Words*. She declares: "The law of equality and the law of freedom of speech are on a collision course in this country."[31]

In fact, though, this line of argument is pernicious and wrongheaded. In our society, founded on the interlinked goals of liberty and equality, we all are entitled to both freedom of speech and equal opportunity under the law. Moreover, these two ideals are mutually reinforcing.

In the women's rights context, freedom of speech consistently has been the strongest weapon for countering misogynistic discrimination and violence, and censorship consistently has been a potent tool for curbing women's rights and interests. Freedom of sexually oriented expression is integrally connected with women's freedom, since women traditionally have been straitjacketed precisely in the sexual domain, notably in our ability to control our sexual and reproductive options.

Accordingly, during the first wave of feminism in this century, Margaret Sanger, Mary Ware Dennett, and other pioneering birth control advocates were prosecuted (and, in some cases, convicted, fined, and imprisoned) for disseminating birth control information. Significantly, this information was held to violate *antiobscenity* statutes. Such laws were used not to promote women's equality, but rather, to erode it (see chapter 11).

Because the American Civil Liberties Union, since its founding, has represented many women's rights activists whose free speech has been throttled—including Sanger and Dennett—its opposition to the antipornography laws endorsed by some feminists is grounded in the organization's long-standing commitment to women's rights, as well as in its consistent defense of free speech. In opposing an antipornography ordinance that Indianapolis enacted in 1984, modeled on one drafted by Dworkin and MacKinnon,[32] the ACLU argued that the law "unconstitutionally introduced gender-based discrimination into the First Amendment." As the ACLU's brief explained:

> The ordinance . . . presumes a natural and inevitable vulnerability of (weaker) women to the unbridled and voracious sexual appetites of (stronger) men and accordingly promises to "protect" all women. As in the past, the cost of "protection" is the perpetuation of gender-based stereotypes and the denial to women of sexually explicit material which may itself benefit women by providing information about sexuality, sexual functions, or reproduction. . . . While it is undoubtedly true that many women are victims of male violence . . . the attempt to [justify] widespread censorship on the false stereotypical assumption that all women are unable to resist male domination . . . is precisely the type of sex-based protectionism that inhibits the evolution of genuine equality between the sexes.[33]

All censorship measures throughout history have been used disproportionately to silence those who are relatively disempowered and who seek to challenge the status quo. Since women and feminists are in that category, it is predictable that any censorship scheme—even one purportedly designed to further their interests—would in fact be used to suppress expression that is especially important to their interests.

That prediction has proven accurate in our neighboring country of Canada, which in 1992 adopted the definition of pornography advocated by MacKinnon, Dworkin, and other procensorship feminists: sexually explicit expression that is "dehumanizing" or "degrading" to women.[34] The Canadian authorities have seized upon this powerful tool to suppress lesbian and gay publications and feminist works, and to harass lesbian and gay bookstores and women's bookstores (see chapter 11).

### With Friends Like These, Who Needs Enemies?

The widespread misperception that Dworkin and MacKinnon speak for feminists generally concerning sexual speech is fostered by their own divisive rhetoric, which suggests that their censorship campaign is the one and only feminist position. Catharine MacKinnon has stated that "Pornography, in *the* feminist view, is a form of forced sex . . . an institution of gender inequality" (emphasis added).[35] Moreover, Dworkin and MacKinnon have charged that those who disagree with them are not true, but "liberal, so-called" feminists.[36] MacKinnon has compared feminists who oppose censorship to "house niggers who sided with the masters," and has denounced a leading feminist anticensorship group, the Feminist Anti-Censorship Taskforce (FACT): "The labor movement had its scabs, the slavery movement had its Uncle Toms and Oreo cookies, and we have FACT."[37] In the same vein, Dworkin has condemned feminists who maintain that the constitutional free speech guarantee extends to sexual speech as "politically self-righteous fellow travelers of the pornographers."[38]

Leanne Katz, executive director of the National Coalition Against Censorship, recently described "the extraordinary name-calling tactics" that the procensorship feminists brandish against anticensorship feminists:

Opposition to their activities is called "slander," and "hate campaigns"; we are charged with being manipulated by "pimps," with being mouthpieces of pornographers. We are accused of being indifferent to violence against women, the Uncle Toms of patriarchy. It is apparently unthinkable that one might care about women and *therefore* oppose censorship.[39]

The procensorship feminists' views that women who disagree with them are being manipulated as tools of "pimps" or "pornographers," and are not thinking for ourselves, conveys at least as subordinating or degrading a view of women as does the pornography they decry. One example of the procensorship feminists' patronizing, "maternalistic" view of their anticensorship counterparts was provided by Norma Ramos, general counsel of Women Against Pornography. Commenting about me in a *Vogue* magazine article in 1992, Ramos said, "The ACLU . . . uses its women to further its antifeminist agenda. When Strossen became an apologist for the pornographers, she passed their litmus test to become president."[40]

In a letter to the editor of *Vogue,* writer Marcia Pally, founder and president of Feminists for Free Expression, responded to Ramos's remarks:

> I was especially edified by comments from Norma Ramos, of Women Against Pornography. Without them, I might never have known that Strossen, a Phi Beta Kappa Radcliffe graduate and editor of the *Harvard Law Review* . . . was a puppet—"used" by ACLU men. . . . Ramos is right: any woman who disagrees with Ramos's own views on sexual material must be a stooge. How foolish to believe that Strossen, a professor at New York Law School, could think for herself, or that her contributions to [various scholarly journals] were anything but sad efforts to pass the "litmus test" of male colleagues. How silly, when it has so long been known that women are muddle-minded pawns. I wonder only that Ramos failed to report that Strossen slept her way to the top.[41]

## The Anticensorship, Prosex Feminists

If you love freedom and like sex, censorship is bad news.

KATHLEEN PERATIS
women's rights attorney[42]

Contrary to the MacDworkinites' image of a unified front, many
feminist women disagree with their implacably negative analysis
of sexual expression, and reject their calls for censoring it.
Moreover, contrary to the MacKinnon-Dworkin line that to dissent from their views reflects an elevation of free speech principles
over principles of women's equality, many feminist women
oppose censoring sexually oriented speech specifically from a
feminist perspective; we believe that censorship would not promote women's rights, but, to the contrary, would undermine
them. Therefore, the proposed feminist antipornography laws are
doubly flawed: they would undermine both free speech and
equality.

Because anticensorship feminists reject the procensorship
feminists' negative views that sex inherently degrades women,
we often are called "prosex" feminists by partisans on both
sides of this debate.

Feminist opponents of censorship include leading activists,
artists, psychologists, scholars, writers, and women (and men)
from all other walks of life. Among the best known are Betty
Friedan, founding president of the National Organization for
Women (NOW); Faye Wattleton, longtime president of
Planned Parenthood; Karen DeCrow, another former NOW
president; and writers Anne Bernays, Judy Blume, Barbara
Ehrenreich, Nora Ephron, Nancy Friday, Mary Gordon, Susan
Isaacs, Molly Ivins, Erica Jong, Jamaica Kincaid, Kate Millett,
Katha Pollitt, Anne Rice, Adrienne Rich, Alix Kates Shulman,
and Wendy Wasserstein.

In the United States, organizations that oppose censoring
pornography specifically from a feminist perspective include the
Feminist Anti-Censorship Taskforce; Feminists for Free

Expression; and the National Coalition Against Censorship's Working Group on Women, Censorship, and "Pornography." (As indicated by its name, the Working Group consistently puts the word "pornography" in quotation marks to underscore the word's inherent ambiguity and subjectiveness.) Although these organizations have slightly different emphases, they and their supporters all share a commitment to both free speech and equality, and a belief that suppressing pornography would subvert, rather than promote, efforts to counter misogynistic violence and discrimination. Feminists have also banded together in other countries—including Canada and Great Britain—to oppose MacDworkinite proposals from a women's rights perspective.

This book focuses on the reasons so many feminists have concluded that censorship would in fact undermine important women's rights goals. Before turning directly to those reasons, though, I will address some related issues to provide a legal and factual context for the feminist anticensorship, prosex position.

First, I will outline the current law governing sexual expression. It is this tired body of law that procensorship feminists seek to resuscitate, and that anticensorship feminists seek to retire. After that, I will sketch the early history of what have been dubbed the feminist "sex wars"—showing how the feminist antipornography movement has sought to change the current law concerning sexual expression, and how its initial efforts were soundly rebuffed by the Supreme Court. Then I will chronicle the alarming recent renaissance of the feminist procensorship faction, and its increasing influence on popular attitudes, public policy, and law.

CHAPTER 2

# Sexual Speech and the Law

Martin Luther King, Malcolm X
Freedom of speech is as good as sex.

MADONNA, performer[1]

Since Christianity . . . concentrated on sexual behavior as the root of virtue, everything pertaining to sex
has been a "special case" in our culture, evoking
peculiarly inconsistent attitudes.

SUSAN SONTAG, writer[2]

While Madonna believes that free speech and sex are equally
good, many other Americans believe that they are equally
bad—at least when the speech is *about* sex. Therefore, just as
the American legal system has outlawed certain types of sexual
activity—even by consenting adults in private—it has outlawed
certain types of sexual expression—again, even by or for consenting adults in private.

This sexual prudery in American law reflects our Puritan
heritage. Garrison Keillor made this point with characteristic
humor in his 1990 congressional testimony supporting the
National Endowment for the Arts, which was embattled
because it had funded certain sexually oriented works, including Robert Mapplethorpe's homoerotic photographs. Keillor
said: "My ancestors were Puritans from England, [who]
arrived here in 1648 in the hope of finding greater restrictions
than were permissible under English law at the time."[3]

The First Amendment's broadly phrased free speech guarantee—"Congress shall make no law . . . abridging the freedom of

speech"—contains no exception for sexual expression.*
Nevertheless, the Supreme Court has consistently read such an
exception into the First Amendment, allowing sexual speech to
be restricted or even banned under circumstances in which it
would not allow other types of speech to be limited. While
American law is, overall, the most speech-protective in the
world, it is far less protective of sexual speech than the law in
some other countries. Our First Amendment jurisprudence,
along with everything else in our culture, as Susan Sontag suggests, treats sex as a "special case."[4]

The very change in current law that procensorship feminists
advocate—that it target sexual expression that "subordinates"
or "degrades" women—highlights the important ideas that
such speech conveys about significant public issues, notably,
gender roles and gender-based discrimination. Consequently,
the courts have recognized that the subset of sexual speech that
the Dworkin-MacKinnon faction seeks to suppress, as distinct
from the subset of sexual speech that is unprotected under current obscenity doctrine, is really "political" speech, which has
traditionally received the highest level of legal protection.

The MacDworkinite concept of pornography, in focusing
expressly on the political ideas conveyed by sexual expression,
would necessarily threaten other forms of political expression,
too. In contrast, the Court's concept of obscene expression focuses specifically on the alleged lack of ideas conveyed by such
speech. At least in theory, then, obscenity is a self-contained category of sexual expression whose unprotected status does not
directly threaten other speech. As I will explain, in practice the
concept of obscenity cannot be cabined, and does threaten valuable expression. But the alternative, more expansive notion of
pornography-as-discrimination even more directly threatens a

---

* Although the First Amendment expressly prohibits only congressional
laws that abridge free speech, the Supreme Court has interpreted it as implicitly prohibiting any government action that abridges free speech. Moreover,
the Court has held that the First Amendment bars private citizens from
invoking the legal system—for example, through private lawsuits—to suppress free speech.

broader range of speech, as well as many core free speech principles.

If we should restrict sexually explicit speech because it purveys sexist ideas, as the feminist antipornography faction argues, then why shouldn't we restrict non–sexually explicit speech when it purveys sexist ideas? And if speech conveying sexist ideas can be restricted, then why shouldn't speech be restricted when it conveys racist, heterosexist, and other biased ideas? These logically indistinguishable applications of the feminist antipornography analysis lead many in the Dworkin-MacKinnon camp, including Dworkin and MacKinnon themselves, to advocate restricting racist and other forms of "hate" speech.[5]

Yet the Supreme Court has repeatedly held that the First Amendment protects not only speech that is *full of hate* on the speaker's part, but also speech that is *hateful* to its audience. As former justice Oliver Wendell Holmes declared, "[I]f there is any principle of the Constitution that more imperatively calls for attachment than any other it is the principle of free thought—not free thought for those who agree with us but freedom for the thought we hate."[6]

Furthermore, the Supreme Court has consistently rejected calls for censoring (nonobscene) speech when there is no demonstrable, direct causal link between the speech and immediate harm. But this is the feminist procensorship argument in a nutshell—that pornography should be suppressed based on speculation that it may lead to discrimination or violence against women in the long run, despite the lack of evidence to substantiate these fears (see chapter 12). If we should restrict pornography on this basis, then why shouldn't we suppress any expression that might ultimately have a negative effect?

If MacDworkinism should prevail in the courts, it would jeopardize all of the foregoing free speech precedents and principles. The government could outlaw flag burning and the teaching of Marxist doctrine because they might lead to the erosion of patriotism and our capitalist system; white supremacist and black nationalist speeches could be criminalized because they might lead to racial segregation; peaceful demonstrations for (or against) civil rights, women's rights, gay rights, and, indeed, any other potentially controversial causes could be banned because they might provoke violent counterdemonstrations; advertising for alcohol, tobacco, and innumerable other products could be prohibited because it might cause adverse health effects; feminist expression could be stifled because it might threaten "traditional family values" and the attendant domestic order and tranquillity; abortion clinic advertising and other prochoice expression could be suppressed because it might lead to the termination of potential life; indeed, feminist antipornography advocacy could itself be suppressed because it could endanger cherished constitutional rights! The list is literally endless.

Make no mistake: if accepted, the feminist procensorship analysis would lead inevitably to the suppression of far more than pornography. At stake is all sexually oriented speech, any expression that allegedly subordinates or undermines the equality of any group, and any speech that may have a tendency to lead to any kind of harm. One might well ask about the feminist procensorship philosophy, not what expression would be stifled, but rather, what expression would be safe.

## The "Preferred" Status of Speech in Our Hierarchy of Constitutional Rights

As noted above, the U.S. Supreme Court has relegated sexual expression to second-class status. To understand the significance of this disparity, we need first to consider the Court's rules concerning freedom of expression in general, and then to consider how the Court has refused to extend these speech-protective general rules to sexually oriented speech.

At the heart of the Supreme Court's extensive free speech jurisprudence are two cardinal principles. The first specifies what is *not* a sufficient justification for restricting speech, and the second prescribes what *is* a sufficient justification. A Dworkin-MacKinnon–style antipornography law violates both of these core principles. Accordingly, for such a law to be upheld, the very foundations of our free speech structure would have to be torn up.

The first of these basic principles requires "content neutrality" or "viewpoint neutrality." It holds that government may never limit speech just because any listener—or even, indeed, the majority of the community—disagrees with or is offended by its content or the viewpoint it conveys. The Supreme Court has called this the "bedrock principle" of our proud free speech tradition under American law.[7] In recent years, the Court has steadfastly enforced this fundamental principle to protect speech that conveys ideas that are deeply unpopular with or offensive to many, if not most, Americans: for example, burning an American flag in a political demonstration against national policies,[8] and burning a cross near the home of an African-American family that had recently moved into a previously all-white neighborhood.[9]

The viewpoint-neutrality principle reflects the philosophy that, as first stated in pathbreaking opinions by former Supreme Court justices Oliver Wendell Holmes and Louis Brandeis, the appropriate response to speech with which one disagrees in a free society is not censorship but counterspeech—*more* speech, not *less*. Persuasion, not coercion, is the solution.

Rejecting this philosophy, the feminist procensorship position targets for suppression a category of sexual expression precisely because of its viewpoint—specifically, a gender-discriminatory viewpoint. Because of this fatal constitutional flaw, all Dworkin-MacKinnon–style antipornography laws will continue to be ruled unconstitutional, as were the two such laws that courts have reviewed to date, as long as our courts continue to enforce the viewpoint-neutrality principle.

The feminist antipornography laws also violate the second cardinal principle that is central to free speech law—that a restriction on speech can be justified only when necessary to prevent actual or imminent harm to an interest of "compelling" importance, such as violence or injury to others. This is often summarized as the "clear and present danger" requirement. As Justice Oliver Wendell Holmes observed in a much-quoted opinion, the First Amendment would not protect someone who falsely shouted "Fire!" in a theater and caused a panic.[10]

This second core free speech principle entails two essential prerequisites for justifying any speech restriction: that the expression will cause direct, imminent harm to a very important interest, and that only by suppressing it can we avert such harm. Each of these requirements is crucial for preserving free expression, and neither is satisfied by advocates of suppressing pornography.

The restricted speech must pose an imminent danger, not an alleged "bad tendency." Allowing speech to be curtailed on the speculative basis that it might indirectly lead to possible harm would inevitably unravel free speech protection. *All* speech might lead to potential danger at some future point. Justice Holmes recognized this fact in an important 1925 opinion. Holmes rejected the argument that pacifist and socialist ideas should be repressed because they might incite young men to resist the draft or to oppose the U.S. system of government—actions and views that many thought might ultimately undermine national interests. As Holmes noted, "Every idea is an incitement."[11]

If we banned the expression of all ideas that might lead individuals to actions that might have an adverse impact even on important interests such as national security or public safety, then scarcely any idea would be safe, and surely no idea that challenged the status quo would be. Judge Frank Easterbrook made precisely this point in holding the Indianapolis version of the Dworkin-MacKinnon model antipornography law unconstitutional. Accepting for the sake of argument the law's cornerstone assumption that "depictions of subordination tend to perpetuate subordination," Easterbrook explained:

> If pornography is what pornography does, so is other speech. . . .
> Efforts to suppress communist speech in the United States were

based on the belief that the public acceptability of such ideas would increase the likelihood of totalitarian government. Religions affect socialization in the most pervasive way. . . . The Alien and Sedition Acts passed during the administration of John Adams rested on a sincerely held belief that disrespect for the government leads to social collapse and revolution—a belief with support in the history of many nations. . . .

Racial bigotry, anti-Semitism, violence on television, reporters' biases—these and many more influence the culture and shape our socialization. . . . Yet all is protected as speech, however insidious. Any other answer leaves the government in control of all of the institutions of culture, the great censor and director of which thoughts are good for us.

Sexual responses often are unthinking responses, and the association of sexual arousal with the subordination of women therefore may have a substantial effect. But almost all cultural stimuli provoke unconscious responses. Religious ceremonies condition their participants. Teachers convey messages by selecting what not to cover; the implicit message about what is off limits or unthinkable may be more powerful than the messages for which they present rational argument. . . . If the fact that speech plays a role in a process of conditioning were enough to permit governmental regulation, that would be the end of freedom of speech.[12]

While Justice Holmes rejected the so-called bad tendency argument—namely, that speech could be suppressed if it might have a tendency to bring about future harm—his Supreme Court brethren accepted that argument in a series of cases during the World War I era and the ensuing "Red Scare." In one of the low points for free speech in this country, they allowed the imprisonment of thousands of political leaders and other citizens who did nothing more than peacefully express views critical of U.S. participation in World War I and other government policies.

The Supreme Court has since repudiated the bad tendency argument in the context of what it calls "political speech," or speech about issues of public policy. But it continues to accept that argument in the context of sexual speech. The Court allows certain sexual expression—"obscenity"—to be restricted merely because of its alleged tendency to undermine community morality, without any evidence of any direct or immediate harm.

The feminist antipornography activists seek to expand the bad tendency rationale to allow suppression of even more sexual speech than is currently restricted under traditional obscenity laws. In 1992, the Canadian Supreme Court adopted the MacDworkinite bad tendency approach. The Canadian court acknowledged that no evidence establishes a direct causal connection between pornography and discrimination or violence against women (as detailed in chapter 12), but it nevertheless ruled that the mere *belief* that such a connection exists is enough to justify suppressing the speech.[13]

In contrast, the U.S. Supreme Court has rejected this censorial notion, maintaining the crucial distinction between *advocacy* of violent or unlawful conduct, which is protected, and intentional, imminent *incitement* of such conduct, which is not. The classic free speech dissents of justices Holmes and Brandeis earlier in this century endorsed this critical distinction as an essential aspect of the "clear and present danger" requirement that they also launched. The Court enshrined the distinction as a cornerstone of contemporary free speech law in a 1969 case, *Brandenburg v. Ohio.*[14] *Brandenburg* upheld the First Amendment rights of a Ku Klux Klan leader who addressed a rally of supporters, some of whom brandished firearms, and advocated violence and discrimination against Jews and blacks. The Court held that this generalized advocacy was neither intended nor likely to cause immediate violent or unlawful conduct, and therefore could not be punished.

The Supreme Court has consistently applied *Brandenburg*'s critical distinction between protected advocacy and unprotected incitement to protect incendiary expression of every stripe. In 1982, it relied on this distinction to protect expression whose thrust was diametrically opposite that of the expression that had been protected in the *Brandenburg* case. The Court held that officials of the National Association for the Advancement of Colored People (NAACP) had a First Amendment right to make speeches advocating violent reprisals against individuals who violated an NAACP-organized boycott of white merchants who had allegedly engaged in racial discrimination. Even though some violence was subsequently committed against blacks who patronized white merchants, it occurred weeks or months after the inflammatory addresses. Accordingly, in a major victory for the civil rights cause, as well as for free speech principles, the Supreme Court overturned a lower-court ruling that had declared the boycott unlawful and held the NAACP responsible for white merchants' large financial losses. The Court explained the fundamental free speech principles at stake:

> The [NAACP leaders'] addresses generally contained an impassioned plea for black citizens to unify, to support and respect each other, and to realize the political and economic power available to them. In the course of those pleas, strong language was used. . . . Strong and effective extemporaneous rhetoric cannot be nicely channeled in purely dulcet phrases. An advocate must be free to stimulate his audience with spontaneous and emotional appeals for unity and action in a common cause. . . . To rule otherwise would ignore the "profound national commitment" that "debate on public issues should be uninhibited, robust, and wide-open."[15]

Procensorship feminists seek to eliminate the fundamental distinction between protected advocacy and unprotected incitement, arguing that sexual expression should be suppressed even if it does not expressly *advocate,* let alone *intentionally incite,* violence or discrimination against women. They want to suppress sexual words or images they interpret as consistent with views that accept violence or discrimination against women, and which might reinforce such views on the part of some audience members.

It has become fashionable among some law professors, of whom Catharine MacKinnon is a prominent example, to question the ongoing relevance of classic First Amendment principles, and I certainly endorse and engage in the constant critical reexamination of all established legal principles. Reexamining the landmark Holmes and Brandeis free speech opinions that I have cited has left me more impressed than ever with their universal, timeless force. They remain relevant and persuasive, specifically in the context of the current pornography debate. Further, the majority rulings that these dissents so powerfully criticize stand as sobering reminders of how much freedom we would lose should we accept the procensorship feminists' call to revive the now discredited "bad tendency" approach that these rulings reflect.

Heed the following passage from Justice Holmes's 1916 dissent in *Abrams v. United States,* in which the majority had upheld prison sentences of up to twenty years for a group of Russian immigrants who had expressed their support for the Russian Revolution and called for a general strike in the United States. It reads as if it were Justice Holmes's answer to contemporary feminists' pleas for censoring pornography—an answer that is understanding of, and even sympathetic to, their reasons for urging such censorship, but that also explains why those reasons are fundamentally at odds with a sustainable constitutional philosophy:

Persecution for the expression of opinions seems to me perfectly logical. If you have no doubt of your premises or your power and want a certain result with all your heart you naturally express your wishes in law and sweep away all opposition. To allow opposition by speech seems to indicate that you think the speech impotent. . . . But when men have realized that time has upset many fighting faiths, they may come to believe even more than they believe the very foundations of their own conduct that the ultimate good desired is better reached by free trade in ideas— that the best test of truth is the power of the thought to get itself accepted in the competition of the market, and that truth is the only ground upon which their wishes safely can be carried out. That at any rate is the theory of our Constitution. It is an experiment, as all life is an experiment. Every year if not every day we have to wager our salvation upon some prophecy based upon imperfect knowledge. While that experiment is part of our system I think that we should be eternally vigilant against attempts to check the expression of opinions that we loathe and believe to be fraught with death, unless they so imminently threaten immediate interference with the lawful and pressing purposes of the law that an immediate check is required to save the country. . . . Only the emergency that makes it immediately dangerous to leave the correction of evil counsels to time warrants making any exception to the sweeping command, "Congress shall make no law . . . abridging the freedom of speech."[16]

Next, listen to Justice Brandeis's powerful opinion in *Whitney v. California,* a 1927 case in which the majority upheld a one- to fourteen-year prison sentence that had been imposed on Anita Whitney merely because she was a member of the Communist Labor Party, whose platform advocated the violent overthrow of the U.S. government. Although Whitney herself unsuccessfully opposed this position, and had called upon the party to pursue its goals through the political process, the Supreme Court majority held that Whitney's mere party membership warranted her criminal punishment.

While Brandeis, like Holmes, is sympathetic to fears about potential speech-induced harms, he eloquently reminds us that our constitutional philosophy reflects and requires not fear, but rather courage, in the realm of ideas. Moreover, directly responsive to the procensorship feminists' concerns about women's relatively powerless status, Brandeis presciently warns that it is precisely those who are relatively weak who will be victimized, not protected, by any fear-based repression:

Those who won our independence . . . believed liberty to be the secret of happiness and courage to be the secret of liberty. . . . They recognized the risks to which all human institutions are subject. But they knew that order cannot be secured merely through fear of punishment for its infraction; that it is hazardous to discourage thought, hope and imagination; that fear breeds repression; that repression breeds hate; that hate menaces stable government; that the path of safety lies in the opportunity to discuss freely supposed grievances and proposed remedies; and that the fitting remedy for evil counsels is good ones. . . .

Fear of serious injury cannot alone justify suppression of free speech and assembly. Men feared witches and burned women. . . .

Those who won our independence by revolution were not cowards. . . . They did not exalt order at the cost of liberty. To courageous, self-reliant men, with confidence in the power of free and fearless reasoning applied through the processes of popular government, no danger flowing from speech can be deemed clear and present, unless the incidence of the evil apprehended is so imminent that it may befall before there is opportunity for full discussion. If there be time to expose through discussion the falsehood and fallacies, to avert the evil by the processes of education, the remedy to be applied is more speech, not enforced silence. Only an emergency can justify repression.[17]

In urging "courageous, self-reliant" individuals to have "confidence" in their own speech as an effective response to "evil counsels," rather than asking the government to protect them by suppressing such evil counsels, Justice Brandeis anticipates an important theme in the current feminist anticensorship movement. Rejecting the procensorship faction's emphasis on women as victims in need of governmental protection through censorship, anticensorship feminists are willing to trust our own voices—as well as those of our antipornography sister feminists—to effectively counter misogynist expression, including misogynist sexual expression. Ironically, the feminist procensorship faction apparently does not view women as capable of such self-help, but instead sees us as helpless.

### *Speech May Be Restricted Only as a Last Resort*

As stated earlier, before the government may restrict expression, it must show not only that the expression threatens imminent serious harm but also that the restriction is *necessary* to avert the harm. This requirement is often described as the "least restrictive alternative" concept: even when a limitation on speech would promote an extremely important goal, if the government could advance that goal by methods that restrict speech less, then it must use those alternative measures.

Undeniably, the interests that procensorship feminists seek to promote, women's equality and safety, are compellingly important. But just as pornography poses no imminent harm to those interests, its suppression is not necessary to promote them. Advocates of MacDworkinite laws cannot even show that these laws would effectively promote women's safety and equality, let alone that they are the necessary and least speech-restrictive means for doing so (see chapters 12 and 13).

In enforcing the preceding principles, which generally permit government to restrict speech only under tightly limited circumstances, American law no doubt provides more protection for speech about most subjects than does the law of any other country. Our legal system protects all manner of controversial, inflammatory, and subversive expression, including speech that is harshly critical of political leaders and policies; speech that is highly provocative or offensive to those who hear it; speech that advocates the overthrow of the existing form of government; and speech that advocates violence or crimes against certain people.

In stark contrast, American law provides far less protection for sexually oriented expression.

### The Second-Class Status of Sexual Speech
### under First Amendment Law

I will not criticize the power of pictures and words to arouse; to arouse passion or ideas, erections or damp panties, fears, curiosities, unarticulated yearnings and odd realizations. Sexual speech, not MacKinnon's speech, is the most repressed and disdained kind of expression in our world, and MacKinnon is no rebel or radical to attack it.

SUSIE BRIGHT, writer[18]

Nor is pornography's purported aim or effect—to excite the reader sexually—a defect. . . . The physical sensations involuntarily produced in the reader carry with them something that touches upon the reader's whole experience of his humanity.

SUSAN SONTAG, writer[19]

Pornography is, again, "designed to cause sexual excitement."[20] Yet the fact that expression arouses feelings and passions does not justify giving it less First Amendment protection than expression that is likely to arouse a more intellectual response. If that were the case, then much literature and art would surely have to join sexually oriented speech as second-class citizens under the First Amendment. But the Supreme Court long has held that the First Amendment extends to all forms of art and entertainment, and has rejected attempts to construe it more narrowly as applying only to ideas or information.[21] Indeed, if all emotion-provoking discourse were relegated to a less protected status, then much political speech—which is at the apex of First Amendment protection—would have to be similarly demoted.

Notwithstanding the Court's appropriate protection of expression that arouses all manner of nonsexual passions and inflames all manner of nonsexual senses, it has consistently given scant protection to sexually oriented expression, without ever offering a coherent explanation of why it is either less important or more dangerous than other kinds of expression. The Court has allowed government to restrict sexually oriented expression on the basis of mere assertions or assumptions about its alleged lack of importance or the purported harms associated with it.

Where sexual speech is concerned, the Court simply fails, without explanation, to enforce its generally applicable, stringent preconditions for restricting expression. The Court never has demanded that the government justify restrictions on sexual speech by showing that they were necessary to avert a "clear and present danger," or to prevent the intentional incitement of imminent violence or illegal conduct, or to promote another goal of compelling importance; if it had, the government would not have been able to satisfy such standards. Instead, the Court allows sexual speech to be suppressed based on vague, unsubstantiated allegations that it is dangerous. Just as our society tends to view sex itself as inherently dangerous, so too our courts view words or images that describe or depict sex.

The "sexual revolution" of the 1960s and 1970s called this view into question, as it ushered in greater societal tolerance for various modes of sexual activity and expression. In 1970, the President's Commission on Obscenity and Pornography (which had been appointed by President Johnson, and submitted its report to President Nixon) recommended the repeal of all laws prohibiting the distribution of sexually explicit materials to consenting adults and advocated a massive sex education program.[22] In the decade that followed, the "women's liberation" movement advocated women's sexual liberation, demanding that women be given information and options that would allow them to break beyond traditional sexual roles. Accordingly, as central aspects of the reenergized women's rights movement, women opened feminist health clinics, provided information and training on women's sexuality, and worked for accessible, safe contraception and abortion.

Although the Supreme Court aided the movement for

increased freedom in the sexual arena by invalidating laws restricting contraception and abortion, the Court did not increase freedom for sexual expression. Ironically, in 1973, the very year that the Court issued its landmark *Roe v. Wade* ruling,[23] which recognized that women have a constitutional right to choose to have an abortion, it also adopted a broader definition of "obscenity," the legal term for sexually oriented speech that the Court deems to be beyond the First Amendment pale and thus subject to prohibition and criminal punishment.

Before its 1973 rulings in *Miller v. California*[24] and the companion case of *Paris Adult Theatre I v. Slaton,*[25] the Supreme Court had held that sexually oriented expression would be constitutionally unprotected only if it were "utterly without redeeming social value."[26] In *Miller,* though, the Court altered that standard so that material could be banned unless it had "*serious* literary, artistic, political, or scientific value"[27]—a standard that lawyers refer to as the "SLAPS" test. Until the *Miller* ruling, *any* literary or other value was enough to redeem a sexually oriented work, whereas after that, only *serious* value would suffice.

In 1973, then, the Court decreased the government's power to curb sexual *conduct,* but it increased the government's power to curb sexual *expression.* In so doing, the Court's majority completely ignored the recommendation of the President's Commission on Obscenity and Pornography that sexually oriented expression should be legalized (for consenting adults) because there is no link between it and criminal or violent conduct. Indeed, the majority acknowledged that "there are no scientific data which conclusively demonstrate that exposure to obscene material adversely affects men and women or their society." Nonetheless, contrary to general First Amendment principles, the Court asserted that such material could be banned based on "unprovable assumptions" about its negative impacts on the moral "tone" of "a decent society."[28]

The Supreme Court's 1973 decisions, as well as its earlier obscenity rulings, failed to provide a clear, objective definition of proscribable obscenity. The justices have wrestled with various definitions over the years, but never have been able to craft one that did not simply call for subjective value judgments. This intractable problem is highlighted by former justice Potter Stewart's well-known statement in a 1964 obscenity case: "I shall not today attempt further to define [obscenity] . . . ; and perhaps I could never succeed in intelligibly doing so. But I know it when I see it."[29]

Justice Stewart's candid statement underscores the inevitably subjective judgment at the heart of any determination that a particular sexually oriented expression is or is not obscene. While none of us could intelligibly articulate a neutral standard for judging sexually oriented works in general, each of us no doubt can recognize particular works that we find less appealing, and more offensive, to our own personal tastes and sensibilities. Each of us, though, including each judge and each juror, sees a different "it."

In its 1973 *Miller* decision, the Supreme Court laid out three criteria for assessing whether any work is obscene, all inescapably vague: (1) the "average person, applying contemporary community standards, would find that the work, taken as a whole, appeals to the prurient interest" in sex; (2) "the work depicts or describes, in a patently offensive way, sexual conduct specifically defined by the applicable state law"; and (3) "the work, taken as a whole, lacks serious literary, artistic, political, or scientific value."[30]

The inherent ambiguity and subjectivity of the *Miller* criteria are underscored by the Court's attempted clarification of the term "prurient," which raised more questions than it answered. The Court explained that a "prurient" interest in sex is a "sick and morbid" one, as opposed to a "normal and healthy" one.[31] Imagine yourself sitting as a judge or a juror attempting to determine whether a particular sexually oriented work appeals to a "sick" interest or a "healthy" one. Can you honestly imagine doing anything other than invoking your own tastes and preferences? Do you want other individuals to judge by their own standards a work that you find interesting or exciting?

As Stanford law professor Kathleen Sullivan memorably

paraphrased *Miller*'s first two requirements, "prurient" means that the expression "turns you on," whereas "patently offensive" means that it "grosses you out."[32] More specifically, Sullivan pointed out, the definition essentially means that material that "turns on" *some* people—namely, those who created, distributed, or viewed it—"grosses out" *other* people—namely, the police, prosecutors, judges, and jurors who found it obscene.

The unpredictability of whether a given work will be determined "obscene" is heightened by the Supreme Court's ruling that the "prurient interest" and "patently offensive" criteria are to be weighed in light of "community standards" in each particular locale where the work might be prosecuted. Consequently, even if the work might not be deemed "prurient" or "patently offensive" in one place, it could well be found to satisfy these criteria in another place.

In reality, the obscenity definition functions more as a Rorschach test for judges and jurors than as an objective legal standard for protecting sexual speech against unwarranted prosecutions or convictions.

## Second-Class Speech Gets Second-Class Law Enforcement Treatment

As with any law whose definition entails subjective determinations, the obscenity criteria give vast discretionary power to law enforcement officials. Such power invites officials to wield it in an arbitrary or discriminatory fashion. Accordingly, obscenity laws can easily become instruments for suppressing the expression of those who are relatively unpopular or disempowered, whether because of their ideas or perspectives, or because of their membership in particular societal groups. Recent major obscenity prosecutions, in fact, have targeted expressions by or about members of groups that traditionally have been victims of discrimination.

The 1991 prosecutions in Broward County, Florida, of 2

Live Crew's song "As Nasty as They Wanna Be" marked the first time in U.S. history that any work of music had been criminally prosecuted under an obscenity law. Likewise, the 1991 prosecutions of the Cincinnati Contemporary Art Center and its director, Dennis Barrie, marked the first time in U.S. history that any art museum or art museum director had been criminally prosecuted under an obscenity law. In the 2 Live Crew case, the targeted musicians and record store owner were African Americans, and in the Cincinnati case, the works of art that triggered the prosecution were homoerotic photographs by the gay photographer Robert Mapplethorpe.

Because of their subjectivity, current obscenity laws offer a license to the police and prosecutors in any community, or the members of any jury, to punish sexual expression that they find distasteful. White middle-class, middle-aged jurors might well be "turned off" by the erotic rap lyrics that "turn on" poor, inner-city black youth. And heterosexual jurors might well be "grossed out" by Robert Mapplethorpe's gay erotica. In our racially polarized society, many jurors might find Mapplethorpe's arresting images of interracial sexuality frightening, and hence also a "turn-off." Indeed, when Senator Jesse Helms attacked the National Endowment for the Arts for having funded Mapplethorpe's photographs, he singled out their interracial, as well as homoerotic, themes, stating: "There's a big difference between 'The Merchant of Venice' and a photograph of two males of different races on a marble table top. . . . This Mapplethorpe fellow was an acknowledged homosexual . . . the theme goes throughout his work."[33]

Because the obscenity laws allow—indeed, *direct*—the majority in any community, and the members of any jury, to criminally punish sexual depictions that they dislike or disapprove, these laws squarely violate the viewpoint neutrality principle that the Supreme Court has called the "bedrock" of our proud American free speech tradition. If the expression concerned any other subject, First Amendment law would protect it against majoritarian sanctions, no matter how hated it might be. This fact is underscored by the Court's recent decisions upholding the First Amendment right to burn both the American flag and a Ku Klux Klan–style cross.[34]

## Sexual Prosecution as Political Persecution

The First Amendment's free speech clause refers unqualifiedly to "the freedom of speech," indicating that *all* speech should be protected equally. Nonetheless, the Supreme Court has deemed some kinds of speech "more equal" than others, creating categories and hierarchies of speech. Sexually oriented expression long has been relegated to the bottom of the Court's First Amendment pecking order. But sex is a vitally important subject, of as much concern to many people as the classically "political" subjects that the Court has placed at the First Amendment apex. The Court itself recognized this in 1957 in *Roth v. United States*: "Sex, a great and mysterious motive force in human life, has indisputably been a subject of absorbing interest to mankind through the ages; it is one of the vital problems of human interest and public concern."[35]

The fact is (and here I agree with procensorship feminists), the sexual *is* political. The Court's bright-line distinction between political and sexual speech, for First Amendment purposes, ignores the significant overlap between those categories made clear by the many major recent political controversies that have centered on sexual issues: the legal rights to be accorded to lesbians and gay men; the protection to be granted to individuals' choices concerning contraception and abortion; the legal, public health, and scientific responses to AIDS and other sexually transmitted diseases; the availability and nature of sex education in public schools; the public funding and display of art with sexual themes; and the legal protection available to women and men from discrimination based on traditional sex roles.

Throughout history, obscenity prosecutions have in fact targeted individuals who have expressed controversial or disfavored ideas about political or religious subjects. One of the earliest British obscenity prosecutions, in the eighteenth century, was instituted by the Tory government to imprison its leading Whig opponent, John Wilkes.[36] In early American experience, antiobscenity laws targeted expression offensive to the prevailing religious orthodoxy and deemed blasphemous or sacrilegious.

The pattern holds today. The so-called NEA Four, performance artists whose NEA grants were denied because of their works' alleged obscenity or indecency, explored themes of domestic violence, the feminization of poverty, homophobia, male dominance, the oppressiveness of traditional gender roles, sexism, and sexual harassment. In the words of one of their lawyers, Marjorie Heins of the ACLU, their work deals with "the politics of sex."[37]

Although a majority of the Supreme Court continues to enforce the *Miller* definition of obscenity, six justices who have sat on the Court during the past quarter century have argued that this definition violates free speech principles. Most recently, in a 1987 dissent, Justice John Paul Stevens, joined by Justices William Brennan and Thurgood Marshall, concluded that all criminal obscenity statutes are unconstitutional, at least as applied to consenting adults.[38] In that same case, moreover, even archconservative justice Antonin Scalia urged the Court to reconsider its *Miller* holding, stating:

> [I]t is quite impossible to come to an objective assessment of (at least) literary or artistic value, there being many accomplished people who have found literature in Dada, and art in the replication of a soup can. Since ratiocination has little to do with esthetics, the fabled "reasonable man" . . . would have to be replaced with, perhaps, the "man of tolerably good taste"—a description that betrays the lack of an ascertainable standard. . . . Just as there is no use arguing about taste, there is no use litigating about it.[39]

The critiques of obscenity law that have been advanced by individual justices on the United States Supreme Court have been adopted unanimously by two state supreme courts: those in Hawaii and Oregon. These courts have invalidated obscenity laws under the free speech guarantees in their state constitutions.[40] Moreover, a number of state legislatures have refused to adopt, or have repealed, antiobscenity laws.

As even the Meese Pornography Commission was forced to recognize, "the bulk of scholarly commentary" has criticized the Supreme Court's obscenity rulings for transgressing First Amendment values.[41] In his authoritative constitutional law treatise, Harvard law professor Laurence Tribe states that the Court's treatment of certain sexual expression as constitutionally unprotected is "incompatible with the First Amendment premise that awareness can never be deemed harmful in itself." He eloquently explains why:

> [I]n the last analysis, suppression of the obscene persists because it tells us something about ourselves that some of us . . . would prefer not to know. It threatens to explode our uneasy accommodation between sexual impulse and social custom—to destroy the carefully-spun social web holding sexuality in its place. . . . [T]he desire to preserve that web by shutting out the thoughts and impressions that challenge it cannot be squared with a constitutional commitment to openness of mind.[42]

Dangerous as the suppression of obscenity under traditional law is to open minds and a free society, the suppression of pornography under MacDworkinite laws poses even greater dangers, as we see in the next chapter.

## CHAPTER 3

# The Fatally Flawed Feminist
# Antipornography Laws

Because of the important respects in which antiobscenity laws endanger free expression, advocates of free speech, including anticensorship feminists, oppose those laws. That should not be surprising. What may be surprising, though, is that this is one issue on which procensorship feminists agree with anticensorship feminists: MacKinnon, Dworkin, and their allies also oppose the concept of obscenity.[1]

Here the agreement quickly ends. Procensorship feminists do not seek freedom for all sexually oriented expression; rather, they would have the law suppress a new and broader category of sexually oriented expression, distinct from the speech that is targeted under the obscenity laws—namely, the ill-defined category for which they have appropriated the term "pornography." (The term "pornography" has no legal significance in the Supreme Court's First Amendment jurisprudence. While the Court has upheld two state statutes that prohibited what each defined as "child pornography," the Court has not itself defined a constitutionally unprotected category of "child pornography." Both state statutes defined the prohibited expression relatively narrowly, as encompassing photographs or films that show actual children either engaging in sexual activities or in a state of nudity.)[2]

As previously noted, the crux of the procensorship feminists' definition of pornography, as set out in a model law drafted by MacKinnon and Dworkin, is "the sexually explicit subordination of women through pictures and/or words,"[3] Obscenity laws, then, do not focus on what procensorship feminists see as the harm that results from certain sexually oriented expression, and they believe that these laws therefore do not target the appropriate subset of such expression. Their own definition of the speech they would censor, however, is so broad as to permit the suppression of virtually all sexually explicit materials, including those encompassed by the obscenity concept.

### First Amendment Infirmities

Ironically, the procensorship feminists' revisionist definition of prohibited sexually oriented expression as speech that conveys a misogynistic message reveals the constitutional Achilles' heel of their antipornography law: its focus on the political dimension of sexual expression. Whatever one's views about what the status of women should be in our society, it is indisputable that such status is a matter of great public and political concern. Therefore, to suppress speech because it depicts the subordination of women would be as antithetical to central First Amendment principles as suppressing speech that depicts—or, indeed, even advocates—the subordination of racial minorities, as in the *Brandenburg* Ku Klux Klan case or the more recent cross-burning case, both referred to in chapter 2. Likewise, suppressing speech that depicts the subordination of women, or any other group, would be as contrary to the First Amendment as suppressing speech that depicts the *equality* or *superiority* of women or others.

In brief, traditional antiobscenity laws differ from the newer antipornography laws some feminists advocate primarily in that the former seek to suppress certain *sexual* expression, whereas the latter seek to suppress certain *sexist* expression. The feminist antipornography laws are another example of the "hate speech" laws that the Supreme Court consistently has held to violate the First Amendment. In accordance with the fundamental viewpoint neutrality principle, the Court long has held that expression may not be restricted simply because it expresses bigoted or discriminatory ideas concerning any individual or group, no matter how offensive, incorrect, or dangerous those ideas may appear to anyone, including even the majority in the community.

The 1992 cross-burning case is the most recent example of the Supreme Court's long-standing refusal to allow society to punish even the most odious, dramatic expressions of group-based hatred—in that case, racism toward African Americans. As Justice Scalia concluded the Court's opinion: "Let there be no mistake about our belief that burning a cross in someone's front yard is reprehensible. But [the government] has sufficient means at its disposal to prevent such behavior without adding the First Amendment to the fire."[4] The Court's unanimous ruling in that case underscores the secure status of the basic principle that expression conveying discriminatory ideas, including sexist ideas, is constitutionally protected. Consistent with this principle, the lower courts have uniformly stricken the "hate speech codes" recently adopted or considered on many college and university campuses, holding that such codes violate the First Amendment. These courts have ruled that the schools' attempts to punish expression that might be offensive or demeaning to members of various groups, including women, breach the free speech guarantee.[5]

Governments have no more constitutional power to restrict speech that advocates *unequal* treatment of certain societal groups, on the ground that it is deemed incorrect or unpopular, than they have to restrict speech that advocates *equal* treatment of those groups on such a ground. If the protectibility of expression about equality issues turned on its acceptance or popularity, then various communities throughout the South and elsewhere would have been allowed to silence the voices of pro–civil rights activists during the 1960s and 1970s. Likewise, the women who advocated the federal Equal Rights Amendment (ERA) during the 1970s and early 1980s could have been silenced because that amendment went down to defeat. Indeed, advocates of women's equal constitutional rights could still be stifled around the country, because voters continue to reject proposed women's equal rights amendments to their state constitutions. In November 1992, Iowa voters became the latest group to do so.

Further cautionary illustrations against allowing views about equality issues to be suppressed based on their unpopularity are provided by the recent epidemic of votes at the city, county, and state levels rejecting legal protections against discrimination on the basis of sexual orientation. If the majority in any community could suppress views about equality issues that they deem incorrect or unacceptable, then advocacy of equal rights for lesbians and gay men would be widely censored around the United States.

In fact, all laws restricting speech—including traditional obscenity laws, laws curbing sexist and other hate speech, and Canada's version of the feminist antipornography law—have consistently been used to suppress speech by members of unpopular or disempowered groups, including political dissidents, feminists, and racial and sexual minorities (see chapter 11). It shouldn't be surprising that government officials and legal institutions would enforce censorship measures in ways that reflect majoritarian biases.

While "tyranny by the majority" is surely to be resisted, as our constitutional framers recognized, tyranny by a minority is hardly more palatable. Thus, the dangers of viewpoint-based speech suppression, which are inherent in MacDworkinite laws, could not be allayed by procensorship feminists' assurances that they would "only" limit speech that conveys "incorrect" ideas about sex, gender, and equality, no matter how (un)popular those ideas might be. Such a "dictatorship of virtue" (in writer Richard Bernstein's apt phrase[6]) is frightening both in the abstract and when we consider the broad range of important expression—including speech by feminist women—that procensorship feminists have actually assailed (see chapter 10).

Beyond suppressing expression because of its viewpoint, the feminist antipornography law's definition of suppressible sexual speech differs from the traditional obscenity concept in two additional respects that make it even more plainly inconsistent with First Amendment values.

First, remember that the Supreme Court's definition of obscenity excludes any material that has serious literary, artistic, political, or scientific value, as discussed in chapter 2. Under the MacDworkin model law, though, there is no such limitation. Sexually explicit material that is "subordinating" to women would be banned no matter how significant its overall literary, artistic, or other value.

Second and relatedly, the Court has held that, to be deemed obscene, works must be considered as a whole. Therefore, isolated passages that meet the obscenity definition will not justify suppressing a work if, overall, it is not obscene. This important qualification is absent from the Dworkin-MacKinnon model law, under which even an isolated sexually explicit, "subordinating" depiction would warrant suppressing an entire work. As MacKinnon has asked, "If a woman is subjected, why should it matter that the work has other value?"[7]

By suppressing works without regard to their overall value, the MacDworkin law reverts to an archaic nineteenth-century obscenity definition that twentieth-century courts have emphatically rejected. For example, in a 1936 ruling, which was subsequently followed by the United States Supreme Court, the great appellate judge Learned Hand explained:

> This earlier doctrine necessarily presupposed that the devil against which the [obscenity] statute is directed so much outweighs all interests of art, letters or science, that they must yield to the mere possibility that some prurient person may get a sensual gratification from reading or seeing what to most people is innocent and may be delightful or enlightening. No civilized community not fanatically puritanical would tolerate such an imposition.[8]

### The Concept of Civil Censorship

MacDworkinite antipornography laws differ from traditional antiobscenity laws in more than content or focus. While the

latter are criminal laws, enforced by police and prosecutors
(sometimes in response to private citizens' complaints), the
former are civil laws, whose enforcement is initiated directly
by private citizens. Under the model law drafted by Dworkin
and MacKinnon, anyone could bring a lawsuit that could lead
ultimately to a court order prohibiting the production, sale,
exhibition, or distribution of pornographic works. In addition,
individuals who claimed that they had been injured by pornography could seek damages. Under a proposed federal antipornography law that was inspired and supported by the
feminist procensorship faction, the Pornography Victims'
Compensation Act (the Senate Judiciary Committee reported
favorably on this bill in 1992, but it died when the full Senate
failed to consider it before recessing), any victim of a sexual
assault could sue those involved in the production or distribution of certain sexual materials for unlimited damages and
could recover if the jury found the materials to be a "substantial cause" of the assault.[9]

No doubt recognizing the stigma that is, appropriately, associated with the term "censorship," Dworkin, MacKinnon, and
other advocates of feminist antipornography laws protest that
these laws do not constitute censorship because they are civil in
nature and do not involve any "prior restraint" on expression.
In seeking to explain away the draconian censorial impact of
the Canadian Supreme Court's 1992 adoption of her pornography concept in construing its antiobscenity law, Catharine
MacKinnon has stressed that the Canadian law is enforced
through criminal prosecutions rather than civil lawsuits.[10] (In
redefining the targeted speech, the Canadian Supreme Court
substituted the MacDworkinite focus on degrading expression
for the traditional obscenity law's focus on immoral expression; the court incorporated that new definition into its preexisting criminal obscenity law.) In short, MacKinnon would
have us believe that if pornography were subject to civil sanctions, rather than criminal, our free speech concerns should
disappear. Andrea Dworkin has revealed similarly constricted
concepts of free speech and censorship. In a 1994 *Ms.* magazine

article, Dworkin asserted, "In legal terms censorship has always meant prior restraint: you pass a law that stops something from being made or being done."[11]

Not surprisingly, Dworkin's and MacKinnon's notions of speech that should be protected and censorship that should be prohibited are unduly narrow. Their protests that their model law does not constitute censorship that violates the First Amendment's free speech guarantee is doubly flawed. First, as the Supreme Court has consistently held, unconstitutional censorship may assume many forms and is not confined either to criminal laws or to formal pre-publication restraints. Indeed, the Court has expressly recognized that civil lawsuits may well have a more devastating censorial impact, as a practical matter, than criminal prosecutions.[12] Second, in any event, the feminist-style antipornography laws do in fact restrain the publication and distribution of many sexually oriented materials; one of the reasons why the trial court judge held the Indianapolis version of the MacDworkin law unconstitutional was her conclusion that it constituted a prohibited prior restraint.[13]

Government-imposed prior restraints violate First Amendment principles in an especially dramatic fashion, as in the U.S. government's attempt to prevent publication of the Pentagon Papers in 1970.[14] But direct, governmental prior restraint is not the only form of censorship that violates the First Amendment. To the contrary, the Supreme Court has recognized that constitutionally prohibited censorship includes any use of government authority—or any threatened use of such authority—to limit the flow of ideas, information, or expression based on their content. Accordingly, the Court has correctly struck down many different types of measures that have prohibited, restricted, regulated, punished, deterred, or threatened expression, regardless of the particular nature or form of such measures. Contrary to the MacDworkinites' semantic quibbling about "criminal" versus "civil" vehicles for suppressing speech, the Court has recognized that censorship in civilian garb is still censorship. In fact, the Court has expressly recognized that "[t]he fear of damage awards" in civil liability actions "may be markedly more inhibiting" upon free expression "than the fear of prosecution under a criminal statute."[15]

In focusing on the actual adverse impact that any particular measure has on expression, the Court correctly refuses to elevate form over substance. Whether the government directly bars the publication of a work through either a criminal conviction or a civil injunction, or whether the work's publication is deterred by the threat or the actuality of damages in a civil lawsuit, the end result is the same.

Of course, private pressure through such vehicles as speaking, writing, and demonstrating may also have the practical impact of deterring a work's publication. Nevertheless, such private pressure not only is not unconstitutional; to the contrary, it is itself a protected exercise of cherished First Amendment rights, precisely the counterspeech that justices Holmes and Brandeis urged as the appropriate response to expression with which we disagree.

The crucial distinction between the constitutionally protected speech-retarding activity of private pressure groups and the constitutionally prohibited speech-retarding lawsuits that would result under Dworkin-MacKinnon–type laws, turns on the role of the government. Thus, those of us who defend free speech rights concerning pornography agree that individuals may raise their voices to denounce it, and may seek to persuade their sister citizens not to produce, pose for, sell, buy, or look at it. (We may, in turn, raise our own voices to counter and criticize such advocacy; see chapter 10.) In contrast, we resist any efforts, through governmental fiat, to remove these choices from individuals. *Private persuasion and counterpersuasion* embody and promote essential human rights values, whereas *governmental coercion* is antithetical to them. This fundamental distinction is recognized even by anticensorship feminists who are critical of pornography—indeed, even by those who believe that pornography may encourage misogynistic discrimination or violence. Writer Molly Ivins, for instance, put it this way, in her inimitable style:

I do not like pornography. In fact, I think it probably does harm people. . . . [P]robably, all those ugly pictures do encourage violence against women. What should we do about it? Well, my answer is: not a goddamn thing. The cure for every excess of freedom of speech is more freedom of speech. . . . I need the First Amendment so that I'll be able to say to people who say things I do not agree with, "Look, you yellow-bellied son of a bitch—you run on all fours, you molest small children, you have the mind of an adolescent tyrant." I need to . . . be able to answer them back. That's what this whole fuss is about.[16]

The MacDworkin model law authorizes civil lawsuits that trespass beyond the permitted realm of private persuasion into the forbidden territory of governmental coercion. Although the government plays a less direct role in civil lawsuits than in criminal prosecutions, that role is still substantial. Most important, judges, as government officials, have a significant impact on the outcome of civil lawsuits through their rulings about the contours of such suits—for example, what evidence should be admitted and how the jury should be instructed. Additionally, civil injunctions can be enforced by police, prosecutors, and sheriffs, and can lead to imprisonment when judges hold defendants in criminal contempt of court.

One of the Supreme Court's landmark free speech rulings, its 1964 decision in *New York Times v. Sullivan*,[17] clearly demonstrates the equivalency between criminal prosecutions and civil damage actions as vehicles for unconstitutional censorship, and how they differ from constitutionally protected private pressure activities. The *Sullivan* decision struck down not a criminal law that barred speech, but rather a civil cause of action that—like MacDworkinite laws—allowed individuals allegedly harmed by the speech to recover damages for it. In the *Sullivan* case, the lawsuit was for libel. Noting that the damages that the jury had awarded dwarfed the maximum fine that the *Times* would have faced in a criminal libel prosecution, the Court held the state's civil libel law unconstitutional because of its "chilling" effect on free speech. In other words, to avoid the economic cost of damages, as well as the economic and intangible costs of defending against a civil damage action, many people would be deterred from saying anything that might result in a successful lawsuit. Indeed, the tangible and intangible costs of defending against a civil damage action—even if the defense is ultimately successful—are so enormous that many prudent people would be deterred from saying anything that might result in a lawsuit, regardless of whether any such lawsuit would be likely to succeed.

In fact, publishers and booksellers have consistently stressed that the only rational response to the threat of expensive litigation and enormous damage awards under Dworkin-MacKinnon–style antipornography laws might well be to avoid creating or distributing any sexually explicit material. Testifying against the proposed Pornography Victims' Compensation Act in 1991, Joyce Meskis, president of the American Booksellers Association, noted that with 700,000 books in print, and about 27,000 book publishers producing more than 50,000 new titles every year, booksellers have no economical way to review all works. Accordingly, she stated, a bookseller's "only real option" under the Act would be "to inform publishers that the store will no longer receive any works with sexual content." Not surprisingly, Meskis therefore concluded that the Act would "produce the most pervasive censorship the U.S. has ever experienced."[18]

In addition to their enormous adverse economic impact, the civil lawsuits that are authorized by feminist-style antipornography laws would be more burdensome on free speech than criminal prosecutions in significant legal respects. Under our legal system, defendants in criminal actions have the benefit of certain constitutionally mandated procedural safeguards. Most important, defendants have the benefit of a presumption of innocence, and cannot be convicted unless the government satisfies a very heavy burden of proof, convincing the jury of their guilt "beyond a reasonable doubt." The standard for establishing civil liability is much lower, requiring only a "preponderance of the evidence." Additional important procedural safeguards in a criminal prosecution are that an indictment must be made by an impartial grand jury, and be carried forward by a prosecutor, whose legal responsibility is to serve the cause of justice neutrally. In contrast, the feminist-style antipornography laws authorize lawsuits to be brought by self-interested parties who hope to secure substantial financial benefits. Yet another important procedural protection available only in the criminal context is the prohibition on "double jeopardy," which means that any publication could produce only one criminal conviction. In contrast, a single publication could lead to an unlimited number of civil actions and damage awards.

### Protecting Endangered Spaces: "Forced" Public Exposure

Feminists who want to restrict sexual expression argue that no one should be forced to see such expression against his or her will. The Dworkin-MacKinnon model antipornography law makes it illegal to "force pornography on a person in any place of employment, education, home, or any public place."

The Supreme Court has recognized that one's right to privacy in one's home affords shelter against being subjected to certain unwanted expression there.[19] But the feminist antipornography law's comprehensive prohibition upon any "forced" exposure, not only in the privacy of one's home but even in "any public place," sweeps far beyond legitimate privacy concerns and intrudes far too deeply into important free speech rights in the public arena. Even in cases concerning private homes, the Supreme Court has been appropriately reluctant to infringe on freedom of expression in order to protect householders' privacy. The Court has held that although some recipients might object to the contents of unwanted mailings to their homes concerning public policy issues, the intrusion was too minimal to warrant curtailing the senders' First Amendment rights. In the Court's words, the involuntary recipients could "escape exposure to the objectionable material simply by transferring [it] from envelope to wastebasket."[20]

As in so many other contexts, the Supreme Court has treated

sexually oriented materials less protectively here too, holding that individuals may prohibit erotic mailings they deem objectionable from being sent to their homes, thereby avoiding even the minimal intrusion that would be involved in disposing of these materials.[21] Even concerning sexually oriented materials, though, the Court has stressed that decisions about which items should not be mailed must be left to the potentially offended individuals, and cannot be made categorically by the government "on their behalf."[22] Accordingly, Judge Frank Easterbrook concluded that the "forced exposure" provision of the Mac-Dworkin law would be unconstitutional even in the context of the home unless it added "a definition of 'forcing' that removes the government from the role of censor."[23]

While certain limitations on expression might be warranted to maintain privacy in the home, there is no sufficiently compelling justification for imposing similar limitations in public places. Therefore, unless the Dworkin-MacKinnon law's prohibition on "forced" public exposure were construed very narrowly, to apply only to intentional, individually targeted, sustained exposure, it would be unconstitutional. To the extent that it purports to outlaw even passing exposure to sexual imagery such as displays outside movie theaters, in bookstore windows, or on newsstands, it violates the First Amendment without sufficient countervailing justification in terms of promoting privacy, gender equality, or other equivalently important interests.

Certainly no one should have to tolerate any unwanted words or images thrust directly at her unwilling eyes and ears repeatedly or for a sustained period, in a deliberate attempt to annoy or upset her; this would constitute harassing or assaultive behavior, which is prohibited under both criminal and civil law. But the situation is different when our contact with unwanted words or images is fleeting. Our fellow and sister citizens' free speech rights to express themselves and to hear or see the expression of others, which is especially important in public places, necessarily means that each of us will occasionally encounter words or images that we may find offensive, obnoxious, and otherwise unpleasant. In a 1975 decision, the Supreme Court recognized this critical distinction and therefore struck down a Jacksonville, Florida, ordinance that barred any nudity from drive-in movie theater screens. Although the law's purpose was to protect those who were driving or walking past the theater from being confronted with images that they might find offensive, the Court held that the fleeting glimpse they might have to endure before realizing they did not want to continue to look, and hence turning away, was only a minor imposition. To bar those images from all who chose to see them, the Court ruled, would be a severe deprivation of First Amendment rights.[24]

We obviously cannot suppress any expression that any passersby might find objectionable, because that would plainly leave us with no free speech in public at all. As Andrea Dworkin walks through the Times Square area in New York, she no doubt is offended by the displays in front of the many "adult" movie theaters, bookstores, and strip joints—not to mention the billboards advertising underwear, jeans, and other merchandise with gigantic seminude, sexually provocative photographs. Some reproductive freedom and gay rights activists who are walking to the ACLU's national headquarters building, which is in that same general area, might well be offended by the rantings against abortion and homosexuality by a soapbox orator who regularly holds forth a few yards away. Others are probably offended by the incendiary messages of African-American men in the vicinity who regularly inveigh against white and Jewish "devils." And, as public opinion polls demonstrate, increasing numbers of passersby are offended by the written or spoken messages of the poor, jobless, and homeless people in Times Square and elsewhere, who describe their dire straits and ask for money, food, or work.

Rather than denude our public square of the diverse, provocative messages that will inevitably offend some who pass through, we have two other remedies, which accord with both common sense and constitutional law. First, we can simply walk on by, averting our eyes, ears, and attention. Second, we can engage in counterspeech. In sum, when confronted in public with speech we find offensive, we should not shut it up; rather, we should either ignore it or answer back.

Procensorship feminists themselves have vividly demonstrated how effective the counterspeech, or "more speech," approach is. By denouncing the misogynistic messages conveyed by some sexual expression, they have made important contributions toward the goal of countering misogynistic attitudes and behavior. But ironically, an essential element of the procensorship feminists' message is conveyed by their own public displays of sexually explicit work that is graphic, violent, and hateful toward women—examples of the very pornography that they seek to ban. Women Against Pornography has compiled a slide show of such images, and its members lead interested observers on tours of the Times Square area and equivalent "red light districts" in other cities. Similarly, Feminists Fighting Pornography (FFP) maintans tables on sidewalks and in other public areas on which members display what they consider to be particularly horrific, violent, misogynistic pornography.

The irony in the procensorship feminists' graphic public exhibitions, aggressively thrusting before passersby the most outrageous examples of the sexual materials they seek to banish from precisely such public displays (as well as from private consumption), was especially acute during an incident in New York City several years ago. When FFP was ordered to remove its display from Grand Central Terminal, on the ground that such material was "disgusting" to commuters, this antipornography, procensorship group promptly sought the assistance of the New York Civil Liberties Union (NYCLU)! Feminists Fighting Pornography asked the NYCLU to champion its free speech right to display pornography—yet the purpose of the display was to persuade viewers that pornography should not be protected speech! Of course, the NYCLU unhesitatingly (and, it should be noted, successfully) sprang to FFP's defense, consistent with the ACLU's policy of defending any private expression, even that which seeks to "constrain the marketplace of ideas," as long as there is no "governmental complicity."[25]

★      ★      ★

MacDworkinite antipornography laws pose an even greater threat to First Amendment values than do traditional obscenity laws. Accordingly, though the Supreme Court has held that obscenity is not entitled to First Amendment protection, it has held that pornography is entitled to such protection. Before looking further at that 1986 ruling, I will briefly outline the events that led to it—the development and enactment of the MacDworkin antipornography law.

## History of the MacKinnon-Dworkin Model Law

In its initial phase in the late 1970s, the feminist critique of sexist, violent imagery in sexual expression was simply a part of a broader critique of sexist, violent imagery throughout our culture and media. The goal was only to mobilize public opinion to persuade the media to revamp their depictions; the feminist cultural and media critics expressly rejected any legal restrictions on expression. In 1979, Women Against Pornography (WAP) was formed in New York. Although WAP advocated education about and protest against pornography, it specifically disavowed censorship: "We . . . are not carving out any new exceptions to the First Amendment."[26]

By the early 1980s, though, a growing faction of feminists began to focus on pornography to the exclusion of other forms of expression that conveyed sexist or violent images, and also began to call for legal restrictions on it. The so-called sex wars within the feminist movement became more polarized, as women who shared other feminist goals became bitterly divided over the pornography issue. This development was described as follows by Columbia University professor Carole Vance, who from the beginning has been a leader of the anticensorship forces and was a founding member of the Feminist Anti-Censorship Taskforce (FACT):

Initially, most feminists could certainly agree with the contention that pornography was often sexist; but before long it became clear that the claims and characterizations of the antiporn groups and leaders were becoming grandiose and overstated. . . . Sexism in sex, or in its substitute, sexually explicit material, was apparently worse than sexism anywhere else. According to its critics, pornography was now the central engine of women's oppression, the major socializer of men, the chief agent of violence against women.[27]

The increasing focus by some feminists on pornography as the preeminent cause of discrimination and violence against women, and on censorship as the corresponding solution, is no doubt linked to frustrations at setbacks in the women's rights cause that began in the late 1970s. Marcia Pally wrote in *The Nation* in 1985:

Few feminists were prepared for the E.R.A. debacle . . . or for Reaganism, with its . . . social service cutbacks. Pro-choice activists found themselves again fighting battles they thought they'd won; women athletes in colleges lost the equal facilities and funding newly guaranteed under Title IX; pregnant women on public assistance could no longer count on supplemental food allowances. . . . Our despair increased and we became desperate for solutions. . . .

Here "cultural feminism" came into play. A strain of the movement since the early 1970s, cultural feminism holds that there exists a benevolent, nurturant female way of being and an aggressive, conquering male approach to life. . . .

By the time feminist politics began to flag, cultural feminism had laid the ground for a new campaign: get at the source of men's mayhem, attack their sexuality and the culture that forms it. Yet it's hard to organize against something as amorphous as sexuality or culture. A focus was needed, a target, a Bastille. Pornography. The changing names of feminist organizations tell the story. Early on, there was Women Against Violence Against Women; then, later, Women Against Violence and Pornography in the Media; and then Women Against Pornography.[28]

In 1983, Andrea Dworkin and Catharine MacKinnon, who were then teaching at the University of Minnesota, drafted a model antipornography law that was passed by the Minneapolis City Council.[29] Declaring that pornography "is a practice of sex discrimination," the law authorizes civil lawsuits for damages and injunctive relief for four offenses: "trafficking in pornography," "coercion into pornography," "forcing pornography on a person," and "assault or physical attack due to pornography." All four offenses are linked by the common—and hopelessly vague—definition of pornography as "graphic sexually explicit subordination of women through pictures and/or words." The definition also lists eight additional criteria purporting to give further specificity to the central notion of "subordination," but these just compound its inherent, intractable vagueness and subjectiveness:

a. women are presented as dehumanized sexual objects, things or commodities; or
b. women are presented as sexual objects who enjoy humiliation or pain; or
c. women are presented as sexual objects experiencing sexual pleasure in rape, incest, or other sexual assault; or
d. women are presented as sexual objects tied up or cut up or mutilated or bruised or physically hurt; or
e. women are presented in postures or positions of sexual submission, servility, or display; or
f. women's body parts—including but not limited to vaginas, breasts and buttocks—are exhibited such that women are reduced to those parts; or
g. women are presented being penetrated by objects or animals; or
h. women are presented in scenarios of degradation, humiliation, injury, torture, shown as filthy or inferior, bleeding, bruised, or hurt in a context that makes these conditions sexual.[30]

Beyond the model law's pervasive chill—if not deep freeze—of free speech resulting from its ambiguous "definition" of pornography, each of the specific offenses that it creates also raises philosophical, practical, and constitutional problems of its own (as treated in more detail elsewhere in this book).

The prohibition on "coercion into pornography" reflects an all-encompassing concept of coercion, effectively decreeing that no woman may ever volunteer or consent to perform in sexually explicit productions, and thus treating women like children, as discussed in chapter 9.

The prohibition on "forcing pornography on a person" reflects a similarly sweeping concept of force. In addition, as discussed earlier in this chapter, this section of the model law purports to limit sexual expression not only in settings such as "a home" or "a place of employment [or] education," where important privacy and equality rights may limit free speech rights, but also "in any public place," where free expression must receive its maximal protection.

The cause of action for "assault or physical attack due to pornography" effectively makes anyone who participates in producing or distributing a sexually explicit work responsible for any assault that might be committed by any individual who happened to see that work, thus deterring the production or distribution of any sexually oriented materials, while displacing legal and moral responsibility from the actual assailant (as explained in chapter 13).

The section of the law that proscribes "trafficking in pornography" is the most frontal attack on constitutional freedoms, because it essentially makes it illegal "to produce, sell, exhibit, or distribute" the targeted sexual speech, decreeing that it constitutes "discrimination against women." This "trafficking" proscription is essentially old-fashioned, moralistic prior restraint dressed in the modern, progressive garb of a private antidiscrimination action, an "empress's new clothes." It can be enforced by "any woman . . . acting against the subordination of women," as well as "[a]ny man or transsexual who alleges injury by pornography in the way women are injured by it." Behind its rhetorical facade, the law empowers *anyone* to bring a lawsuit to halt *any* production or distribution of sexual materials. Even libraries, including college and university libraries, may be sued under this breathtakingly broad provision, for any "special display presentations."

Laws based on this model have been considered in the following locations throughout the United States: Bellingham, Washington; Cambridge, Massachusetts; Indianapolis, Indiana; Los Angeles County, California; Madison, Wisconsin; the State of Massachusetts; Minneapolis, Minnesota; and Suffolk County, New York. As already noted, in 1992 the Senate Judiciary Committee approved the Pornography Victims' Compensation Act (which died when the full Senate failed to consider it before recessing), and the Canadian Supreme Court has incorporated the Dworkin-MacKinnon concept of pornography into Canadian obscenity law. According to a letter MacKinnon wrote to *The New York Times* in 1994, versions of her antipornography legislation also have been introduced in Germany, the Philippines, and Sweden.[31] In addition, feminist antipornography activists have advocated these laws in Great Britain and New Zealand.

The Minneapolis City Council, the first government body to consider a MacDworkin-style law, adopted it twice in 1983. On both occasions, however, Minneapolis's liberal Democratic mayor Donald Fraser vetoed the law on the ground that it violated the First Amendment. Significantly, Fraser had championed women's rights throughout his distinguished government career, and his wife, Arvonne Fraser, long had been an internationally recognized leader of the women's rights movement. (After serving many years as mayor of Minneapolis, Fraser did not run for reelection in 1993. Shortly after his successor took office, an antipornography feminist issued a call for the city's renewed consideration of the MacDworkin law.)[32]

In 1984 (in an appropriately Orwellian twist), the same law was enacted in Indianapolis with the support of conservative Republican politicians and right-wing groups that had consistently opposed women's rights. One leading supporter, Baptist minister Greg Dixon, had been an official in the Moral Majority. Every Democratic member of the Indianapolis City Council voted against the law, while every Republican member voted for it. This ostensibly feminist law received no support from local feminist groups; the local chapter of the National Organization for Women (NOW) opposed it, while it was endorsed by the prominent antifeminist Phyllis Schlafly. Catharine MacKinnon's closest ally in securing the law's passage was a conservative Republican woman who had been a leader of the Stop ERA movement, former Indianapolis City Council member Beulah Coughenour.[33]

Testifying in support of her antipornography law before the Indianapolis City Council, MacKinnon described Indianapolis as "a place that takes seriously the rights of women and the rights of all people. . . . "[34] This description came as a shock to the Indiana women who had lobbied unsuccessfully for the ERA, as well as to the gay men who had been beaten by Indianapolis police only weeks before MacKinnon's testimony, in an ugly episode that happened to be caught on videotape. Sheila Suess Kennedy, a Republican feminist attorney whom MacKinnon's antipornography ally Coughenour had attacked in a 1980 political race specifically for her pro-ERA and other feminist positions, stated in her written testimony to the council:

> As a woman who has been publicly supportive of equal rights for women, I frankly find it offensive when an attempt to regulate expression is cloaked in the rhetoric of feminism. Many supporters of this proposal have been conspicuously indifferent to previous attempts to gain equal rights for women.[35]

As Kathy Sarris, president of an Indiana lesbian and gay rights organization, asked, "It has not occurred to Mayor Hudnut to put women in leadership positions in city-county government; why is he now so concerned with the subordination of women in pornography?"[36]

These key aspects of the Indianapolis situation—MacKinnon's unholy alliance with opponents of women's rights, and her disregard for both the local political reality and the views of local feminist leaders—presaged what have since become patterns in the feminist antipornography movement. From its support of the 1986 Meese Pornography Commission, which was dominated by right-wing opponents of women's rights, to its support for the 1992 Canadian Supreme Court decision that has wreaked havoc on feminist bookstores and lesbian literature, the feminist pro-censorship movement has repeatedly overlooked the actual concerns of the real women who are most directly affected by its initiatives. These tendencies are at best politically naive and at worst cynically opportunistic.

Less than ninety minutes after the Indianapolis version of the Dworkin-MacKinnon law was signed by Mayor William Hudnut (a conservative Republican who was also a minister), it was challenged in federal court by a coalition of booksellers, publishers, and others involved in creating, distributing, and reading or viewing the types of materials that the law targeted. This coalition argued, and in a case entitled *American Booksellers Association v. Hudnut,*[37] the courts agreed, that the feminist antipornography law violated the First Amendment's free speech guarantee.

### The Courts Call It Censorship

The law was struck down originally by the federal trial court judge in *Hudnut*; her ruling was affirmed by a panel of the U.S. Court of Appeals for the Seventh Circuit; and the U.S. Supreme Court affirmed that ruling. Indeed, the law so plainly violated fundamental free speech principles that the Supreme Court affirmed the Seventh Circuit's holding through a procedure called "summary affirmance," under which the Court did not even receive briefs, hear oral arguments, or issue an opinion.

The Seventh Circuit's ruling stressed that, by singling out only depictions or descriptions that subordinate women, the feminist antipornography law violates the cardinal free speech principle of content or viewpoint neutrality (discussed in chapter 2). In an opinion by Judge Frank Easterbrook, who was a law professor at the University of Chicago before President Ronald Reagan nominated him to the Seventh Circuit, the court explained:

The ordinance discriminates on the ground of the content of the speech. Speech treating women in the approved way—in sexual encounters "premised on equality"—is lawful no matter how sexually explicit. Speech treating women in the disapproved way—as submissive in matters sexual or as enjoying humiliation—is unlawful no matter how significant the literary, artistic, or political qualities of the work taken as a whole. The state may not ordain preferred viewpoints in this way. The Constitution forbids the state to declare one perspective right and silence opponents.[38]

Both the American Civil Liberties Union and the Feminist Anti-Censorship Taskforce (FACT) filed briefs in the *Hudnut* case arguing that the Indianapolis antipornography law violated women's constitutional equality rights, as well as free speech rights. Because the trial and appellate courts invalidated the law on First Amendment grounds, they did not need to address the other issues raised in these briefs. Nevertheless, the opinion of the trial judge—who happened to be a woman, Sara Evans Barker—referred to a defect in the law that was one of the bases for the conclusion by both the ACLU and FACT that it undermined women's equality. Judge Barker observed:

> It ought to be remembered by . . . all . . . who would support such a legislative initiative that, in terms of altering sociological patterns, much as alteration may be necessary and desirable, free speech, rather than being the enemy, is a long-tested and worthy ally. To deny free speech in order to engineer social change in the name of accomplishing a greater good for one sector of our society erodes the freedoms of all and . . . threatens tyranny and injustice for those subjected to the rule of such laws.[39]

Although MacKinnon has decried the *Hudnut* case as "the *Dred Scott* of the women's movement,"[40] referring to the Supreme Court's justly maligned 1856 decision upholding slavery and racial discrimination,[41] *Hudnut* is in fact more like the *Brown v. Board of Education*[42] of the women's movement. Just as *Brown* recognized that racially separate schools are inherently unequal, *Hudnut* recognized that any separate concept of free speech for expression by or about women or sexuality is also inherently unequal.

The Supreme Court's 1986 summary affirmance in the *Hudnut* case seemed to seal the constitutional doom of any attempt to embody the feminist antipornography analysis in law. Following *Hudnut,* a federal court struck down another law based on the MacDworkin model, which had been enacted by voter referendum in Bellingham, Washington, in 1988 and was promptly challenged by the ACLU.[43] Likewise, in 1989, the U.S. Court of Appeals for the Ninth Circuit rejected an argument by Andrea Dworkin (in a lawsuit she had brought against *Hustler* magazine, based on unflattering statements it had published about her) that it should hold pornography to be constitutionally unprotected expression; the court stated that this argument was "contrary to fundamental First Amendment principles."[44]

In the wake of this string of judicial defeats for the feminist procensorship position, the feminist anticensorship advocates relaxed their organized efforts. A 1986 news story about the Supreme Court's ruling in the Indianapolis case quoted New York University law professor Sylvia Law, a founder of FACT and coauthor of FACT's brief in that case, as stating, "It's over. We've won."[45] Indeed, FACT became inactive shortly after this ruling, but reorganized in 1992, in response to the Pornography Victims' Compensation Act and other signs of the resurgence of the feminist procensorship forces, which I discuss in the next chapter; these developments also prompted the 1992 formation of two new feminist anticensorship organizations, Feminists for Free Expression and the National Coalition Against Censorship's Working Group on Women, Censorship and "Pornography."

## Strange Bedfellows Make Gains

Just as the Supreme Court's 1973 abortion rights ruling in *Roe v. Wade*[46] galvanized the antiabortion movement, so the Court's

1986 ruling in the Indianapolis case motivated the feminist antipornography faction. For the time stymied in the courts, the procensorship feminists redoubled their efforts in other forums.

Even during the year of its Supreme Court setback, the MacDworkinite movement was given a second wind when the Meese Pornography Commission co-opted its feminist rhetoric to camouflage the reactionary nature of its report. Following the pattern that had been set in Indianapolis, the feminist anti-pornography faction worked closely with, and provided strategically important support for, the right-wing conservatives and fundamentalist Christians who spearheaded the report.

Feminist opponents of pornography recently have secured new restrictions on sexual speech, even beyond such speech in the traditionally unprotected category of obscenity. Here in the United States, they have persuaded courts, as well as other decision makers, that a wide range of sexually oriented expression may constitutionally be banned from workplaces and campuses, on the pretext of protecting women from sexual harassment.

Buoyed by the acceptance of its doctrine in the Canadian Supreme Court in 1992, the feminist antipornography faction recently has introduced and supported various versions of the Dworkin-MacKinnon law in the U.S. Congress and in state legislatures. Although these laws will be held unconstitutional as long as the Supreme Court continues to adhere to its 1986 ruling in the *Hudnut* (Indianapolis) case, it cannot be taken for granted that the Court will do so, given the appointment of new members and some post-*Hudnut* rulings that indicate an unwillingness to protect sexual speech even outside the traditional obscenity category.[47] Alarmingly, *The New York Times Magazine* reported in 1991 that "a few leading constitutional theorists now predict that, within a decade, [MacKinnon] will have carved out a new exception in constitutional protection of speech."[48]

As a result of the renewed efforts by the feminist-fundamentalist alliance against sexual speech, we recently have witnessed an all-out—and increasingly successful—war on sexually oriented expression, an across-the-board suppression of "sexpression." In the next chapter, we take a closer look at each front in this war.

## CHAPTER 4

# The Growing Suppression
## of "Sexpression"

The Dworkin-MacKinnon approach to pornography enjoys an enormous intuitive appeal to many feminists and liberals, as well as to many conservatives and moderates; it offers political advantages to a wide spectrum of government officials and politicians; it is disproportionately covered, and hence strengthened, by the media; it has dominated many segments of academia, including elite law schools and women's studies programs; and it accordingly exerts a significant impact on public opinion.

It is not surprising that proposals to censor words and images that are claimed to foster discrimination and violence against women would meet with broad acceptance. After all, proposals to censor words and images that are associated with any troubling societal issue are always popular, for they hold out the alluring promise of a cheap "quick fix" for seemingly intractable problems. It also is no wonder that such proposals inevitably meet with broad support among politicians, who then can tell their constituents that they are "doing something" about pressing problems but not causing attendant tax increases.

### Public Perception, Public Permission

We might expect that feminist proposals to suppress pornography would be supported by the many conservative and moderate members of the public who often are enticed by what Marcia Pally has termed "the great soothing appeal of censorship."[1] But it is disturbing that these proposals have been sympathetically received among sectors of the public that traditionally have

resisted calls for censorship, including liberals, the media, and
academia. The reason so many individuals in these groups are
willing to overcome their normal predisposition against censorship in this context no doubt stems from their well-intentioned
desire to support measures that would advance women's rights
and interests, and to be aligned with the feminist movement.
Consequently, the widespread misconception that feminists
generally support censorship of pornography is very influential—and very damaging—among these groups. As writer Anne
Rice has noted:

> I think they're [MacKinnon and Dworkin] absolute fools. If
> two Baptist ministers from Oklahoma came up with their argu-
> ments, they would have been immediately laughed out of the
> public arena. They got away with their nonsensical arguments
> because they were feminists, and because they confused well-
> meaning liberals everywhere.[2]

The media magnification of MacDworkinism has done its
share to perpetuate the misperception that most or all feminists
consider pornography harmful and want it to be censored. A
statement by a female *New York Times* reporter in a 1993 article
is symptomatic. She simply asserted, without explanation, that
"virtually all feminists agree that pornography is detrimental to
women."[3] Yet this statement is patently untrue, as this book
demonstrates.

Also symptomatic is the fact that, while MacKinnon's 1993
book *Only Words* received many critical reviews, most mainstream publications carried reviews either by men or by women
who are not associated with the feminist anticensorship movement. Noted Alice Echols, a women's studies professor and one
of the few anticensorship feminists to write such a review (in
the *Voice Literary Supplement*): "Most reviews of *Only Words* fail to
register that MacKinnon's views on pornography are by no
means gospel among feminists."[4]

The media give disproportionately extensive coverage to the
procensorship faction of feminism. As one commentator wrote
in 1992:

Catharine MacKinnon is on a roll. A cover story [about her] in *The New York Times Sunday Magazine* coincided with the Thomas confirmation debacle. Suddenly she is everywhere, identified as "a national expert on sexual abuse," "a brilliant political strategist," or "the Meese Commission's favorite feminist." Peter Jennings anointed her as "the country's most prominent legal theorist in behalf of women, whose dedication to laws which serve men and women equally has made it better."[5]

The common misperception that MacKinnon, Dworkin, and other leading procensorship feminists speak for women's rights advocates generally has been fueled by their refusal to debate feminist women who disagree with them about pornography. Catharine MacKinnon has said, "I do not allow myself to be used to orchestrate and legitimate a so-called 'debate within feminism' over whether pornography harms women. It is my analysis that that is the pimps' current strategy for legitimizing a slave trade in women. I do not need to be sucked into the pornographers' strategy, period."[6]

Leading feminist anticensorship advocates repeatedly have been invited to participate in such debates, only to have the invitations rescinded because of MacKinnon's and Dworkin's refusal to share the podium with them. By accepting similar invitations when the anticensorship position is presented by men, though, or by traditional First Amendment advocates, the feminist censorship proponents perpetuate the misconception that women and feminists support censorship, with the opposition coming only from men and nonfeminists. The media, as well as other institutions that arrange for speakers, too often abet this strategy by capitulating to the procensorship feminists' dictates about whom they will or will not debate.

This tactic is vividly illustrated by MacKinnon's diametrically different responses to two invitations for debates on the same day in the same city. She was invited to debate me on NBC's *Today* show in New York City on December 20, 1993, but declined. She accepted, however, an invitation for another debate on that very same date, also in New York City, against a male First Amendment champion and opponent of censoring pornography, Floyd Abrams. (Portions of this debate were published in *The New York Times Magazine*.[7])

When MacKinnon refused to debate me on the *Today* show, the show simply tabled its plans to cover the important pornography debate within feminism. Disappointing as that was, it was less disappointing than the decisions that others have made to stage completely one-sided presentations on the issue, showcasing only the procensorship view.

Although MacKinnon does not expressly acknowledge that she has a policy of refusing to debate feminists in the anticensorship camp, her apparent practice has been so consistent that it is now well known; many people simply assume that she would be unwilling to participate in such a debate, and hence do not even seek to arrange one. As noted by *New York Times* legal columnist David Margolick in 1993, "So eager are interviewers and conference organizers to mollify [MacKinnon] that feminists who consider her views censorious and harmful to women have grown used to being unceremoniously dropped from programs at which she is scheduled to appear."[8]

This type of capitulation to MacKinnon's often unspoken, but still widely understood, practice of not sharing the podium with anticensorship feminists apparently afflicted the women judges who organized the 1993 conference of the National Association of Women Judges (NAWJ)—an especially influential audience, and one that should particularly value the exchange of ideas on a legal issue as important as the First Amendment status of sexual expression.

In early 1993, a federal district court judge, on behalf of NAWJ, wrote me a letter inviting me to address the Association's annual convention in November on the pornography issue. I gladly accepted the invitation. When my assistant called several months later to finalize travel plans, though, she was told that I would no longer be needed. This summary disinvitation was hardly the height of professional courtesy, but I attributed it to an administrative error and dismissed the incident from my mind.

It rudely resurfaced in November 1993. At that time, an

ACLU colleague of mine, Deborah Leavy—who knew nothing about my retracted speaking invitation—told me that she had attended the NAWJ convention and that Catharine MacKinnon had addressed it for almost an hour. There was no opposing speaker, and only a few minutes were allowed for audience questions. I suddenly had a very strong hunch as to why my invitation to address the convention had been rescinded, and why that development had been communicated to my assistant with a great deal of embarrassment and apology, but with no explanation.

Although MacKinnon apparently did not tell the women judges who were organizing the convention that she refused to debate me or another anticensorship feminist, they evidently understood this to be her position, and acted on it. One of the judges who organized the conference admitted as much to the *Times*'s David Margolick: "I had heard [MacKinnon] was not very receptive to be with women who disagree with her. The general feeling was that MacKinnon would be less than pleased to be on the program with Strossen, so we had no choice."[9] MacKinnon, in answer to Margolick's question about whether she would have accepted an invitation to debate me or another anticensorship feminist, commented that participating in such debates played into what she called "a pimp strategy to hide behind feminist women."[10] (She elaborated on that "analysis" in the statement I quoted earlier.)

Similarly, when arguing against including anticensorship voices in another discussion of pornography, MacKinnon asked, "When world hunger is discussed, is it necessary to have the pro-hunger side present?"[11]

(Thanks to the intervention of some prominent female judges, who were upset about the 1993 NAWJ incident, I was invited to address the 1994 NAWJ convention. In contrast with MacKinnon's invitation, mine was to debate women with differing viewpoints, something I am always happy to do.)

### One-Sided Legal Forums

Recently, two leading law schools hosted conferences that featured *only* the procensorship perspective in the feminist debate over pornography. In March 1993, the University of Chicago Law School hosted a conference that brought together advocates of censoring pornography and advocates of censoring racist, sexist, and other forms of biased speech, in an effort to forge a common strategy for overturning traditional constitutional protections for both types of expression. The conference attracted a very large and enthusiastic group of participants, including many law students from all over the country. Notwithstanding the conference's relatively neutral, academic title—"Feminist Legal Perspectives on Pornography and Hate Propaganda" (although the term "propaganda," along with the term "pornography," has pronounced negative connotations)—it included only a single feminist perspective on pornography and eschewed rational, academic discourse. As the National Coalition Against Censorship's executive director, Leanne Katz, commented: "Feminists who disagreed were brushed aside and insulted away."[12]

*New York Times* correspondent Isabel Wilkerson, who attended the event, reported that the atmosphere was at times more appropriate for a "revivalist meeting" than an academic conference.[13] Feminists who disagreed with the procensorship perspective were constantly and viciously reviled by speakers throughout the proceedings. One conference attendee, who left reprints of an article criticizing the procensorship feminist position on an information table, was spat upon by conference participants, who ripped up the reprints. Madonna's book *Sex*[14] was also ritually torn to shreds, and speakers trumpeted—to cheering crowds—that no evidence that pornography harms women was needed as a prerequisite for censoring it, since "*we know* it causes harm." A lawyer who works for the ACLU of Illinois, Jane Whicher, likened her attendance at the conference to "combat duty," saying she feared physical violence if other conference participants discovered her ACLU affiliation.[15]

One flier that was produced and distributed to conference

participants by a procensorship feminist group showed a picture of a woman in panties and bra, with nipples clearly visible, who was bound, gagged, and lashed to a chair with multiple straps, her arms pinioned behind her. The caption read: "A free speech message brought to you by the American Civil Liberties Union." Ironically, this flier would fall squarely within the procensorship feminists' conception of proscribable pornography and hence could well be subject to suppression should their own views prevail. Of course, though, the ACLU would defend the conferees' right to produce and distribute this flier (notwithstanding its defamatory nature), should it be challenged under MacDworkinite laws or any others; in that sense, the flier does indeed convey an ACLU free speech message.

As journalist Maureen Dezell noted, the Chicago conference, as the first official gathering of leaders from both the antipornography and the anti–hate speech movements, was widely perceived as "mark[ing] a turning point in the feminist anti-porn movement, increasing its respectibility by dint of its association with scholars" such as University of Chicago law professor Cass Sunstein and Stanford University law professor Charles Lawrence, its being hosted by the prestigious University of Chicago Law School, and its funding from the MacArthur Foundation.[16]

Another conference, held at the University of Michigan Law School during the fall of 1992, further demonstrates the extent to which feminist proponents of censoring sexual expression have silenced those who disagree with them within the legal academy. (For the details of that episode, see chapter 10.)

Just as some feminists' attempts to censor sexually oriented expression have dominated law school conferences, such views have dominated academic law journals in recent years. A survey of all law review articles about the feminist controversy over this issue, which law students conducted under my supervision in 1994, revealed both that a majority of these writings advocated censorship, and that almost all that were written from a feminist viewpoint did so. Because most of the law review literature that refutes the MacKinnon-Dworkin analysis does not do so from an acknowledged feminist perspective, it does not counter the misperception that feminist values necessarily weigh in favor of censoring pornography.[17]

## Strength in Numbers:
## The Feminist–Fundamentalist Axis

The persistent conservative, fundamentalist sentiment in favor of censoring sexually explicit work that propelled the Meese Pornography Commission also has fueled the feminist censorship movement. Traditionalist crusaders against sexual speech such as Jesse Helms, Ed Meese, Phyllis Schlafly, and Donald Wildmon seek on one level to distance themselves from what they describe as "radical feminists," and the procensorship feminists likewise seek distance from such conservatives. Yet these feminists, fundamentalists, and conservatives all reinforce each others' mutual pursuit of largely overlapping goals concerning sexual speech. Underscoring this point, writer Susie Bright calls MacDworkinites "fundamentalist feminists,"[18] and others have aptly labeled them "reactionary" or "right-wing" feminists. Political scientist Jean Bethke Elshtain elaborates:

> Feminist antipornographers vehemently deny any mutual interest with conservative campaigners. In their view . . . conservative groups have the heaviest interest of all in maintaining male dominance. . . . But if, as feminists claim, the explicit intent of pornography is to keep women in a subordinate position . . . it is hard to figure out why "right-wing men" wouldn't . . . favor pornography. . . . Despite disavowals from both sides, the right-wing and radical feminist efforts do converge. The rationales may differ, but the ends sought—the elimination of pornography as defined by each group—are identical.[19]

The mutually reinforcing relationship between the Dworkin-MacKinnon attacks on pornography and those of extreme conservatives undermines women's equality because it strengthens the right wing, with its antifeminist agenda.

The mutuality of interest between "traditional family values" conservatives and antipornography feminists is illustrated by a 1992 campaign against sexual expression. The National Coalition Against Pornography undertook this well-publicized campaign under the slogan "Enough Is Enough." Although the program's leaders were mostly conservative women with ties to such right-wing organizations as Phyllis Schlafly's Eagle Forum and Beverly LaHaye's Concerned Women for America, the group's promotional materials, including billboards throughout the Midwest, prominently featured quotes from Andrea Dworkin.[20]

As feminist anthropologist Carole Vance has shown, right-wing and fundamentalist organizations around the country "have mastered the sound bite that pornography 'degrades women' and contributes to an 'inequality' that they otherwise favor."[21]

The allies in the feminist–fundamentalist axis are united by many substantive, as well as strategic, bonds—most importantly, their use of the stigmatizing term "pornography" to condemn an increasingly broad range of sexual expression, extending far beyond the scope of constitutionally unprotected obscenity to encompass virtually all sexual imagery. As Vance says, "Both groups are skilled in deploying demagogic charges of 'pornography' and mobilizing sex panics in order to eliminate expression, images and perspectives that counter their own agendas."[22]

History shows that when women's rights advocates form alliances with conservatives over an issue such as pornography, prostitution, or temperance, they promote the conservatives' antifeminist goals, relegating women to traditional sexual and gender roles. Historian Judith Walkowitz emphasized this conclusion in her 1980 book *Prostitution and Victorian Society: Women, Class and the State,* which documented the antifeminist impacts of such a misalliance in Victorian England: "As late as 1914, feminists were rediscovering once again that the state 'protection' of young women inevitably led to coercive and repressive measures against those same women."[23] Yet, eighty years later, the procensorship feminists still have not learned this historical lesson.

## Government Assaults on Sexually Explicit Speech

Beginning with the 1980 Reagan election, the conservative
censorship forces have had the necessary political power to
implement their views—and, indirectly, those of their procensorship feminist sister travelers—through increased government efforts to curtail or punish sexually explicit speech. The
climate of hostility to sexual expression—especially any branded
with the inflammatory epithet "pornography"—which the
feminist antipornography movement had played a key role in
creating, was exploited by reactionary right activists and their
representatives in the Reagan and Bush administrations, as well
as in local and state governments around the country. In turn,
their stepped-up assaults on sexual expression contributed to the
recent resurgence of the procensorship feminists.

Because these government assaults were influenced by, and
reflect, the feminist procensorship rhetoric, and because the
targeted works could all be pursued under the capacious
MacDworkinite concept of pornography, these government
attacks provide strong indications of the actual impact that a
MacDworkin-style antipornography law would have if it were
directly adopted. Therefore, it is important to examine them in
some detail. They include both direct law enforcement actions
and indirect government pressures—notably, through the
power of the purse.

The Justice Department's National Obscenity Enforcement
Unit was formed in 1986 in response to the Meese
Commission's call for renewed enforcement of obscenity laws.
This Unit has done lasting, irreparable damage by forcing
many sellers of sexually oriented materials out of business.

The activities of this zealous Justice Department operation
were not widely known prior to the 1991 publication of *Above
the Law: The Justice Department's War against the First Amendment*,[24]
an exposé by the ACLU Arts Censorship Project. That report
documented the unlawful, improper tactics that the Obscenity
Unit deployed in its concerted campaign to drive constitutionally protected sexual expression from the market. Several

courts held that these tactics did indeed violate constitutional guarantees, strongly criticizing the Unit's abuse of prosecutorial powers.

Under the Unit's direction, government agents raided businesses, entrapped previously law-abiding individuals into violating the law, and instituted multiple prosecutions against distributors of sexually oriented work in carefully selected forums where the juries were expected to be less tolerant and the defense to be more expensive and burdensome. Even if the defendants ultimately were likely to win these legal battles on the ground that the targeted material was not constitutionally unprotected obscenity, many could not afford the economic, psychological, and other costs involved in mounting defenses, especially in multiple cases and in courts far from their homes and places of business.

To short-circuit the Unit's harassing law enforcement strategies, distributors of sexually oriented works were forced to enter into settlements that imposed sweeping limitations on their future activities. Under the coercive pressure of avoiding the Unit's heavy-handed prosecutorial tactics, some distributors agreed not to distribute even works that are clearly eligible for constitutional protection, including popular materials such as *Playboy* and *The Joy of Sex*.

Even some law enforcement agents with experience in combating obscenity denounced the extremist goals and tactics of the Obscenity Unit. Robert Marinaro, who ran the FBI's antiobscenity operations, denounced the Unit's leaders as religious zealots who suppressed much constitutionally protected material: "[T]hey became zealots about . . . pornography, and their religious beliefs overstepped good judgment."[25]

The Obscenity Unit's misplaced zealotry fomented an atmosphere in which all sexual expression was suspect, even works by respected artists. One of the best-known victims of this sexual hysteria is the San Francisco-based, internationally renowned photographer Jock Sturges. The *Los Angeles Times* vividly described his nightmarish ordeal at the hands of the Obscenity Unit, which began in 1990, as follows:

The doorbell rings. You open the door. Standing on your front porch are six FBI agents and plainclothes police officers with guns and badges. They force their way into your apartment and begin canvassing the place, observing everything you own. Your address books. Your clothes. The art on your walls. Every page of your personal diaries.[26]

That is what happened to Sturges, whose portraits of nude families appear in the permanent collections of many museums, including the Metropolitan Museum of Art and the Museum of Modern Art in New York, and the Bibliothèque Nationale in Paris. Claiming that photographs of "partially disrobed juveniles" in Sturges's possession might violate child pornography laws, the agents turned his apartment upside down; seized all his photographic prints, negatives, equipment, and business records; and drove off. Moreover, according to Sturges, about six dozen of his clients, friends, and family members across the United States and Europe were telephoned or visited by law enforcement authorities. Agents demanded that art galleries representing Sturges turn over their customer lists.

It took Sturges almost two years to get his property back after a grand jury that the Justice Department had impaneled to investigate his case failed to find evidence that he had committed any crime. Sturges and his associates were made to suffer through this prolonged nightmare simply because he had taken nude photographs of children, many in nudist colonies or on nude beaches in Europe. As indicated by the grand jury's refusal to indict Sturges, the children had not been abused or exploited. Sturges had releases from their parents, and the resulting photographs, characteristic of Sturges's portfolio, were works of art, not "child porn."

Abusive prosecutorial efforts, allegedly directed at child pornography, even resulted in a reversed conviction at the hands of the Rehnquist Supreme Court, despite that Court's strong proprosecutorial leaning and routine affirmances of criminal convictions. The federal government's antipornography tactics went too far even for the Rehnquist Court, which in 1992 held that the U.S. Postal and Customs Services (which worked with the Obscenity Unit) had unconstitutionally "entrapped" a Nebraska farmer, Keith Jacobson, into buying sexually explicit photographs of minors through a concerted campaign to lure him into making the purchase.[27] As the Court ruled, Jacobson had not been "independently predisposed to commit the crime" of buying the photographs. Moreover, there was no evidence that Jacobson had any pedophiliac interests, let alone that he had ever had any sexual contact with minors.

The kind of relentless sting operations that U.S. officials aimed at Jacobson and thousands of other individuals who had never displayed any interest in such materials made the federal government one of the major marketing forces of child porn in the U.S., according to one commentator.[28] Invalidating some of these operations, the U.S. Court of Appeals for the Ninth Circuit noted that the government authorities were seeking to entrap "individuals possessing . . . a broad range of legal sexual and non-sexual interests."[29]

Tragically, these stings led at least five targeted individuals to commit suicide. One was thirty-four-year-old Robert Brase, another Nebraska farmer. There was no evidence that he had ever molested a child. But, after his arrest for receiving a "kid-porn" videotape in the mail, in response to the government's sustained solicitations, Brase parked his pickup truck on a country road and shot himself. He left a widow and two sons.

The court rulings denouncing the Obscenity Unit's overzealous attacks on sexual expression came too late to protect Brase and countless other victims. Given the stigma that is now associated with the term "pornography," the mere charge that someone has produced or distributed an allegedly pornographic work could lead to more unfortunate and tragic consequences—including some individuals being driven out of business and others being driven to commit suicide. If that charge carried with it the threat of a lawsuit for potentially unlimited damages, as under MacDworkinite laws, the resulting fear and pressure would no doubt increase the desperate responses.

Seizing upon the porn panic inspired by Meese and Mac-

Kinnon in recent years, state and local governments also have increased the number of arrests and prosecutions under obscenity laws, protection-of-minor laws, and newly enacted laws designed to impose additional restrictions on sexually oriented expression. In 1992, for example, the legislature in the State of Washington passed a law banning the sale to minors of recordings containing "erotic" lyrics. In our erotophobic era, almost no members of the Washington legislature dared to vote against this sweeping censorial measure, whose vague terms barred minors from purchasing an enormously broad spectrum of vocal music. Dealers who violated the law could be fined up to five hundred dollars and sentenced to six-month jail terms.[30]

Frightening as it is to contemplate the wide-ranging "erotic" lyrics—from country western to opera—that would be off-limits to young people under a law such as Washington's, it is yet more frightening to contemplate the devastating impact on music that might result from the antipornography feminist philosophy. Susan McClary, a musicologist at the University of Minnesota, has described some classical music masterpieces as conveying the sort of sexually violent messages that would run afoul of the Dworkin-MacKinnon model law were they transmitted through words or images. Given that many believe music to be an even more powerful medium in influencing our emotions and impulses, it is not unthinkable that antipornography activists might seek to control it as well. If so, Professor McClary's description of Beethoven's symphonies affords a somber warning of the works that would be embattled:

> Beethoven's symphonies add two other dimensions to the history of style: assaultive pelvic pounding . . . and sexual violence. The point of the recapitulation in the first movement of the Ninth is one of the most horrifying moments in music, as the carefully prepared cadence is frustrated, damming up energy which finally explodes in the throttling, murderous rage of a rapist incapable of attaining release.[31]

In another type of assault on sexual expression by state and local governments, law enforcement authorities have sent out lists of "suspect," purportedly obscene videotapes to video store owners, strongly hinting that they might well face criminal charges if they continued to sell or rent these tapes.[32] In some cases, police and prosecutors had obtained the videotape blacklists from right-wing, fundamentalist organizations. Perhaps because neither the citizens' organizations nor the law enforcement officials wanted to actually look at these allegedly "dirty" videotapes, they seemed to conclude rather casually that the tapes should be off-limits. In a variation on Justice Stewart's famous dictum, "I know it when I see it," these law enforcement officials and their citizen-informants "knew it when they *heard* it"—they claimed to be able to ascertain a work's obscenity from its title!

The flaw in this overly aggressive approach is illustrated by the fact that one of the tapes that was blacklisted in some Ohio communities, *Doing It Debbie's Way,* turned out to be not a sequel to the erotic videotape *Debbie Does Dallas,*[33] but rather an exercise video featuring Debbie Reynolds, icon of traditional, "all-American" femininity.

Feminist antipornography activists might well concur with the right-wing organization that attempted to suppress Debbie Reynolds's exercise videotape, Citizens for Community Values. In a 1987 study, University of Southern California professor Margaret Morse, taking a feminist perspective, criticized many aerobics videos for depicting women as sexual objects and for their allegedly "soft-porn" content. Morse cited heavy breathing; revealing exercise clothing; sexy stares; close-up shots of breasts, legs, and thighs; and "camera action that seems to simulate sexual activity." According to Morse, even Debbie Reynolds's video, which was aimed at the over-forty audience, presented her as a sex object. Under feminist-style antipornography laws, all these tapes could be suppressed as "subordinating" or "degrading" to women. Even the popular exercise tapes of Jane Fonda, a prominent spokeswoman on women's rights issues, might well be vulnerable under the MacDworkin regime. As Morse commented:

> I see poses of Jane Fonda sitting on her buttocks with her legs raised in the air in a V. On the one hand, that looks powerful.

But on the other, it completely immobilizes her and forces her into a submissive posture. The message clearly is, "I'm powerful but I'm still a woman who needs a man."[34]

Some of these attacks on sexual expression have been successfully challenged by the ACLU and others.[35] But they and the many other, similar attacks that they typify still have an ongoing adverse effect on free speech. Many individuals and organizations are unwilling to endure the controversy, let alone the more tangible costs, associated with even a successful resistance to threatened criminal charges or civil sanctions against sexual speech. For each record, video, or book dealer who defends against accusations of handling suppressible sexually oriented materials, there are many others who respond to such accusations—or even the possibility of such accusations—by refraining from handling sexually oriented materials.

The many recent attacks on sexual expression that have been carried out under current law are only a mild foretaste of the wide-ranging assaults that would be launched under feminist-style antipornography laws, given their more open-ended definition of sanctionable sexual speech. Therefore, recent efforts to pass such laws are cause for alarm.

Although the U.S. Congress has not—yet, at least—passed the Pornography Victims' Compensation Act, in 1990 the State of Illinois enacted a similar law.[36] Moreover, other laws based on the MacDworkin model are also being considered in other states and localities. For example, the Massachusetts legislature considered such a law in 1992. Underscoring the infantilizing outlook of all these feminist antipornography laws, the Massachusetts bill was tellingly entitled *An Act to Protect the Civil Rights of Women and Children*.[37]

The feminist procensorhip perspective, blaming books and images for misogynistic violence, also has infiltrated federal and state legislation in more subtle guises. For example, both House and Senate versions of the Violence Against Women Act, which was considered in 1993–1994, originally allocated funds to train state court judges and other personnel about misogynistic violence, including "current information on the impact of pornography on crimes against women, or data on other activities that tend to degrade women"; concerted lobbying by anticensorship feminists led to the deletion of this language from the final law.[38] Similarly, a bill filed in the Oregon legislature in 1993 would impose a 30 percent "sin tax" on sales and rentals of X-rated videos, with proceeds going to rape and child sexual abuse counseling programs. As anticensorship feminists have noted, such bills reflect the unproven—and counterproductive—procensorship feminist assumption that erotic material can be blamed for sexual violence, thereby exonerating the flesh-and-blood men who actually assault women (see chapters 12 and 13).

### Indirect Pressure: The Power of the Purse

In addition to direct threats and prosecutions, the government recently has used funding cutbacks and other limitations on grants from the National Endowment for the Arts (NEA) to curb sexual expression. The procensorship feminists did not explicitly endorse these efforts; nonetheless, their antipornography crusade and their collaboration with the Meese Pornography Commission and other right-wing censorship initiatives had laid the groundwork for the vicious—and in key respects victorious—attack on the hitherto respected NEA.

Of course, no artist has a First Amendment right to government funding, so the government's denial of an NEA grant would not ordinarily implicate constitutional rights. If, though, the government uses its funding policies to exert impermissible pressure on the content of an applicant's work, the courts have rightly recognized that this is unconstitutional censorship. Just as the Supreme Court has been alert to curb other indirect governmental restraints on speech, such as the civil lawsuits discussed in chapter 3, it has said that the government may not use the funding "carrot" to silence certain messages any more than it may use the prior restraint "stick" to achieve such a result.

Obviously, the government has some legitimate concern with the content of artwork for which NEA funding is sought, to the extent that it reasonably seeks to fund only work that has artistic merit. Accordingly, since the NEA's inception, "peer review" panels of recognized artists have made recommendations about which grant applications reflect artistic quality. Such a limited, ideologically neutral consideration of a work's content raises no First Amendment problems.

But if the government seeks to impose limitations on the content of a work that go beyond a politically neutral concern with its artistic quality, and if the government funds only works that conform to some prescribed ideological or moral agenda, it transgresses free speech rights. Specifically, it violates the core First Amendment requirement of content or viewpoint neutrality, discussed in chapter 2. To take an extreme example, the government clearly could not decide to fund only art with a political message supportive of the current administration, or of the party that currently has a congressional majority.

Although the recent restrictions on NEA funding are not so blatantly partisan, they do in fact seek to impose an ideological and moral orthodoxy, deterring sexually oriented works that are not obscene, and therefore are constitutionally protected. The special targets of the new NEA funding restrictions have been artists who explore sexually related themes that challenge "traditional family values"—in particular, themes of homosexuality and of feminism. Several lower federal courts have held that these restrictions violate the First Amendment (the Supreme Court has not yet ruled on this issue).[39]

As with the direct government crackdowns on sexually oriented expression already discussed, these indirect assaults reflect the extensive influence that the procensorship feminists have already exerted. The NEA experience also highlights the types of sexual speech that would be even more endangered should the procensorship feminists' own laws be enacted. The feminist antipornography leaders have neither disavowed the onslaught against the NEA nor supported its many female, feminist victims. As performance artist Holly Hughes, who (with the ACLU's assistance) sued the NEA over an ideologically motivated grant denial, remarked:

> In this, the most censorious period since McCarthy, when the term "pornographer" is being used to silence people as "Communist" was then, I hoped that prominent feminists . . . might protest. . . . Instead there has been a huge deafening silence that I have found not only painful but complicitous.[40]

The attacks on the NEA were spearheaded by North Carolina senator Jesse Helms and by citizens' groups from the far right, including Donald Wildmon's American Family Association and Pat Robertson's Christian Coalition. They targeted grants that supported art concerning mainly homosexual or feminist themes, but any sexual themes or references—indeed, even any nudity—came under suspicion. One lightning rod for the right-wing, fundamentalist NEA bashing was the work of photographer Robert Mapplethorpe. The attacks against Mapplethorpe's work extended not only to explicit homoerotic images but also to works whose sexual connotations were, at most, subtle and implicit, including studies of calla lilies.

The NEA's entire annual budget has always been less than the Pentagon's yearly allotment for military bands, and in 1994, at the level of $170.2 million,[41] it amounted to a trifling two one-hundredths of 1 percent of the national budget, an expenditure of about sixty-five cents per American. Moreover, only a handful of the more than 100,000 grants that the NEA has given have ever raised questions of "decency."[42] Nevertheless, shell-shocked by recent right-wing attacks on a few such grants, Congress has repeatedly subjected the agency to difficult reauthorization struggles and further trimmed its budget. As NEA chair Jane Alexander has noted, the combined impact of congressional cutbacks and inflation made the NEA budget effectively 46 percent lower in 1994 than it had been in 1979.[43]

Despite Alexander's entreaties, in 1994 Congress voted to slash the NEA's budget still further, yet again in response to protests over a grant for a sexually and politically controversial work—this time, a $150 grant that indirectly supported a performance by Ron Athey, a gay, HIV-positive man, whose piece dealt with public anxiety about AIDS.[44] Significantly, the epithet "pornography" was hurled against this disfavored work during the congressional debate about the NEA's budget. Referring to Athey, Representative Robert K. Dornan exclaimed, "I can't comprehend . . . how these porno freaks keep getting this money."[45]

In 1989, Congress further hamstrung the NEA and its grantees (as well as would-be grantees) by imposing unprecedented restrictions on the content of funded art, aiming at certain sexually oriented art. It barred the NEA from supporting any art that it "may consider obscene," including "depictions of . . . homoeroticism." In 1990, Congress attached another unprecedented restriction on NEA funding, requiring all grant applications to be evaluated in light of "general standards of decency and respect for the diverse beliefs and values of the American people." In a 1992 ruling in a case brought by the so-called NEA Four—four performance artists whose grants had been denied (and who were represented by the ACLU, the Center for Constitutional Rights, and the National Campaign for Freedom of Expression)—a federal trial court held that these kinds of restrictions violated the First Amendment. Noting the "close relationship between academic freedom and artistic expression," Judge A. Wallace Tashima commented:

> [T]he fact that the exercise of professional judgment is inescapable in arts funding does not mean that the government has free rein to impose whatever content restrictions it chooses, just as the fact that academic judgment is inescapable in the university does not free public universities of First Amendment scrutiny. The right of artists to challenge conventional wisdom and values is a cornerstone of artistic and academic freedom. . . . [46]

Unfortunately, these controversies are not remote relics of the Reagan-Bush era. While campaigning for the presidency, Bill Clinton said he opposed conditioning NEA grants on criteria unrelated to artistic merit. He vowed to depoliticize the agency; criticized the Bush administration's defense of the vague, open-ended decency standard; and specifically praised Judge Tashima's

First Amendment ruling in the NEA Four case. However, in March of 1993, in a dramatic about-face, the Clinton Justice Department filed a brief asking a federal appellate court to overturn that very ruling. As noted by an attorney for an artist whose NEA grant had been withheld under the decency standard, the Clinton administration's position in the brief is "indistinguishable from the arguments by the Bush administration."[47]

Whether or not the executive branch continues to advocate politically and ideologically driven restrictions on NEA grants, influential members of Congress no doubt will. Even absent future attempts to impose limitations on NEA grantees, the persistent criticism of certain controversial NEA grants in the past has already created a chilly artistic climate that cannot quickly be thawed. Ellen Stewart, founder of the La Mama Experimental Theatre in New York City, told the press that in response to the attacks on the NEA, she had instructed her troupe members "to clean up their acts."[48] In the words of performance artist Karen Finley, one of the NEA Four: "It's the biggest form of censorship, where you question yourself. When people are attacked it stops the creativity from growing."[49]

The sustained attack on sexual content in works for which artists are seeking NEA grants has had a spillover effect far beyond the government funding context. Support from the NEA has served as a seal of approval for art, which in the past had been seen as a "safe" investment or contribution for conservative corporate and individual donors. Accordingly, NEA grants had a catalytic effect, spurring private sector funding of the arts. Now, would-be patrons recognize that art, no matter how dimly or subtly touching on sexual themes, is hardly a noncontroversial object of support.

Just as there is no longer any safe sex, there is no longer any safe art about sex. Artists all over the country are suffering from decreased financial support from the private sector as well as from the government. Judy Blume, whose candid novels about adolescent sexuality have made her beloved among young readers but also one of the most widely banned writers in school and public libraries around the country, made a poignant observation. If she were starting out as a writer today, she said, "I might find it impossible to write honestly about kids in this climate of fear."[50] The tragic overall consequence of this fearful sex panic, in the words of theater director and critic Robert Brustein, is that art in the United States is "inadequately evaluated, published, produced, [and] disseminated."[51]

Art would be even more embattled if the procensorship feminists had their way. For example, the performance art of Karen Finley includes exhibition of her own body and smearing food on herself. Although Finley's performance pieces are angry protests against sexual abuse, violence, and discrimination against women, they could well be regarded as in themselves sexually degrading under the MacDworkin model law. Nor would other, less avant-garde art be any less endangered. Not only would all depictions of women be threatened—recall the protests over Goya's *Nude Maja* and the *Venus de Milo* described in chapter 1—but so would even abstract works, as indicated by the following passage in Marilyn French's 1992 book *The War against Women:* "Visiting galleries and museums (especially the Pompidou Center in Paris) I feel assaulted by twentieth-century abstract sculpture that resembles exaggerated female body parts, mainly breasts."[52]

## Targeting Lesbian and Gay Expression

Almost all of the recent anti-NEA initiatives have targeted works that are by or about gay men, lesbians, and feminists. As Judge Tashima noted in upholding the NEA Four challenge to the "decency" requirement for all funded art, "At least since 1989 . . . the NEA has been the target of congressional critics . . . for funding works . . . that express women's anger over male dominance in the realm of sexuality or which endorse equal legitimacy for homosexual and heterosexual practices."[53]

The actual and threatened NEA cutbacks for art exploring feminist or homoerotic themes demonstrate a major danger of any restrictions on free expression: they will be enforced against the ideas and expressions that are least popular with the community at large and with the political establishment. Unfortunately, in many communities and political bodies, such unpopular themes include feminism and homosexuality.

As this book was going to press, yet another government attack on sexual speech dramatically displayed the usual hallmarks of all such attacks, including the singling out of expression with an unpopular political message and the persecution of gays and lesbians. During the summer of 1994, the City of Cincinnati brought obscenity charges against a gay and lesbian bookstore, the Pink Pyramid, and its owner, manager, and clerk. These individuals, who were arrested and handcuffed, face sentences of up to six months' imprisonment and fines up to $1,000. Their "crime"? They had rented out a video of the film *Salò, 120 Days of Sodom*, by Pier Paolo Pasolini, a world-renowned Italian filmmaker, novelist, and poet. The film's sexual-political subject is the dark aspect of sexuality that had served Italian fascism. In the words of American film critic Peter Bondanella, *Salò* "is a desperate . . . attack against . . . a society dominated by manipulative and sadistic power."[54]

Just as the allegedly obscene video itself had a deeply political message, so too did the charges against those who rented it out. These prosecutions were announced on the opening day of a federal lawsuit (brought by the ACLU and Lambda Legal Defense & Education Fund, Inc.) challenging a referendum that had overturned gay and lesbian civil rights legislation. As the National Coalition Against Censorship commented: "At best, the timing suggests indifference to the possibility that these prosecutions would exacerbate already existing prejudices and intolerance."[55] At worst, given the frivolous nature of obscenity charges based on a film of such indisputably serious value (see chapter 2), the prosecution was a calculated act of harassment. Accordingly, the ACLU filed a brief on behalf of an impressive array of individuals and organizations from the worlds of film, art, and academia, urging the court to dismiss these charges before subjecting the defendants to a pointless and chilling criminal trial. Unfortunately, though, the municipal court judge rejected this argument.

The feminist procensorship movement provides still further tools and tactics that can—and, given our society's persistent homophobia, inevitably will—be seized upon to suppress the already embattled writings and artworks of lesbians and gay men. (This danger, which has been both clear and present in Canada since it adopted the procensorship feminists' concept of pornography, is detailed in chapter 11.)

Although the Dworkin-MacKinnon model law defines pornography as the "sexually explicit subordination of *women* through pictures and/or words" (emphasis added), it expressly stipulates that even images of men could be interpreted as portraying the subordination of women: "The use of men, children, or transsexuals in the place of women . . . is pornography for purposes of this law." Moreover, prominent procensorship feminists have made clear that they view depictions of lesbian and gay sexuality as indistinguishable from heterosexual depictions in their alleged subordination of women (see chapter 8). In a statement that sounds frighteningly similar to some homophobic rhetoric—and is also a wholesale condemnation of all forms of intercourse—Andrea Dworkin has written: "Fucking requires that the male act on one who has less power. . . . [T]he one who is fucked is stigmatized as feminine during the act even when not anatomically female."[56]

Alongside the recently growing suppression of "sexpression" is an attack on sexuality on another front: "sexistence," the sexuality that is part of being alive and human in public, at work, and in school. To fathom this attack, which I describe in chapter 6, you first must understand the antisex attitudes behind it. These attitudes, which Andrea Dworkin has expressed in particularly vivid language, underlie the entire feminist campaign against sexual expression. It is important to air the procensorship feminists' negative views toward sex, which is the purpose of the next chapter, precisely because these views are not as well publicized as the antipornography theory and laws to which they have given rise.

## CHAPTER 5

# Revealing Views of Women, Men, and Sex

Unambiguous conventional heterosexual behavior is the worst betrayal of our common humanity.

ANDREA DWORKIN[1]

The procensorship feminists' effort to extirpate sexually explicit expression that, in their view, perpetuates demeaning stereotypes about women, itself perpetuates such demeaning stereotypes. The most important such subordinating stereotype, which is central to the feminist antipornography movement, is that sex is inherently degrading to women. Of course, this is the very same conclusion that long has been advocated by traditional conservatives and right-wing fundamentalists, although for somewhat different reasons.

To emphasize that the feminist procensorship position rests upon traditional, stereotypical views disapproving sex and denying women's sexuality, many have characterized the procensorship feminists as being antisex, while labeling anticensorship feminists as prosex. The basic contours of these opposing positions are delineated by feminists Lisa Duggan, Nan Hunter, and Carole Vance as follows:

Embedded in [the feminist procensorship] view are several . . . familiar themes: that sex is degrading to women, but not to men; that men are raving beasts; that sex is dangerous for women; that sexuality is male, not female; that women are victims, not sexual actors; that men inflict "it" on women; that penetration is submission; that heterosexual sexuality, rather than the institution of heterosexuality, is sexist. . . . It's ironic that a feminist position on pornography incorporates most of the myths about sexuality that feminism has struggled to displace. . . . [2]

While the procensorship feminists' negative, traditional attitudes toward sex are on one level ironic—as noted by Duggan, Hunter, and Vance—on another level, these attitudes are completely expected. After all, it should not be surprising that advocates of banning sexual expression would view sexuality itself with such suspicion.

### The Antisex Thrust of the Procensorship Position

Intercourse with men as we know them is increasingly impossible. It requires an aborting of creativity and strength, a refusal of responsibility and freedom: a bitter personal death. It means remaining the victim, forever annihilating all self-respect. It means acting out the female role, incorporating the masochism, self-hatred, and passivity which are central to it.

ANDREA DWORKIN[3]

Compare victims' reports of rape with women's reports of sex. They look a lot alike. . . . [T]he major distinction between intercourse (normal) and rape (abnormal) is that the normal happens so often that one cannot get anyone to see anything wrong with it.

CATHARINE MACKINNON[4]

I am inclined to worry that . . . after the feminist revolution, "approved" sex will consist of everyone joining hands and circling round until we all simultaneously fall asleep.

CARLIN MEYER, professor
New York Law School[5]

If I can't dance, I don't want your revolution.

EMMA GOLDMAN[6]

The antisex position of the procensorship feminists essentially posits a mutual inconsistency between a woman's freedom and her participation in sexual relations with men. Both Dworkin and MacKinnon, for example, have argued that, in light of society's pervasive sexism, women cannot freely consent to sexual relations with men. Accordingly, as Cardozo Law School professor Jeanne Schroeder has observed, their analysis of pornography "functions as a critique of sexuality as such, not of violence, violent sex or sexualized violence."[7]

The equation of all heterosexual intercourse and rape, which underlies the feminist antipornography analysis, is articulated in especially dramatic terms in Dworkin's 1987 book *Intercourse*. According to that book, "[I]ntercourse remains a means or the means of physiologically making a woman inferior."[8] The book argues that the physical "invasion" of a woman's body, which is the essential, physiological aspect of heterosexual genital inter-course, inevitably entails the same kind of loss of freedom and subjugation that occurs when the armed forces of one country invade and occupy another: "The political meaning of inter-course for women is the fundamental question of feminism and freedom: can an occupied people—physically occupied inside, internally invaded—be free?"[9]

In *Pornography: Men Possessing Women* (1979), Dworkin states:

> The penis causes pain, but the pain enhances the pleasure. It is as if the ability of the penis to cause pain were an intrinsic qual-ity of the penis, not a use to which the penis is put. . . . As a result, fucking is inherently sadistic because it is necessarily both pain and pleasure; and when penile pain is supplemented by purposeful cruelty, it occasions the highest sexual ecstasy, emotional love, or both.[10]

In her 1988 book *Letters from a War Zone*, Dworkin essentially equates marriage and romance with prostitution and rape, in the following pithy phrases: "One of the differences between marriage and prostitution is that in marriage you only have to make a deal with one man," and "Romance . . . is rape embellished with meaningful looks." Likewise, "Marriage . . . is a legal license to rape" and "In seduction, the rapist bothers to buy a bottle of wine."[11] In Dworkin's novel *Ice and Fire* (1987), she writes: "Coitus is the punishment for the fear of being alone. . . . [C]oitus is the punishment for being a woman: afraid to be alone."[12]

As for those poor benighted women who believe that they actually choose to engage in intercourse with men and that they enjoy doing so, Dworkin has not only pity, but outright contempt. According to Dworkin, women who say they enjoy heterosexual lovemaking are "collaborators, more base in their collaboration than other collaborators have ever been, experiencing pleasure in their own inferiority, calling intercourse freedom."[13]

Catharine MacKinnon's writings offer ample variations on this same antisex theme. According to MacKinnon, feminism "sees sexuality as a social sphere of male power of which forced sex is paradigmatic."[14] Her observations about heterosexual intercourse include the following: "If there is no inequality, no violation, no dominance, no force, there is no sexual arousal";[15] "Women share . . . degradation in intimacy";[16] "[T]hey just want to hurt us, dominate us and control us, and that is fucking us";[17] "To be about to be raped is to be gender female in the process of going about life as usual";[18] rape and intercourse "express the same power relation";[19] "sexuality is itself violating";[20] "[H]eterosexuality . . . institutionalizes male sexual dominance and female sexual submission";[21] "[T]he degradation and violation and domination of women . . . defines the social meaning of female sexuality in societies of sex inequality";[22] "[A] women [*sic*] is . . . one whose sexuality exists for someone else";[23] and "Women's sexuality is, socially, a thing to be stolen, sold, bought, bartered or exchanged by others."[24]

As the foregoing statements indicate, MacKinnon views even nonviolent, consensual sex as inherently degrading to women; it isn't surprising, then, that she apparently considers any depiction of sex—not just images of violent, forced sex—to be oppressive. Indeed, she is at least as eager to suppress images suggesting that women welcome and enjoy sex as images showing women resisting and suffering from it. One of the specific indicia of subordination under the MacDworkin model law is that "women are presented as . . . inviting penetration."[25] MacKinnon has condemned pornography specifically because it shows that women "desire to be fucked."[26] One of the most popular sex manuals in our country, *The Joy of Sex,* which has been suppressed in right-wing antisex campaigns, would clearly be just as vulnerable under a MacDworkinite regime; the book not only shows that women, in MacKinnon's condemnatory phrase, "desire to be fucked," but worse yet, it attempts to stimulate that desire in them.

MacKinnon also echoes Dworkin's thesis that women who believe they voluntarily engage in, and enjoy, heterosexual sex are victims of "false consciousness." She has said that women who believe in their sexual agency are merely denying the "unspeakable humiliation" of having been "cajoled, pressured, tricked, blackmailed, or outright forced into sex."[27] In the same vein, she has written: "Faced with no alternatives, the strategy to acquire self-respect and pride is: I chose it."[28] Denying that women can give meaningful consent to sex, MacKinnon asks: "If you feel that you are going to be raped when you say no, how do you know that you really want . . . sex when you say yes?"[29] According to MacKinnon, women who believe they are free sexual agents are, instead, the dupes of men: "The so-called sexual agency people insult women by assuming that living out a role men have assigned women in sex—the 'wallow in filth' whore as opposed to the 'violate the pure' madonna—amounts to sexual freedom."[30]

The condemnation of sex, or at least heterosexual sex, by Dworkin and MacKinnon is also expressed by other procensorship feminists. Dorchen Leidholdt, a founder of Women Against Pornography, has stated that "under male supremacy . . . women's . . . denigration and abuse *is* sexual pleasure," and that male "sexual pleasure . . . is usually achieved through women's subordination and violation." Likewise, Leidholdt has denounced the "prosexism" among anticensorship feminists as "embrac[ing] pleasure in our degradation and pacifying lies."[31]

Since the pornophobic feminists' negative views of heterosexual sex flow from their critique of pervasive societal sexism, it would seem to follow that heterosexual sex is verboten until that sexism is eliminated. This presents a serious dilemma for those who deplore sexism but not sex. As New York Law School professor Carlin Meyer asked:

> Even if it were desirable, can we eliminate inequality in the realm of the intimate? Can we do so before we eliminate pervasive economic and social inequality? And if not, what do we do in the meantime? Eschew all sex? Heterosex only?[32]

The only "solution" consistent with the antipornography feminists' worldview was aptly summarized by one group of such feminists who participated in a conference at New York University in the early 1980s; the group's acronym, WAS, stood for Women Against Sex. This same "solution" to the challenge of fulfilling female sexuality in a sexist world was offered by Sally Cline's 1993 book *Women, Passion, and Celibacy.* Cline argues that sexual intercourse, and even female orgasm, are essentially forced on women through media manipulation in order to please men. She therefore concludes that genuine female liberation can be found through celibacy. Cline decries women's orgasms as "a form of manipulated emotional labour which women worked at in order to reflect men and to maintain male values." In the same spirit, she disparagingly dismisses sexual intimacy by declaring, "Like militarism today, fur coats the day before, sexual intercourse and general genital thrashing about, are things a woman is expected to purchase—if she can afford the price."[33]

## The Anti-Male Angle
## in the Feminist Procensorship Position

An integral element of the procensorship feminists' hostility toward both heterosexual sex and pornography is their view that men are essentially bestial, like the attack dogs to which MacKinnon has compared them. (In *Only Words,* she argues that showing pornography to men is less like protected speech and "more like saying 'kill' to a trained guard dog, and the training process itself."[34]) For this reason, Katie Roiphe refers to MacDworkinism as the "zookeeper school of feminism—training the beasts to behave within 'acceptable parameters.'"[35]

In this respect, too, the procensorship feminist philosophy is a carbon copy of the right-wing view of sexuality and gender roles. An important theme in sex education materials that the extreme right has been pushing in many public schools around the country is that, by nature, females are nonsexual, whereas males are sexually aggressive and manipulative. When such ideas are touted by conservatives, liberals appropriately denounce them as retrograde sexist stereotypes, but when such ideas are touted by so-called radical feminists, too many liberals do not respond, at best, or acquiesce, at worst.

That men are innately violent, and that they instinctively use sex as an instrument of violence, was repeatedly emphasized in Dworkin's book *Pornography: Men Possessing Women.* Here's one illustrative passage:

> Force—the violence of the male confirming his masculinity—is seen as the essential purpose of the penis, its animating principle as it were. . . . This penis must embody the violence of the male in order for him to be male. Violence is male; the male is the penis. . . . What the penis can do it must do forcibly for a man to be a man.[36]

In *Letters from a War Zone,* Dworkin added to this invective, "For fun they rape us or have other men or sometimes animals, rape us and film the rapes and show the rapes in movie theaters or publish them in magazines."[37] Echoes MacKinnon: "[W]hat men want is: women bound, women battered, women tortured, women humiliated, women degraded . . . women killed."[38]

Ironically, since the feminist antipornography law is written in gender-neutral terms, many of the writings of those who advocate the law would be subject to censorship under it, because of their dehumanizing depictions of men. (As noted in chapter 11, the Canadian version of the MacDworkinite law has in fact been used to suppress feminist works, including nonsexual works, because of their critical views about men.)

### Two Steps Backward

For those who view feminism as an inclusive movement to end all gender-based discrimination and all gender stereotyping, the feminist antipornography movement is doubly distressing: it perpetuates negative, demeaning, disempowering stereotypes of both men and women, and hence deeply damages the cause of gender equality. In the words of the ACLU brief challenging Indianapolis's antipornography law: "A statute that formally equates women with children and men with satyrs is hardly a step toward sexual equality."[39]

In asserting that sex and sexual expression degrade women, procensorship feminists not only repudiate central tenets of 1970s-era feminism, but also revive traditional, patriarchal, subordinating stereotypes that the feminism of the 1970s had in turn sought to repudiate. In this respect, the feminist antipornography movement is a throwback to the archaic stereotypes that underlay nineteenth-century-vintage laws prohibiting "vulgar" or sexually suggestive language from being used in the presence of women and girls, as well as statutes and judicial decisions "protecting" women from exposure to such language in the courtroom by barring them from practicing law or serving on juries. These stereotypes—not pornography—have traditionally been used to subjugate women.

In *The Female Eunuch,* published in 1971, Germaine Greer emphasized that the repression of women's sexuality was integrally bound up with women's second-class political and economic status, and thus that reclaiming women's sexuality was an essential aspect of advancing women's societal status more generally. In words that are at least as relevant today as they were in 1971, Greer powerfully rebutted the antisex feminist position:

> It is often falsely assumed, even by feminists, that sexuality is the enemy of the female who really wants to develop . . . her personality. . . . It was not the insistence on her sex that weakened the American woman student's desire to make something of her education, but the insistence upon a *passive* sexual *role*. In fact, the chief instrument in the deflection and perversion of female energy is the denial of female sexuality for the substitution of femininity or sexlessness.[40]

Learning how to derive greater sexual pleasure in a greater variety of situations was a major theme of the women's movement during the early 1970s, as indicated by the following events of central importance to the then-new second wave of feminism:

- In 1971, the Boston Women's Health Book Collective published the first edition of *Our Bodies, Ourselves,* a guide to women's sexuality and sexual health;
- In 1972, Shere Hite embarked on her study of women's sexuality, sending detailed questionnaires on sexual practices and preferences to thousands of women;
- In 1973, prostitutes formed COYOTE (Call Off Your Old Tired Ethics), an organization advocating the decriminalization of prostitution and seeking to end the stigma attached to working in the sex business;
- In 1974, Betty Dodson self-published *Liberating Masturbation* after five thousand women responded to a notice in *Ms.* magazine offering a booklet on women and masturbation.

At its outset, then, the modern women's movement considered sexual liberation to be an essential aspect of what was then commonly called "women's liberation." Just as feminists then sought to be freed from confining social stereotypes and legal restrictions concerning other aspects of their personal and professional lives, they sought to be freed from limiting, conventional stereotypes concerning their sexuality. Aptly capsulizing the contrast between her prosex, anticensorship perspective and MacDworkinite views, writer Ann Snitow stated: "Ti Grace Atkinson [a procensorship feminist] says, 'I do not know any feminist worthy of that name who, if forced to choose between freedom and sex, would choose sex.' While women are forced to make such a choice we cannot consider ourselves free."[41]

The misogynistic stereotypes to which contemporary procensorship feminists revert, and which they perpetuate, are throwbacks to earlier eras and their archaic, repressive views about women, men, and sexuality. While commentators have aptly compared MacDworkinism to nineteenth-century Victorianism and seventeenth-century Puritanism, Cardozo Law School professor Jeanne Schroeder has unearthed the even deeper historical roots of this contemporary antisex movement. Comparing MacKinnon's writings to those of St. Augustine and other early Christian philosophers, Schroeder observed:

> Catharine MacKinnon is widely considered to be one of the most radical . . . feminist theorists writing today. . . . [T]hat perception is incorrect. In her antipornography analysis, MacKinnon . . . embraces a deeply reactionary theory of the flesh—the very approach to sexuality that has served to underpin American gender roles. What at first blush appears to be a postmodern sociological theory . . . is actually a modern liberal theory of the individual grafted onto a premodern Christian concept of the body. MacKinnon's . . . . analysis devolves into a conservative paean to the potency of masculinity as traditionally conceived.[42]

MacKinnon's views, Schroeder concludes, are "radically traditional."[43] It is not surprising, then, that these theories closely parallel those of contemporary Christian fundamentalists, as mentioned previously. Marcia Pally has noted the substantial overlap between the views of the "Religious Right" and those of procensorship feminists, whom she accordingly labels "right-wing" feminists:

> Both groups propose that ridding society of sexual words and images will reduce rape, incest, and battery. Right-wing feminists would add sexual harassment to the list; religious fundamentalists would add interracial sex, homosexuality, AIDS and feminism.[44]

Just as the procensorship feminist faction views women as inevitably being victims in sexual matters, that faction also perpetuates the stereotype that women are victims in a more general sense. This constitutes a fundamental reorientation from the conception of women that animated feminism in the 1960s and 1970s, when "assertiveness" was the watchword.

As writer Cathy Young has observed, from some perspectives it is considered strategically advantageous to depict women as victims: "Victimhood is powerful. Both feminists and antifeminists see advantages in keeping women down."[45]

On the other hand, though, growing numbers of feminists are recognizing that purveying the view of women as victims can backfire against gender equality. This is the theme, for example, of two 1993 books: Katie Roiphe's *The Morning After: Sex, Fear, and Feminism on Campus,* and Naomi Wolf's *Fire with Fire: The New Female Power and How It Will Change the 21st Century,* in which she criticizes what she calls "victim feminism" and advocates instead "power feminism."[46]

The growing rejection of the victim-centric view of women among many feminists is now being mirrored in some feminist art and fiction, with depictions of women as aggressive avengers against male violence and sexism. Ironically, many of these works could well fall prey to the MacDworkinite antipornography law. Consider, for example, a comic strip from a 1993 issue of an underground feminist magazine called *Frighten the Horses,* described in Wolf's book. Entitled "Penis Envy II," the strip shows a man reading violent erotica until he turns into a gigantic penis that devours women he picks up in bars. After destroying several women, though, the penis-man gets his comeuppance:

he meets a woman who becomes a huge vagina dentata, completely consuming him.[47] Recall that the MacDworkin law prohibits "women's body parts—including . . . vaginas" from being "exhibited such that women are reduced to those parts." The law contains no exception for depictions of women's body parts that, as in this strip, in turn reduce men to *less* than *their* body parts!

The courageous "vagina-woman"—whose sexuality is synonymous with her strength—contrasts dramatically with the procensorship feminists' image of the cowering, cringing female whose sexuality is synonymous with her weakness. The procensorship feminists' archetype of the chronically vulnerable, victimized woman is further perpetuated through their views on sexual harassment, as described in the next chapter.

## CHAPTER 6

# Defining Sexual Harassment

## SEXUALITY DOES NOT EQUAL SEXISM

Although pornophobic feminists have not succeeded in purging pornography from our public sphere, as the Dworkin-MacKinnon model law would do directly, they recently have made significant strides toward that goal through an alternative strategy. They have used the concept of sexual harassment as a Trojan horse for smuggling their views on sexual expression into our law and culture. By influencing the legal and societal understandings of this concept, procensorship feminists have been alarmingly successful in effectively outlawing *all* sexual expression in many sectors of our society, even without any claim that the particular expression is subordinating or degrading.

The serious problem of sexual harassment, and how it should be defined, recently has been at the forefront of public consciousness and public policy. Building on the theory that sexual speech necessarily degrades women, antipornography feminists have argued that it should be deemed sexual harassment and accordingly prohibited, at least in workplaces and on campuses.

This distorted concept of sexual harassment reflects two false assumptions: first, that all sexually oriented expression is gender discriminatory; and second, that all such expression is harassing. The false equation of sexuality and sexism, which lies at the core of the procensorship feminist philosophy, is as dangerous to women's rights as it is to free speech. As discussed in the previous chapter, the notion that women are inherently demeaned by sex and sexual expression reflects archaic, infantilizing stereotypes that long have been used to deny women full equality, not only in employment and education, but also in our society at large.

The second MacDworkinite false equation—of sexual expression and sexual harassment—has unfortunately been widely accepted by employers, employees, campus officials, students, and policy makers, too often without any serious examination. Given the special importance of free expression in an academic setting, this stifling of sex-related speech on campus is particularly frightening.

Even more ominously, as explained later in this chapter, the procensorship feminists have also experienced some success in attempting to leverage their malleable, expansive harassment concept into a general proscription on sexual expression not only in all public spaces, but worse yet, in some private spaces too.

It is not surprising that the concept of sexual harassment has proven a fast-lane vehicle for transporting the feminist anti-pornography analysis into our law, since Catharine MacKinnon has been a leading theorist and activist in both areas. Her 1979 book *Sexual Harassment of Working Women: A Case of Sex Discrimination*[1] is widely credited with having pioneered the notion that sexual harassment constitutes a form of gender-based employment discrimination. She also successfully argued the first sexual harassment case that the Supreme Court decided, in which the Court unanimously adopted this notion.[2]

Our society's recent concern about promoting gender-based equality in education and employment by preventing actual sexual harassment in those settings is commendable. However, in the wake of such widely publicized events as the Anita Hill–Clarence Thomas confrontation and the Tailhook scandal, thoughtful concern too often has degenerated into unthinking overreaction. Too many policy makers and citizens have uncritically accepted the overly expansive MacDworkinite conception of harassment, to the detriment of women's rights as well as free expression.

To date, the procensorship feminists' notion that pornography *is*—not just causes, but *is*, in and of itself—gender-based discrimination,[3] has been universally dismissed by the courts as the hyperbolic rhetoric it is. But, as just noted, the Supreme Court has unanimously accepted the argument that sexual harassment is gender-based discrimination. Therefore, when employers, campus officials, judges, and other policy makers accept the argument that pornography, in turn, *is* sexual harassment—as distressingly many have done—then, in effect, they have accepted the claim that pornography is gender-based discrimination. This is a backdoor way into the procensorship feminist camp. It illustrates the most insidious threat posed by MacDworkinite ideas, to which Katie Roiphe astutely pointed in her 1993 book: "The threat is that MacKinnon's radical premises are absorbed into our culture: her pure, crystalline politics is distilled into other, less strident forms."[4] But only slightly less strident.

Although the Supreme Court has not yet ruled on the burgeoning claims, reflecting the antipornography feminist worldview, that virtually all sexually oriented expression may be deemed proscribable sexual harassment, some lower courts have upheld these claims. Furthermore, many employers and campus officials have accepted and enforced these claims in situations that are not subject to judicial review.

Once again, I want to stress that eliminating gender-based discrimination in employment and education, and promoting equality of opportunity in those important spheres, are critically important goals, and that eliminating sexual harassment is an essential element of these goals. The incorporation of the antipornography feminist analysis into the concept of sexual harassment, however, has severely undermined not only free speech, but also the very gender equality concerns that the procensorship (and anticensorship) feminists seek to advance. The misguided emphasis on sexually oriented expression has diverted the attention of policy makers from *sexist conduct* to *sexual speech,* and has shifted their focus from gender-based discrimination to sexual expression. By presuming that all sexual expression constitutes or leads to gender-based discrimination, this distorted approach also has revived outmoded, confining stereotypes about women's alleged sexual purity and vulnerability that will perpetuate rather than eradicate gender-based discrimination in employment and education.

As Feminists for Free Expression stated in a brief challenging a workplace rule that treated *all* sexually oriented expression as sexual harassment:

> It is ironic that just as women are finally making inroads into such male-exclusive venues as handling a skyscraper construction crane, a hostile corporate takeover attempt, and an Air Force fighter plane, we are being told we cannot handle dirty pictures, and certainly that we would never enjoy them.[5]

In chapter 1, I described some examples of the proliferating situations in which any sexual reference to a woman has been deemed to be proscribable harassment and therefore subject to banishment from work, school, and other settings. Now I will outline the legal standards governing sexual harassment, explain how these standards and actual current practices reflect and perpetuate the feminist antipornography philosophy, and elaborate on the resulting dangers to both free speech and equality.

## The Legal Definition of Sexual Harassment

The concept of sexual harassment has mushroomed—in both its legal elaboration and its practical implications—since the Supreme Court's 1986 ruling on the Indianapolis version of the MacDworkin antipornography law. When the Court issued that decision, it had not yet decided any case concerning sexual harassment. Since then, it has ruled in two such cases—the first in 1986, and the second in 1993.

In 1986, the Supreme Court held that sexual harassment in the workplace violates Title VII of the 1964 Civil Rights Act, which prohibits various types of employment discrimination, including discriminatory "terms" or "conditions" of employment, because of an employee's "sex."[6] The Court endorsed guidelines that the Equal Employment Opportunity Commission (EEOC) had issued in interpreting Title VII, which recognized two types of sexual harassment: first, "quid pro quo" harassment, which occurs when an employment opportunity or benefit is conditioned on an employee's granting sexual favors to a supervisor; and second, "hostile environment" harassment, which occurs when "verbal or physical conduct of a *sexual* nature has the purpose or effect of unreasonably interfering with an individual's job performance or creating an intimidating, hostile or offensive work environment"[7] (emphasis added).

The EEOC's definition of "hostile environment" harassment, consistent with MacKinnon's writings on the subject,[8] targets conduct that is sex*ual* rather than sex*ist*. Yet since Title VII's goal, appropriately, is to protect women from gender-based discrimination, this EEOC focus is misplaced; in legal terminology, it is both "underinclusive" and "overinclusive." It is underinclusive insofar as it does *not* encompass *non*sexual conduct that *is* gender discriminatory. It is overinclusive insofar as it *does* encompass *sexual* conduct that is *not* gender discriminatory.[9]

Discussion and controversy concerning the appropriate scope of prohibited sexual harassment have focused on the "hostile environment" branch of harassment, given its relatively vague, subjective contours. It was this aspect of harassment that the Court revisited in its second decision on the subject, its 1993 ruling in *Harris v. Forklift Systems, Inc.,*[10] in which Justice Sandra Day O'Connor wrote an opinion for a unanimous bench. Specifically, the Court rejected the employer's argument that no conduct could rise to the level of hostile environment harassment unless it caused a demonstrable psychological injury to the employee. The Court likewise rejected the employee's argument that any conduct that she found "offensive" should be deemed hostile environment harassment.

Beyond rejecting these two extreme positions, though, the Court provided scant additional guidance. It said only that, to constitute hostile environment harassment, conduct has to be "severe or pervasive enough" that it would be perceived as abusive or hostile by both a hypothetical "reasonable person" and the actually affected employee.[11] This leaves enormous discretion to the corporate and academic officials who implement harassment policies.

The Court acknowledged in *Harris* that the standard it had adopted was imprecise, and emphasized the necessarily factbound nature of the determination in any particular case:

> [W]hether an environment is "hostile" or "abusive" can be determined only by looking at all the circumstances. These may include the frequency of the discriminatory conduct; its severity; whether it is physically threatening or humiliating, or a mere offensive utterance; and whether it unreasonably interferes with an employee's work performance. . . . [W]hile psychological harm, like any other relevant factor, may be taken into account, no single factor is required.

As Justice Scalia commented in his separate concurring opinion, the Court's unclear standard, "[a]s a practical matter . . . lets virtually unguided juries decide whether sex-related conduct" in the workplace constitutes prohibited sexual harassment. He confessed, however, that he was unable to formulate an alternative, more precise, standard. Accordingly, he endorsed the openended, contextual approach laid out in O'Connor's opinion. I also believe that whether conduct is sexually harassing must be determined on a case-by-case basis, as Justice O'Connor's majority opinion stipulates. Consistent with this approach, Justice Ginsburg suggested a helpful definition of hostile environment harassment in her concurring opinion: "The critical issue . . . is whether members of one sex are exposed to disadvantageous terms or conditions of employment to which members of the other sex are not exposed."

The difficulty of constructing a precise legal definition of sexual harassment is compounded when the alleged harassing behavior consists of expression that would be entitled to First Amendment protection in other contexts. The Supreme Court's two sexual harassment decisions did not discuss such expression. But extrapolating from those cases, as well as from free speech rulings, it is clear that protected expression can be distinguished from proscribable harassment only on an ad hoc basis, turning on all the facts and circumstances of each particular case.

When employees work for a government agency, or when faculty or students are at a public educational institution, their expression is constitutionally protected. In private sector workplaces and campuses, the First Amendment does not literally bar employers and academic officials from regulating expression.* Nevertheless, consistent with our society's general commitment to First Amendment values, employers and campus officials should respect free expression even in the private sector. Given the importance of free speech and academic freedom in any educational setting, many experts and groups of experts, including the American Association of University Professors, persuasively argue that the First Amendment should be honored in spirit on all campuses, even if it is not literally binding. Likewise, given the central role that work plays in the lives of so many Americans, advocates of workers' rights, including the American Civil Liberties Union, maintain that all employees should enjoy freedom of expression while at work, as long as that expression does not substantially interfere with workplace operations. In any event, when private employers or campus officials adopt censorial policies to comply with anti-discrimination laws, then such government-mandated policies should be subject to First Amendment constraints.

## The Practical Definition of Sexual Harassment

The process of distinguishing workplace or campus expression that constitutes punishable sexual harassment from workplace or campus expression that constitutes protected free speech—

---

*The First Amendment provides that "Congress shall make no law . . . abridging the freedom of speech. . . . " Although the Supreme Court has interpreted this language to bar any action by the government (or with significant government involvement) that infringes on free speech—not just congressional enactments—the Court has never extended this provision to nongovernment actions.

parallel to the process of defining hostile environment sexual harassment generally—turns on no precise, generally applicable formula; rather, it requires a fact-specific examination of each particular situation. In some cases it might be difficult to draw this line, so that even two individuals who are equally committed to both free speech and gender equality might well disagree about the proper outcome. For purposes of the present discussion, though, it is not necessary to address such potentially problematic situations, because so many employers, universities, courts, and other policy makers have drawn the line far beyond any legitimately proscribable harassment—and thus have egregiously violated not only free speech principles but also equality principles.

The many sexual harassment rules in place in America today that have too broadly condemned sexual expression have done so because they have not complied with the Court's essential requirement, sensibly emphasized in its unanimous 1993 *Harris* decision, that *any* expression or conduct must be evaluated in its overall context. Too many rules have treated sexually oriented expression in an acontextual fashion, concluding that, no matter what the surrounding facts and circumstances, such expression automatically constitutes sexual harassment. Worse yet, some lower courts have endorsed this approach.

Sexual expression—along with all other expression or conduct—might well constitute sexual harassment, *if*—but only if—it is used in a certain way. A case entitled *Robinson v. Jacksonville Shipyards, Inc.*[12] makes this point. In that case, there was some evidence that male coworkers had forced sexually explicit photographs upon a female welder, Lois Robinson, in situations designed to make it more difficult for her to work, with apparent gender-discriminatory intent.

For example, a picture of a nude woman, with her knees drawn up to her chest and exposing her genitals, was left on a toolbox where Robinson had to return her tools. Several male coworkers were present when she did so and laughed at her when she became visibly upset by the picture. Similarly, one of Robinson's coworkers waved around a picture of a nude woman with long blond hair holding a whip, in an enclosed area where he and Robinson were working with about five other men. Robinson said she felt particularly targeted by this action, because she has long blond hair and worked with a welding tool known as a "whip."

The foregoing treatment was appropriately deemed sexual harassment. But Robinson's complaint, as well as the federal trial judge's order, went much further. Robinson sought, and the judge issued, a total ban on *all* "sexually suggestive" pictures, regardless of how they were used. Thus, the court banished from the workplace not only the sexually oriented images that some employees used to harass Lois Robinson, but also sexually oriented images that employees used for their own private enjoyment, in places and at times that interfered with neither their own work nor that of any coworkers. Under the court's sweeping order, no employees could bring any sexually suggestive pictures to work, even if they only kept the pictures in their own lockers, or discreetly looked at them during their lunch breaks, without showing them to any other employees.

The *Robinson* judge's expansive definition of proscribed images included any picture of a woman "who is not fully clothed or in clothes that are not suited to . . . routine work in and around the shipyard and who is posed for the obvious purpose of . . . drawing attention to private portions of . . . her body."[13] The appellate brief that the ACLU filed in the *Robinson* case in 1992, challenging the trial judge's overbroad purge of sexually oriented expression, noted that this prohibition could well encompass fashion magazines, family photographs, and classic works of art. Defenders of the *Robinson* order pooh-poohed these fears as speculative. But they proved sadly prophetic in 1993, when officials of the University of Nebraska at Lincoln ordered a graduate teaching assistant to remove from his desktop a photograph of his wife in a bathing suit. They claimed that this photo constituted hostile environment sexual harassment of female faculty, students, and staff.[14] Although overbroad, the *Robinson* order at least was predicated on the court's conclusions that there had been some intentionally harassing acts, and that there was a pervasively gender-discriminatory atmosphere, in the Jacksonville Shipyards; in contrast, neither factor was found to be present in the University of Nebraska situation.

Because the *Robinson* case was settled while on appeal, the Supreme Court will not rule on it. Nor has the Court ruled on any other case involving similar facts. Therefore, we do not know whether the Court would accept the procensorship feminists' equation of sexual expression and sexual harassment. In any event, this false equation has inspired rules in many workplaces and campuses that are not subject to judicial review, because there are no legally enforceable free speech rights on many campuses and most workplaces. As previously pointed out, the First Amendment protects speech only from government-imposed restrictions. While some employees are covered by collective bargaining agreements negotiated by their unions that may extend some protection to their expression, only a small and shrinking percentage of America's workforce is in this category. Though most private employers and universities have no legal obligation to respect the free speech rights of their employees, faculty, or students, they do have legal obligations to protect these individuals from sexual harassment under civil rights laws. Employers and campus officials thus have legal and practical incentives to err in favor of overbroadly defining sexual harassment and overzealously enforcing antiharassment policies, rather than the opposite. (As I noted above, speech-restricting harassment policies that are adopted in order to comply with antidiscrimination laws could fairly be viewed as government-imposed and hence subject to First Amendment challenge. As of this writing, though, I am unaware of any such challenge.)

As Nat Hentoff remarked when Penn State officials removed a reproduction of Goya's *Nude Maja* from a classroom in response to professor Nancy Stumhofer's complaint (as recounted in chapter 1), "It was either Goya or Stumhofer. And Title VII does not protect dead Spanish painters."[15] Ironically, shortly after this incident, and as a direct result of it, Professor

Stumhofer herself was accused of sexual harassment because of the false equation between sexual expression and harassment. Here's her own account of what happened:

> In an effort to explain some nontraditional ways of seeing art to the faculty . . . I distributed a portion of John Berger's book *Ways of Seeing,* and invited people to read the article and discuss it with me. . . . Berger looks at representations of the female figure as the eternal object of the male gaze, and shows various paintings of naked or nude females. My attempts to increase people's awareness of how women are represented in art had an unexpected result. Two men on campus—one faculty member and one maintenance person—filed a complaint of sexual harassment with the Affirmative Action Office. They claimed I was harassing them with pictures of nude women.[16]

Referring to the burgeoning attacks on campus art inspired by MacDworkinite perspectives, Marjorie Heins, director of the ACLU's Arts Censorship Project, has said: "Students are increasingly seduced by these code-word excuses. There's a tendency to describe anything you don't like in a work of art as sexual harassment, so that it becomes a civil rights violation."[17]

The all-purpose epithet "pornography" has been joined by a functional synonym, "sexual harassment," to stigmatize, and hence suppress, seemingly any expression that even hints at sexual themes. This decontextualized, demonized approach to art and expression betrays a fundamental misunderstanding of images and words. As Columbia University professor Carole Vance has noted:

> [T]he idea that an image per se is harassing . . . is totally incompatible with how we normally think about images. Context matters, so does interpretive frame, and viewers differ in how they interpret an image. If the question is posed as, Which images are sexually harassing? half of an important question has already been ceded to those who have a reductionist, simplified view of art and culture.[18]

A growing body of sexual harassment rules are expressly barring much, if not all, sexual expression from workplaces and campuses, even when such expression is not targeted at, or even seen by, any objecting female employees, students, or faculty members. Many workplaces have now been declared off-limits for materials with any sexual content. In 1992 the Los Angeles County Fire Department issued a sweeping sexual harassment policy that bans all "sexually-oriented magazines, particularly those containing nude pictures . . . posters or calendars which display nudity or are overtly sexual, [and] . . . [a]ll other material . . . of a clear sexual connotation"[19] from the entire workplace, including dormitories, restrooms, and lockers. All firefighters are forbidden to read these materials or even just to bring them to the firehouse. Similarly, the Ventura County Fire Department in California has banned the Playboy Channel at fire stations.

These total bans on sexual speech are especially onerous for firefighters, whose workplace functionally doubles as a home for long periods. Firefighters, for all intents and purposes, often live at their stations, serving many round-the-clock shifts each month, and regularly staying there for several days in a row. They have individual rooms or privately partitioned sleeping quarters in the dormitory section of the firehouse, and unless there is an emergency, are considered to be on "personal time" after the normal working day.

Given the extent to which the firehouse serves as their "home away from home," to forbid firefighters from looking at certain materials there, when they are on personal time and in their private quarters, is tantamount to prohibiting them from enjoying these materials alone in the privacy of their homes. As former justice Thurgood Marshall wrote in a Supreme Court opinion upholding the right to read or view obscene materials in one's home, "If the First Amendment means anything, it means that the State has no business telling a man, sitting alone in his own house, what books he may read or what films he may watch."[20] Accordingly, on behalf of Captain Steven W. Johnson, the ACLU challenged the Los Angeles County Fire Department's sweeping restraints as violating the firefighters' rights of free speech and privacy.

In June 1994, the trial court held that the rules were unconstitutional,[21] and Los Angeles officials subsequently adopted a policy acceptable to Johnson and the ACLU. The Johnson/ACLU position was supported by Feminists for Free Expression, which has emphasized that the mere possession of any materials, including sexually oriented materials, should never be deemed sexual harassment unless, at the very least, such expression was intended to discriminate. The Feminists for Free Expression brief, written by Cathy Crosson, also made the important point that overly broad sexual harassment rules undermine privacy principles that are pillars of the women's rights cause, with no countervailing gain for that cause:

> This case critically implicates the privacy rights which have been a fountainhead of protections for women's sexual and reproductive freedom. Without the privacy doctrine . . . women's access to abortion and contraceptives today could be dramatically curtailed at the whim of local legislators. . . . The [Los Angeles Fire Department] rules are entirely antithetical to this line of cases so crucial to women's interests, because they assail the basic premise that government has no business intruding into one's bedroom and into intimate personal decisions such as the choice to read or view sexual materials. . . . The defense of [privacy] rights should be high on the feminist agenda; the notion that women should be willing to trade them away for empty gestures like these repressive workplace rules is pure folly.[22]

Employers' moves toward broadly banning sexual expression as sexual harassment have been matched by similar moves on campuses. Author and Princeton graduate student Katie Roiphe reports, "Like most common definitions Princeton's definition of sexual harassment includes 'leering and ogling, whistling, sexual innuendo, and other suggestive or offensive or derogatory comments, humor and jokes about sex.'" Likewise, an American College Health Association pamphlet characterizes "unwanted sexual comments, jokes or gestures" as "a form of sexual assault."[23] As previously noted, these types of behavior could be deemed sexually harassing if they were part of a sufficiently severe or pervasive pattern of conduct, but isolated incidents of such behavior should not be considered sexual harassment.

In its 1993 statement on "Sexual Harassment and Academic Freedom," the National Association of Scholars (NAS), while recognizing that sexual harassment "constitutes a serious violation of an educator's responsibilities and is morally wrong," also warns that "[t]oo many [higher educational] institutions have adopted vague definitions of harassment that may all too easily be applied to attitudes or even to a scholar's professional views," thus inducing "a chill . . . on academic discussions of sensitive but legitimate topics, such as human sexuality, sex differences, and sexual roles." For example, the NAS statement points out that the University of Minnesota's official definition of sexual harassment provides that it "often consists of a callous insensitivity to the experience of women."[24]

The notion that sexual harassment extends to all manner of expression with any sexual connotation has reached the high school and grade school levels, too. In collaboration with the National Organization for Women's Legal Defense and Education Fund, researchers at Wellesley College's Center for Research on Women designed a survey on sexual harassment in schools, which included within the definition of sexual harassment student-to-student sexual "comments" or "gestures." In the same vein, the State of Minnesota recently adopted guidelines defining the student-to-student conduct that will be deemed sexual harassment. Students from kindergarten onward may now face expulsion for virtually every imaginable expression with any iota of sexual connotation or innuendo, including: "students 'rating' other students"; "sexually descriptive notes and letters"; "dirty jokes"; "spreading sexual rumors about other students"; "teasing students about their sexual activities or lack of sexual activity"; "students giving other students the finger"; and "displays of affection between students."[25]

## The Expanding Definition of Sexual Harassment

Sweeping as the foregoing rules are in banning sexual expression from employment or educational settings, an even more capacious concept of sexual harassment is emerging that would make sexual expression unavailable to members of the general public. The charge has been made in both the United States and Canada that the sale of sexually oriented magazines such as *Playboy, Penthouse,* and *Playgirl* constitutes sexual harassment of female employees and customers. Such complaints have been leveled against a variety of outlets, including convenience stores and campus bookstores.

Since 1985, the Ontario Human Rights Commission has been investigating claims by antipornography feminists that the availability of such magazines in any stores other than "adult" bookstores creates an environment that is "hostile and discriminatory against women."[26] The complainants were not satisfied by the fact that, in accordance with local laws, all erotic magazines are displayed unobtrusively, behind opaque barriers that reveal little more than titles.

Similarly, in 1991, when Dolores Stanley was promoted to manager of the Ohio Dairy Mart C-Store where she worked, she yanked copies of *Playboy* and other adult magazines, even though they were covered in sleeves and concealed behind counters. Although Dairy Mart offered Stanley a job at the same pay in a store that did not sell these magazines, she sued for the "right" to run a "pornography-free store."[27] Stanley's objections to sexually oriented magazines were based on her Christian beliefs; other employees might well make the same claim based on their adherence to MacDworkinism. Indeed, MacKinnon served as a consultant to Stanley's counsel, the American Center for Law and Justice, which was founded by Pat Robertson. For instance, in 1992, with the support of antipornography feminists, some female students at Carleton College filed a complaint under the college's sexual harassment code against the campus bookstore because of its sale of sexually oriented magazines.[28]

If complaints of this sort prevail, sexually explicit material will be available only in specialty, "adult" stores. This development would not only make sexual material much less accessible to many would-be purchasers, but it also would allow the sex police to operate more effectively—there would be just a few retailers in any given locale for them to harass.

Procensorship feminist theories have engendered efforts to ban sexually oriented expression from the entire spectrum of public places—including the streets, sidewalks, and parks that the Supreme Court has deemed "traditional public forums" where free speech should be especially safe.[29]

In 1991, a waitress at Bette's Oceanview Diner in Berkeley, California, refused to serve a journalist who was reading an article in *Playboy* magazine on the ground that this constituted "sexual harassment in the workplace and a threat to women's self-esteem," hence violating Title VII of the 1964 Civil Rights Act. Ironically, the article he happened to be reading was about the Bill of Rights.[30] Suppose a customer had been reading a newsletter from the National Organization for Women or from Planned Parenthood, and the waitress was a Catholic who believed that abortion is murder. Should she be permitted to deny service to the customer on the ground that this reading material constituted religious harassment, in violation of Title VII's prohibition on religious discrimination in employment? The 1964 Civil Rights Act barred discrimination not only in employment, but also in access to public accommodations.[31] What a setback that this Act should be invoked to deny equal access to public accommodations!

Harassment rules such as those adopted by the Los Angeles and Ventura County Fire Departments essentially assume that free speech need not be protected in workplaces. As previously noted, though, employees should indeed have free speech rights at work. Moreover, the Bette's Oceanview Diner scenario raises an additional reason for protecting expression in workplaces, even beyond a concern for employee free speech: one person's workplace is another person's public accommodation. And in the case of streets, sidewalks, and parks, one person's workplace may be another person's traditional "public forum," where free speech receives the greatest protection. As Cathy Crosson explained in the Feminists for Free Expression brief in the Los Angeles firefighters case:

> [T]he argument that the workplace can be simply excised from free speech protection ignores the reality that *every conceivable location* constitutes the workplace for some group of workers. . . . [E]ven these quintessential public fora [streets and parks] are workplaces for maintenance crews, garbage collectors, postal carriers, and an endless array of other employees. These workers surely have an equal claim to protection from a "hostile work environment." . . . In short, we cannot afford to exclude so pervasive a realm of life as the workplace from First Amendment protection, without rendering free speech a nullity.[32]

Crosson's warnings are realistic. As journalist Mark Schapiro reported in 1994, "In more than a dozen recent cases, allegations of sexual harassment have been used to force removal of artwork from classrooms, municipal buildings, and public art galleries."[33] To add insult to injury, some of these incidents have involved works by women artists and with feminist themes.

One such victim of this misconceived notion of sexual harassment was Brazilian artist Zoravia Bettiol, an outspoken proponent of artistic freedom under that country's former military dictatorship. How sad that her artistic freedom has now been stifled by government officials right here in the United States! In 1993, the Menlo Park, California, City Hall presented an exhibit of Bettiol's woodcuts that featured Greek gods and goddesses and scenes from *Romeo and Juliet*. City officials abruptly terminated the exhibit a few weeks after it opened in response to a female worker's complaint that the nude bodies portrayed in some of these works made her feel "violated." Alluding to the liberal bent of the Menlo Park area, an editorial in the conservative *Washington Times* offered the following sarcastic, but sobering, comment:

> [O]ne wonders what would have happened had [the employee's] protest been made on the grounds of public decency? The response would no doubt have been very different. Now, if

someone could please make a case that the "performance art" of [lesbian and feminist artists] Holly Hughes and Karen Finley are a form of sexual harassment, too.[34]

Alas, Hughes's and Finley's work, as well as much other art, *will* apparently be off-limits in the public spaces of Menlo Park from now on. In the wake of the Bettiol imbroglio, Menlo Park City Attorney William McClure said that in the future the city planned to display only "pleasant, non-controversial art," such as "landscapes, holiday pictures, and children's handiwork."[35]

The campus sexual harassment codes that expansively prohibit sexual "looks" and "gestures" would also be extended to public streets and sidewalks if the feminist antipornography activists and their supporters have their way. In an article published in the prestigious *Harvard Law Review* in 1993, Northwestern University law professor Cynthia Grant Bowman urged cities to pass ordinances that would treat sexual harassment on public streets as a misdemeanor, punishable by a fine of up to $250.[36] Her proposed ordinance sweepingly defines punishable harassment as any intrusion upon a woman's attention "in a manner that is unwelcome to [her] with language or action that is explicitly or implicitly sexual." It proscribes "wolf-whistles, sucking noises and catcalls," as well as comments that range from "Hello baby" to "vulgar" suggestions. Bowman's idea has been incorporated into a proposed sexual harassment bill that California state senator Tom Hayden has sponsored in the California legislature. He commented that her proposal was "on the cutting edge of a problem that needs to be addressed."[37]

The notion that *all* expressions, looks, or gestures that recognize a woman's sexuality are somehow antithetical to her personhood and equality, is *itself* inconsistent with personhood and equality. Surely men can be *sexual* beings at the same time that they are *human* beings with other attributes and potentialities. Why not women too? Marcia Pally, founder and president of Feminists for Free Expression, refutes the notion that viewing women as "sexual objects" necessarily undermines their full humanity:

As a political condition, objectification is a frightful state. . . . In the realms of art, games, and sex, objectification is one of life's charms. . . . At times, one wants to be appreciated for all one's aspects by those who know one thoroughly. At times, one wants to be desired by total strangers, to grab the attention of a room. . . . Without the distinction between the worlds of money and power and those of art, games, and sex, image-blamers will deny women the thrill of admiration in a bogus bargain for safety. Women will deny themselves admiration in a mistaken ploy for respect. . . . One wants to be the author of one's life, its subject, but one also wants to be the object of irrepressible lust. . . . It cannot be the goal of feminism to eliminate moments during the day when a heterosexual man considers a woman . . . to be sexually desirable. Feminism seeks to expand the roles accessible to women, including the role of voyeur and sexual subject.[38]

## Beyond Victorian Views

The growing presumption that a woman is demeaned or harassed by any sexual reference to her, or in her presence, hardly advances women's rights. To the contrary, it has the opposite effect, for three important reasons. First, when women, employers, or campus officials cry "sexual harassment!" at any passing reference to sex, they trivialize the issue, make it a laughingstock, and deflect attention and resources from the serious ongoing problems of gender discrimination in employment and education, including the many instances of quid pro quo harassment and the many instances of intentionally discriminatory, targeted, and persistent sexist conduct, which clearly give rise to legitimate claims of hostile environment harassment.

Second, and more fundamentally, the accelerating presumption that the mere presence of sexual words or pictures in the workplace or on campus is somehow inherently incompatible with women's full and equal participation in those arenas, resurrects the very traditional, and very disempowering, notion that sex is intrinsically demeaning to women.

Under this same rationale, nineteenth-century state laws prohibited "vulgar" and sexually suggestive language from being used in the presence of women; women, along with children, were deemed too fragile to be subjected to such language. Indeed, some of these laws relegated women to a status even below male children. Until recently, a South Carolina state law prohibited "any obscene, profane, indecent, vulgar, suggestive or immoral message" that was addressed to a "woman or woman child." At the behest of women's rights activists, in 1993 the South Carolina Supreme Court ruled:

> Statutes . . . that distinguish between males and females based on "old notions" such as a belief that females should be afforded special protection from "rough talk" because of their perceived "special sensitivities" can no longer withstand equal protection scrutiny.[39]

Likewise, in 1991, in a suit brought by the ACLU, a Michigan judge struck down that state's sixty-year-old law prohibiting the use of "indecent, immoral, obscene, vulgar or insulting language" in the presence of women or children. While the judge held that the law unconstitutionally infringed on free speech, Susan Fall, the ACLU attorney who challenged the law, noted that it was also a "discriminatory, paternalistic approach to protecting women."[40] Once again, suppression of sexual expression retarded, rather than advanced, gender equality.

Nineteenth- and early-twentieth-century judicial rulings— previous incarnations of the procensorship feminists' current view that women need to be protected from sexually oriented language—asserted that, in the words of former Supreme Court justice Joseph Bradley, women's "natural and proper timidity and delicacy" not only disabled them from entering into contracts, but also made them unfit "for many of the occupations of civil life."[41] In ruling that states could bar women from practicing law or serving on juries, for example, judges expressly cited the need to "protect" women from vulgar or sexual language. As recently as 1949, the Arkansas Supreme Court rejected a challenge to a statute that allowed women to serve on juries only if they specifically volunteered, on the ground that "[c]riminal court trials often involve testimony of the foulest kind, and . . . the use of filthy and loathsome words, references to intimate sex relationships, and other elements that would prove . . . degrading to a lady."[42]

Now procensorship feminists seem determined to reinstate such misguided protectionism through an overly expansive concept of sexual harassment. As Wayne State University law professor Kingsley Browne has commented: "The assumption that women as a group may be more offended by profanity than men as a group seems like just the sort of stereotype that Title VII was intended to erase."[43]

Third, procensorship feminists' concepts of sexual harassment subvert women's rights by making it harder for women to get jobs and to succeed in those jobs. The antipornography feminists seek to protect women from the rigors of the marketplace of ideas; numerous laws enacted during the nineteenth and early twentieth centuries sought to protect women from the rigors of the economic marketplace by limiting their hours and days of work, and the tasks that they would be allowed to perform on the job. Upholding one such piece of legislation, a 1908 Supreme Court decision compared women to children in their purported need for special government protection.[44] As a later Supreme Court recognized, though, in a 1973 decision that struck down a law reflecting such gender-based, ultimately incapacitating stereotypes, these allegedly protective laws "reflected an attitude of romantic paternalism that put women not on a pedestal, but in a cage."[45] (Ruth Bader Ginsburg, then director of the ACLU Women's Rights Project, successfully argued this case.)

Any doctrine resting upon the incomparability of women and men cannot be confined to circumstances that may at first appear "beneficial" to women; the principle can always then be used to "justify" denying rights to women. By invoking women's special reproductive role, some employers have excluded women from high-paying jobs that involve exposure to certain substances that might impair their potential fetuses, even if the women do not intend to have children, and even though there is evidence that these substances could damage the male reproductive functions as well.

In occupations and professions that depend heavily on mentor relationships, women are being penalized, since the men who predominate in the upper echelons are deterred from mentoring them by exaggerated concepts of sexual harassment; on campus, many female students say they are especially hard-hit by this problem. I know from my own involvement in professional legal organizations that many female lawyers believe that, because of hyperbolic harassment charges, they are being denied travel, social, and other opportunities for informal interaction with male partners and clients that would help them to rise to leadership positions at their firms.

Pittsburgh restaurateur Sarah J. McCarthy has said that the overly broad concept of sexual harassment as all speech with sexual connotations has made even her, an avowed feminist, "fearful of hiring women." Speaking both as the owner of a restaurant and bar who makes many hiring decisions, and as a longtime women's rights advocate, McCarthy berated proponents of the MacDworkinite sexual harassment concept:

> You do women a disservice. . . . You have made us ladies again.
> . . . [Y]ou are frightening managers into hiring men over women. . . . You have installed a double pane of glass on the glass ceiling. . . . Men and women who wanted to work shoulder to shoulder with you are now looking over their shoulders. You have made women into china dolls. . . . We women are not as delicate and powerless as you think. We do not want victim status in the workplace. Don't try to foist it on us.[46]

As the preceding discussion makes clear, in recent years the feminist procensorship faction has enjoyed growing influence on many fronts in the escalating war against sexual expression. It is past time to turn back the troops that are trampling freedom of sexual speech. In the remainder of this book, I elaborate on the critical weaknesses in the feminist procensorship analysis, beginning with its fatally flawed foundation: simplistic demonization of sexual expression.

# *"Different Strokes for Different Folks"*

## THE PANOPLY OF

## PORNOGRAPHIC IMAGINATION

> I do not know what has caused MacKinnon to become, and, more surprisingly, to remain, so obsessed with pornography, and so zealous for censorship. But let us not sacrifice our civil liberties on the altar of her obsession.
>
> JUDGE RICHARD POSNER
> U.S. Court of Appeals for the Seventh Circuit[1]

In our pervasively sexist society, it should be expected that some expression in every genre, including sexually explicit speech, may convey, at least to some viewers, ideas about women (and men) that are antithetical to gender equality. By heightening public awareness of this dimension of some sexually oriented speech, the feminist antipornography movement has had a valuable educational impact. The American Civil Liberties Union's brief in the Indianapolis case lauded Dworkin, MacKinnon, and their allies for this contribution:

> By emphasizing the degree to which sexually explicit speech glorifying humiliation and violence is fundamentally inconsistent with our national commitment to equality, proponents of the Indianapolis ordinance contribute to public understanding of the need to eradicate sex discrimination and violence against women from American life.[2]

What distinguishes the procensorship faction from other

feminists, however, is its obsessive, oversimplified demonization of sexually explicit expression. This pornocentric tunnel
vision distorts the reality of sexist imagery in our society in two
important ways.

First, it ignores the many other words and images that
reflect women's second-class status in our society, many of
which are no doubt more important and influential because of
their mainstream status. Based on her recent comprehensive
survey of the views of women's sexuality and gender roles that
are purveyed in nonpornographic media, New York Law
School professor Carlin Meyer has concluded that the mainstream media—television, film, advertising, music, art, and
popular literature—have a far greater impact in shaping these
views than does pornography. As she explains, not only do we
encounter mainstream language and imagery more often and at
earlier ages than we do most sexual representation, but also,
because mainstream imagery is ordinary and everyday, "it more
powerfully convinces us that it depicts the world as it is or
ought to be."[3]

Even if we could wave a magic wand and eliminate all sexually explicit sexist images from our culture, our social environment would still be pervaded by sexist and violent images.
Thus, to end the purported "cause" of misogynistic discrimination and violence, we would have to ban virtually all communications. (And what, then, could be done to the sexist and
violent *thought* that "caused" the communications?)

Second, the feminist antipornography movement's insis-
tence that *all* pornography conveys misogynistic messages to *all*
viewers—or at least to all male viewers—ignores the complex,
variegated nature of sexually explicit expression and the subjective, nuanced nature of any viewer's interpretation of such
expression. To categorically condemn all sexual expression is as
inane as categorically condemning all nonsexual expression or
all expression in any other category, as if responses to anything
were uniform, rather than totally individualized and unique.

Those who pillory all sexually explicit expression promote
another common misconception—that it appeals only to men,

and that women, or at least feminists, find nothing of any redeeming value in such expression. These generalizations belie reality. In fact, many who categorically castigate sexually explicit magazines and films as misogynistic are unfamiliar with these materials, perhaps assuming that the overtly violent, sexist samples that are selectively presented in displays and slide shows mounted by feminist antipornography groups are typical. But the opposite is true, as writer Sallie Tisdale has concluded from her extensive viewing of commercial erotica: "Women who have seen little pornography seem to assume that the images in most films are primarily, obsessively, ones of rape. I find the opposite theme in American films: that of an adolescent rut, both male and female. Its obsession is virility, endurance, lust."[4] Consistent with Tisdale's account, surveys indicate that depictions of violent sexual encounters—rape or sadomasochism—account for only 3 to 8 percent of commercially available erotica.[5]

Lisa Palac, then editor of *Future Sex* magazine, recounted in a 1994 *Esquire* magazine interview how she had converted from a devout disciple of Catharine MacKinnon to an avid enjoyer of pornography simply by actually looking at some examples of this hitherto despised, but unseen, genre. Now, far from preaching against the perils of pornography, Palac proselytizes for the pleasures it can provide:

When I was at the University of Minnesota in 1983, where Catharine MacKinnon taught in the law school, I was a devout follower of hers and a real antiporn feminist. . . . One day at my boyfriend's house I opened his closet to get a sweater and *hundreds* of hardcore-porn magazines came tumbling out. I was disgusted, livid. I wanted him to burn them in a cleansing bonfire. . . . But a couple of days later he said, "Just watch one video, and if you still feel the same way, I'll get rid of them all." We watched *Sleepless Nights,* and it sparked some honest dialogue— I told him my "sick" sexual fantasies, and we rented more movies. The watershed event was when I was able to watch a movie—*Aerobisex Girls*—by myself and get so turned on I had to masturbate right away. Then I wanted to tell everyone how to use pornography. . . . [6]

The fact that many women find much that excites or otherwise pleases them in commercial erotica is indicated by their large and growing share of the burgeoning market for such imagery. Women, either singly or as part of a couple, constitute more than 40 percent of the adult videotape rental audience; to put this number in perspective, it should be noted that 410 million adult videos were rented in 1991 alone, and that adult video sales and rentals have soared since then.[7] In 1987 two social scientists conducting a survey of over 26,000 female readers of *Redbook* magazine found that nearly half the respondents said they regularly watch pornographic films.[8]

Women also make up a growing portion of those who produce erotic materials. Increasing numbers of women writers, filmmakers, and magazine editors have been producing sexually explicit materials, many expressly aimed at a female audience. These include Marianna Beck, copublisher of *Libido: The Journal of Sex and Sensibility*; author Susie Bright, whose many writings include the "Cliterati" column in the *San Francisco Review of Books* and three books entitled *Herotica,* annual collections of erotic writings by and for women; filmmaker Candida Royalle, who heads Femme Productions; the Kensington Ladies Erotic Society, which has published anthologies of women's erotica; and the editors of *Bad Attitude* and *On Our Backs,* two lesbian feminist erotic magazines. In the words of Marianna Beck, who estimates that *Libido*'s readership is 40 percent female, "We're . . . depicting sex as not just something that men engage in actively while the woman somehow endures while thinking of Catherine [*sic*] MacKinnon."[9]

Pornography also has literary value. In "The Pornographic Imagination," a 1967 essay, Susan Sontag analyzes and debunks the various assumptions underlying the view that pornography can be categorically distinguished from "authentic literature":

The ratio of authentic literature to trash in pornography may be somewhat lower than the ratio of novels of genuine literary merit to the entire volume of subliterary fiction produced for mass taste. But I doubt that it's any lower than, for instance, that of another somewhat shady subgenre with a few first-rate books to its credit, science fiction. (As literary forms, pornography and science fiction resemble each other in several interesting ways.) Anyway, the quantitative measure supplies a trivial standard. Relatively uncommon as they may be, there are writings which it seems reasonable to call pornographic—assuming that the stale label has any use at all—which, at the same time, cannot be refused accreditation as serious literature.[10]

Procensorship feminists argue that they would ban only sexual materials that are violent or subordinating. But no consensus is possible concerning which pornography can be described with such reductionist, subjective labels. By ascribing to any sexually oriented work one meaning only, and by imposing that construct on the rest of us, the feminist antipornography movement is profoundly antithetical to individualism, denying autonomy both to all the people who create expressive works and to all the people who see their works.

As writer Sallie Tisdale has stated:

> Always, the [feminist] censors are concerned with how men *act* and how women are portrayed. Women cannot make free sexual choices in that world; they are too oppressed to know that only oppression could lead them to sell sex. And I, watching, am either too oppressed to know the harm that my watching has done to my sisters . . . or else I have become the Man. And it is the Man in me who watches and is aroused. (Shame.) What a misogynistic worldview this is, this claim that women who make such choices cannot be making free choices at all. . . . Feminists against pornography have done a sad and awful thing: *They* have made women into objects.[11]

The antipornography feminists rigidly presume that all viewers, or at least all male viewers, will interpret sexual speech as conveying misogynistic messages. But many other feminists view much such speech as conveying to many viewers messages that are at worst ambiguous and at best positive. Ambiguous and positive interpretations apply to the full range of sexual speech, including violent imagery and imagery that might well be labeled "subordinating" or "degrading," such as rape scenes and scenes dramatizing the so-called rape myth— namely, that women want to be raped. As I show below, women have found affirmations of eroticism and empowerment in all such images, and feminist women have seen them as exploring such pro-feminist themes as liberation from conventional sexual conduct and from traditional gender roles.

## Pornography and Poststructuralism

The concept that no text or image has any objective, fixed meaning, but rather has a different meaning for each member of its audience, is an integral aspect of the poststructuralist, or deconstructionist, movement that has been so influential in the humanities and social sciences in recent years. Professor Thelma McCormack, director of the Centre for Feminist Research at York University, notes that, under the influence of poststructuralism, "pornography began to slip quietly away as a younger generation of feminist literary critics deconstructed it, scooping out its literal meanings and leaving behind an empty shell with no fixed meaning."[12]

The reductionist approach of the procensorship feminists denies the existence of ambiguity, subtlety, and irony in the interactions between all individuals and a text or image. It overlooks the boundary between fantasy, imagination, and ideas, on one hand, and behavior, on the other. As writer Pete Hamill remarked, "In a way, the work of MacKinnon and Dworkin is some of the saddest writing I've ever read. . . . There is no fantasy or magic."[13]

The feminist antipornography faction disavows individual control over thoughts and actions, assuming that viewers of pornography will react to it in a simplistic, "monkey-see, monkey-do" fashion. This debased view of humanity is invoked to justify legal controls. Procensorship feminists "reject the distinction between thought and deed which is both the cornerstone of liberal democracy and the foundation of a humanistic model of human nature," writes Thelma McCormack. Elaborating on their error, she explains:

> Typically, [Dworkin and MacKinnon] disregard the work of social psychologists for whom the relationship between attitudes and behaviour, between what we think and what we do is the problematic. According to social psychologists, the relationship is . . . largely indeterminate; there is no way of specifying what the behavioral outcomes are of specific attitudes, especially when we live in a world of contradictory messages. . . .
>
> Our distinctively human capacity is to think, select, interpret and reinterpret content, to read texts on different levels and in different ways. The result is a broad spectrum of possible attitudes which loop back to shape how we read future texts. . . .
>
> Thus, when Dworkin-MacKinnon collapse the distinction between dream and deed, fantasy and act, thought and behavior they construct a Skinnerian model of human nature which, in turn, justifies an elaborate system of social control.[14]

The individualized interaction that viewers have with imagery and words in general certainly exists when the imagery and words concern sexual themes in particular. Just as sexuality and sexual relationships are themselves inherently individualized, tied to the most intimate, personal aspects of each human being's pysche and life, so one's interpretations of and reactions to sexually explicit expression are uniquely subjective and individualized. As observed by feminists Lisa Duggan, Nan Hunter, and Carole Vance:

> To some, *any* graphic sexual act violates women's dignity and therefore subordinates them. To others, consensual heterosexual lovemaking within the boundaries of procreation and marriage is acceptable, but heterosexual acts that do not have reproduction as their aim lower women's status and hence subordinate them. Still others accept a wide range of nonprocreative, perhaps

even nonmarital, heterosexuality but draw the line at lesbian sex, which they view as degrading.[15]

An image that one woman views as misogynistic discrimination may for another reaffirm her desires and her equality; an image that one woman views as subordinating, another may view as liberating. Based on extensive discussions of sexual imagery with other women, as part of a sex and history study group, Columbia University anthropologist Carole Vance has formulated what she dubs "Vance's One-Third Rule": "Show any personally favored erotic image to a group of women, and one-third will find it disgusting, one-third will find it ridiculous, and one-third will find it hot."[16]

A 1992 editorial cartoon by Mike Mereu well captured the same idea by showing three different people's reactions as they all look at a sculpture of a naked female torso in an art museum; the thought-bubbles above each of their heads reveal the following responses, in order: "SMUT!," *"Art!,"* and "An insult to headless quadruple amputees."

Life does indeed imitate art—or, depending on your perspective, smut or insults. Two years after the Mereu cartoon was published, it seemed to serve as the script for a real-life scenario, described as follows in the April 16, 1994, *San Francisco Chronicle*:

> Pulitzer-Prize-winning author Alice Walker was pleased to be named a "state treasure" by Governor Wilson, until she got a glimpse of the gilded statuette of a naked female torso that went with the prestigious award.
>
> The hefty art piece, nearly a foot high, features the headless and limbless body of a woman mounted on a bronze base.
>
> Walker's most recent work is "Warrior Marks," a film and companion book of the same title on female genital mutilation.
>
> "Imagine my horror when, after four years of thinking about the mutilation of women, I was presented with a decapitated, armless, legless woman, on which my name hung from a chain," said Walker earlier this week.
>
> "Though these mutilated figures are prized by museums and

considered 'art' by some, the message they deliver is of domination, violence and destruction," she said.[17]

And, in the never-ending spiral of one person's art being another's degradation or dirt, Walker's own work—while recognized as art by those who awarded her the Pulitzer Prize and many others—has itself been decried as pornographic and degrading. Even before she was presented with the sculpture she found so offensive, Walker had already had hesitations about accepting the California "state treasure" award, because California education officials had treated two of her own works as offensive. In 1993, in response to complaints from religious conservatives, state educators had pulled two of Walker's stories from a pool of writings used in state reading tests of public school students. (Following an ACLU protest, on behalf of Walker and various writers' groups, the state restored Walker's stories to the testing pool.)[18]

Commenting on these two incidents, Los Angeles writer David Link noted that the statue that Walker found so revolting—and which would be considered taboo pornography under the MacDworkin law—"was designed by one of the most gifted sculptors of our time, Robert Graham," whose work is in museums worldwide. Observing that "[t]he paradox of Walker's offended sensibilities is breathtaking," Link underscored why we must never allow expression to be stifled—as it is under antiobscenity and antipornography laws alike—because it is offensive to someone's sensibilities: "Offense is a purely subjective experience, an entirely solipsistic exercise."[19]

In 1993, one group of lesbian feminists sought to suppress the magazine of another group of lesbian feminists because the first group saw the publication's cover photograph of a woman as degrading, whereas the second saw it as empowering. The magazine in question was the May-June 1993 issue of *On Our Backs,* a San Francisco–based lesbian erotic magazine. The cover photograph showed model Dawn Wan, an Asian- American woman, fully covered in body paint portraying flames, with images of fire all around her. The caption says, "Dawn Wan in Flames."

A Seattle organization, Dykes Against Porn (DAP), ripped

the covers off copies of this magazine in bookstores, spray painted protest messages on the sidewalks and walls of bookstores that carried it, and picketed outside one of the bookstores. Spokeswomen for DAP explained that they saw the Wan photograph as racist and as promoting violence against Asian women. A leader of the demonstration outside Red and Black Books—a leftist bookstore collective that specializes in multicultural and politically progressive titles—shouted: "*On Our Backs* glorifies and promotes violence against Asian women; what it basically says is that white dykes should be getting off on setting Asian girls on fire."[20]

Other feminists had very different, less literal, interpretations of the Wan photograph. Wan herself, who had had the idea for the body paint and the photograph, expressed "shock" that her choice was construed as racist and sexist, stressing that she had defined for herself how she wanted to look.[21] When informed that Wan had taken the lead in constructing this image, a DAP spokeswoman displayed the disrespect that procensorship feminists typically show toward anyone who chooses to pose for or look at images of which they disapprove: "I think she's a fucking sellout, and that's all I have to say about it."[22]

The editors of *On Our Backs* explained the positive associations that inspired the Wan cover photograph:

> When stripper Dawn Wan danced at the [*On Our Backs*] Christmas party last year, her body painted in flames, the room got so hot we decided that not sharing the heat with our readers would constitute cruel and unusual punishment. When she's all painted, says Dawn, she feels like she's in a wet suit. . . .[23]

And then–managing editor Heather Findlay explained her reaction to the end result:

> I *liked* how [the cover] portrayed an Asian-American woman complete with attitude and sexual assertiveness—a departure, in my opinion, from the stereotype of the passive "oriental" lady—so I didn't feel we had any apologies to make to anyone, especially to Dawn, who came up with the cover concept herself.[24]

In the same spirit, Christine Wenz, editor of the Seattle-based *Stranger* magazine, said that she saw the photograph and its caption as "a metaphor for [Wan's] being really hot and turned on."[25]

Similarly, a letter to *Seattle Gay News* commented: "The woman looks empowered, for she has her head high with her hands on her hips. It is art! We interpret the fire-woman as a goddess, or a flame nymph. She is beautiful and strong."[26]

Antipornography feminists contend that women have historically and consistently been subjugated in the realm of sexuality, yet that view is contestable. In her book *Swept Away,* sex researcher Carol Cassell writes: "Sex has historically been a commodity. It's a valuable source of power. . . . Sexual power is . . . the female commodity."[27] In the same vein, author Nancy Friday has said that "women have always derived power from withholding sex."[28] Echoes former porn star Veronica Vera: "A dominant patriarchy? Wake up folks. . . . [A]s any good whore can tell you, it never existed in the bedroom."[29]

Even erotica that superficially depicts female subjugation can be understood as acknowledging, but seeking to overturn, women's greater power in the sexual arena and as advocating more equalized male-female sexual relationships. So, images that on their surface portray a sexually subordinate female may be interpreted as protesting *any* inequality in the sexual domain. Thus, men's rights activist Jack Kammer contends, "Ms. MacKinnon's efforts to suppress men's pictorial fantasies of reversing their sexual subjugation can be supported only by those who fail to acknowledge women's control of sex or by those who seek to preserve it."[30]

## Wide-Ranging Reactions to Rape Scenes

Scenes of rape, which some viewers might well understand as showing a woman's subordination, nevertheless may be viewed by others, including some feminist women, very differently.

For some women, scenes that would be real-life nightmares could be fantasy-life daydreams. Anaïs Nin's diary reveals her erotic excitement in fantasizing about violent, forced sex:

> Sometimes in the street, or in a cafe, I am hypnotized by the "pimp" face of a man, by a big workman with knee-high boots, by a brutal criminal head. I feel a sensual tremor of fear, an obscure attraction. The female in me trembles and is fascinated. . . . A desire to feel the brutality of a man, the force which can violate? To be violated is perhaps a need in women, a secret erotic need.[31]

As noted by feminist artist and writer Sara Diamond:

> [M]any women . . . fantasize about being ravished. It is not surprising that women daydream about being uncontrollably desired in a culture in which our value as human beings is based on our attractiveness, and in which we are constantly prevented from acting out our desires. If we fantasize a partner taking complete control of a sexual encounter, then we are absolved from responsibility for our abandoned behavior. In this way we can mentally break sexual taboos that still remain in place in practice.[32]

The impossibility of proscribing all overtly violent, sexist depictions, or of agreeing on which overtly violent, sexist depictions should be banned, is illustrated by the fierce debates that have swirled around *Swept Away,* Lina Wertmuller's provocative and artistically acclaimed 1975 film, released at precisely the historical moment when the then–newly revived women's movement had focused on rape and the rape myth (that women really want to be raped) as major symbols and instruments of women's oppression. With a story line that, on its surface, was a classic embodiment of the rape myth, the film set off an avalanche of controversy. *Swept Away* (its full title is *Swept Away by an Unusual Destiny in the Blue Sea of August*) would be a prime target for censorship under the MacKinnon-Dworkin model law. Yet consideration of both its story and the manifold reactions to it, including among feminists, underscores the hopelessly simplistic and surface-obsessed nature of the MacDworkin definition—and of any definition—of "sexually incorrect" expression.

The heroine of *Swept Away* is a wealthy socialite, haughty in general but particularly arrogant and condescending in her treatment of the members of the crew on her yacht. She taunts them with her sexual unattainability, prancing around in a tiny bikini while alternately completely ignoring them or treating them as near-animals or near-slaves—in either case, not as men who could possibly have any sexual response to her. After she is marooned on an uninhabited island with one of her former crew members, the tables are turned, as she becomes completely dependent on him, his virtual slave. He rapes her, beats her, and abuses her verbally. Nevertheless, she develops not only passion but also love for him.

Some feminists denounced *Swept Away* as a classic rape myth that allegedly perpetuated violence and discrimination against women. Others praised Wertmuller for spotlighting and exploding the false assumptions that have anchored women's second-class citizenship. Some thought the film propounded traditional and demeaning stereotypes about women's sexuality. Others thought it explored novel, liberating, alternative views. Some believed it celebrated the triumph of sexism. Others believed it celebrated the downfall of classism. Some considered it a glorification of violence. Others considered it a condemnation of violence. Some understood the film literally. Others viewed it symbolically. Some interpreted it straightforwardly; others construed it ironically. Some found its sex scenes aesthetically revolting; others disagreed. Some were turned off; others were turned on.

And so forth. The countless varying, even contradictory, reactions that the film engendered among its viewers—including its female, feminist viewers—simply mirrored the wonderfully infinite variety in the human mind, imagination, and emotions.

## Degradation or Delight (or Both)

The inescapably individualized, and hence wildly divergent, interpretations that all persons bring to all sexual expression can be illustrated further by considering another type of such expression that, along with rape scenes, is commonly cited as a paradigmatic example of the subordinating imagery that would be banned under the antipornography feminist regime: the "come shot," in which a man ejaculates on a woman's body. In many such scenes, the woman then smears the sperm over her body and licks it. Although procensorship feminists routinely cite these as archetypal images of female degradation, this characterization is as oversimplified as every other aspect of their approach to sexual expression.

Canadian writer Wendy McElroy has suggested other interpretations of these scenes. She notes that makers of commercial erotic films often insert "come shots" simply to prove that the male *did* ejaculate, that he was "into" the sex. Likewise, the woman's response of spreading the sperm over her body or tasting it would simply demonstrate that she, too, was fully, enthusiastically involved in the sexual encounter.[33]

Many women viewers may be particularly interested in seeing come shots because men's ejaculations are usually hidden from them, occuring inside the woman's own body. As McElroy observes, to such women, the sight of male ejaculation "is as elusive as a glimpse of breast or lace panty must be to a pubescent boy. In this context, the come-shot can be interpreted in an almost romantic way: the woman wishes to share, as much as possible, in her lover's orgasm."[34]

In the introduction to *Perspectives on Pornography: Sexuality in Film and Literature,* Gary Day offers a more Freudian analysis of the come shot, which construes it as conveying pro-female messages:

A feminist interpretation of this might be that it shows the subordination of a woman to a man's pleasure, thereby presenting him in a dominant role. However, if . . . pornography in part involves a realization of the incestuous phantasy, then the "come" shot takes on a very different meaning. For what the man does in ejaculating over the woman is in a sense to replicate the role of the mother giving milk to the infant. . . . If this analysis is accepted, then pornography does not show, as some feminists have claimed, a hatred of women but rather a desire to become like them.[35]

Accept these interpretations or don't, but my point is that they prove that when we look at sexually explicit depictions alleged to be misogynistic, violent, and subordinating—the quint-essential examples of what procensorship feminists label as the pornography that should be banned—diverse interpretations are possible; *no* sexual imagery can be given one universal meaning. Each individual must make her—or his—own choices about what to read or view, and how to understand and respond to the material. To accept the MacDworkinite concept of "subordinat-ing" sexual imagery would be, as Judge Richard Posner observed (see the epigraph at the beginning of this chapter), to elevate the "obsession" of some women above all other women's—and men's—civil liberties.[36] The procensorship feminist faction posits a false choice between free speech and women's equality. The true choice is between civil liberty and no liberty.

## Do As They Say, Not As They Do

Procensorship feminists perforce must concede the oversim-plified nature of their rhetoric denouncing the inherent dan-gers supposedly caused by exposure to pornography; their own experience proves that some individuals may survive exposure to pornography without any adverse impact on their attitudes and behavior toward women. Probably very few men have examined the volume of violent, misogynistic pornography with the attention that Dworkin, MacKinnon, and other pro-censorship advocates have lavished upon it. Katie Roiphe reports that when MacKinnon lectured at Princeton University in 1992, she "assure[d] the audience that she's seen more porn than any of us."[37] As Pete Hamill wrote:

> MacKinnon and Dworkin . . . [have] obviously pored over more pornography than the ordinary man sees in a lifetime. . . . If human beings are so weak and pornography so powerful, why aren't MacKinnon and Dworkin playing the Krafft-Ebing Music Hall with the rest of the perverts?[38]

Dworkin, MacKinnon, and their allies still maintain respect for women's equality, as they envision it, and for women's safety. Their proposed censorship regime thus is predicated on a double standard: that *they* can withstand the allegedly pernicious influence of exposure to pornography, but *others* cannot.

This double standard is typical of censorship advocates generally. Noting that "those who would suppress pornography often betray a mighty fascination with the subject of their condemnation," Marjorie Heins, director of the American Civil Liberties Union's Arts Censorship Project, pointed out:

> In 1990, Donald Wildmon's American Family Association [AFA] reproduced portions of artworks that it viewed as scandalously homoerotic, then mailed them by the truckload to its membership list, with a fund appeal letter noting that if contributions were sent, the AFA would supply more of this awful stuff. A 1992 Christian Coalition newsletter described in juicy detail a lesbian film that it simultaneously excoriated the NEA for having funded.[39]

Likewise, in a widely publicized television ad during his 1992 bid for the Republican Presidential nomination, Pat Buchanan's voice lambasted the NEA's funding of "filthy and blasphemous art, too shocking to show," while images from that very same, assertedly too-shocking art were simultaneously rolling across the screen! (The NEA-funded art that was pilloried in this case, true to the common pattern described in chapter 4, explored themes concerning sexual and racial minorities; it was a documentary film called *Tongues Untied,* about African-American gay men.)[40]

One of the most recent examples of crusaders against sexually explicit speech themselves perusing—and, moreover, purveying—such materials is the Meese Pornography Commission. Its voluminous report contained so many vivid descriptions of the sexual materials it ostensibly condemned that *Newsweek* labeled it "the Attorney General's dirty book."[41] Cardozo Law School professor Edward de Grazia reported that more than 300 of the report's 1,976 pages—a full 15 percent—were dedicated to "detailed descriptions of the plots, images, and ideas disseminated by 725 books, 2,325 magazines, and 2,370 films of the hard-core pornographic type."[42] No wonder "sexpert" Susie Bright exclaimed that she "came three times" while reading the Meese Commission Report![43]

In his thorough study of pornography in modern culture, Fordham University professor Walter Kendrick described the Meese Commission's report as "blatantly pornographic":

> [T]he Commission provided three hundred pages of summaries and descriptions, some with dialogue: "I want to taste your cum. I want you to come in my mouth. I want to feel your hot cum squirt in my mouth," and much, much more in the same vein. No doubt this established a landmark in the history of government publications.[44]

Mirroring the Meese Commission in this respect, as in so many others, MacKinnon and Dworkin have published and distributed graphic, sexually explicit descriptions that fall squarely within their own definition of pornography, because it depicts the "subordination" of women. As Carole Vance has commented:

> Ironically, in a culture where it was increasingly costly for feminists to present erotic images or speak in an erotic language, only the antipornography movement could publicly revel in the most graphic sexual images and lurid sexual language, all acceptable because their purpose was condemnation.[45]

Here, for example, is the opening passage of MacKinnon's 1993 book *Only Words*:

Imagine that for hundreds of years your most formative traumas, your daily suffering and pain, the abuse you live through, the terror you live with, are unspeakable—not the basis of literature. You grow up with your father holding you down and covering your mouth so another man can make a horrible searing pain between your legs. When you are older, your husband ties you to the bed and drips hot wax on your nipples and brings in other men to watch and makes you smile through it. Your doctor will not give you drugs he has addicted you to unless you suck his penis.[46]

As political scientist Walter Berns commented about MacKinnon: "Obsessed with pornography, yes, but does she really hate it? . . . As she puts it [in *Only Words*], talking sex is having sex, and the fact is, Catharine MacKinnon talks a lot of sex. She talks sex right off and never lets up. And some sex!"[47]

Dworkin's writings, too, are laced with passages that would violate her own concept of prohibited pornography. In a survey conducted by University of Pennsylvania professor James Lindgren, 63 percent of the respondents found that Dworkin's 1991 novel *Mercy* is "pornographic" under the criteria she and MacKinnon advocate.[48] Likewise, Dworkin's 1987 novel *Ice and Fire* contains much pornographic prose, as indicated by the following samplings:

She is lean and tough. She fucks like a gang of boys. . . . She fucks everyone eventually, with perfect simplicity and grace. She is a rough fuck. She grinds her hips in. She pushes her fingers in. She tears around inside. She is all muscle and jagged bones. She thrusts her hips so hard you can't remember who she is or how many of her there are. The first time she tore me apart. I bled and bled.

*          *          *

We are on the beach. Mister wants some sex. N whispers to me that she can't fuck, she is bleeding again. All summer she has this mysterious bleeding. . . . [S]he is bleeding, not menstruating, hemorrhaging; she can't be fucked. She and I make love for him on the beach. It is not enough. He is wired, tense, has spasms of violence, shows us his knife. N holds me down from behind, both arms. . . . She grins ear to ear. I try to get loose watching her grin. She is strong and I can't. She holds me down. He pulls down his pants. He fucks me.

\* \* \*

He tears into me. He bites my clitoris and bites it and bites it until I wish I was dead. He fucks. He bites my clitoris more, over and over, for hours, I want to die. The pain is shooting through my brain. I am chewed and bitten and maimed. I am bleeding. He leaves. I hurt so bad I can't even crawl.

\* \* \*

I teach him not to be afraid of causing pain. Not to be afraid of hurting me. . . . I teach him not to be afraid of piss and shit, human dirt. . . . I scratch, I bite, I tie him up, I hit him with my hand open, with my fist, with belts: he gets hard. He does each thing back to me. . . . I ended up cowering, caged, catatonic. . . . I wanted to help: but this was a hurricane of hate and rage let loose: I wanted to help: I saved him: not impotent, not suicidal, he beat me until I was a heap of collapsed bone, comatose, torn, bleeding, bruised so bad, so hard: how it will end, I don't know.[49]

With passages like these, it is hardly surprising that two of Dworkin's books have been seized at the Canadian border, where customs inspectors determined that they violated the Canadian version of the MacDworkin antipornography law.[50]

Simultaneously condemning pornography while engaging in pornographic expression themselves, procensorship advocates, from the Meese Commission members to Catharine Mac-Kinnon, simply mirror the hypocrisy of much of the general public regarding sexually explicit material. In 1989, Americans bought 9 million copies of *Playboy, Penthouse,* and *Hustler* magazines *each month*.[51] Pornographic videos are widely credited with helping to make the VCR a household appliance; recent surveys indicate that "adult videos" constitute 30 percent of all rentals; adult video sales and rentals in general-interest video stores alone soared 75 percent between 1991 and 1993, when they reached $2.1 billion (adult-only outlets are estimated to take in hundreds of millions of dollars more).[52]

Now sexual words and images are burgeoning on the newer communications frontiers, in cyberspace, on computers.[53] Indeed, the human desire for sexually oriented words and images is so consistently strong that some experts see it as a major motivating factor behind the development and usage of all new communications media, throughout history. As John Tierney noted in a 1994 *New York Times* article aptly entitled "Porn, the Low-Slung Engine of Progress": "Sometimes the erotic has been a force driving technological innovation; virtually always, from Stone Age sculpture to computer bulletin boards, it has been one of the first uses for a new medium."[54]

In a 1994 interview, MacKinnon described the pornography business as a $10 billion annual enterprise,[55] and that figure is corroborated by the Justice Department.[56] This number underscores the fact that many members of the American public enjoy sexual materials. Yet public opinion surveys regarding such works indicate ambivalent attitudes; most people believe it's okay for People Like Us to see this material, just as long as we keep it away from People Like Them. In her essay "The Pornographic Imagination," Susan Sontag criticizes "this chronic mutual suspicion of our neighbor's capacities" to view sexual materials without sociopathic effects, because it "suggest[s], in effect, a hierarchy of competence with respect to human consciousness."[57]

In an important 1971 free speech decision (overturning the defendant's breach-of-peace conviction for wearing a jacket that said on its back, "Fuck the draft"), Supreme Court Justice John Marshall Harlan wrote, "One man's vulgarity is another man's lyric."[58] In the context of the feminist debate about pornography, Justice Harlan's famous epigram could be paraphrased as: "One woman's subordinating scene is another woman's liberating scene."

When writer Ntozake Shange posed for this photograph that appeared on the cover of *Poets & Writers* magazine, some readers complained that the publication was degenerating into a "flesh magazine." During a *Ms.* magazine panel discussion on pornography in 1994, Shange described the incident, exclaiming, "Bare shoulders are exploitation now?" Andrea Dworkin responded, "It's very hard to look at a picture of a woman's body and not see it with the perception that her body is being exploited." [© ADÁL, 1993]

This ad for *Libido: The Journal of Sex and Sensibility,* copublished by Marianna Beck and Jack Hafferkamp, has been denounced as pornographic, and some magazines, including *The Atlantic Monthly,* have refused to run it (it has appeared in *Harper's* and *The Nation*). The photograph is of Beck herself, and the other hands are those of Hafferkamp (who is Beck's life partner, as well as her business partner) and the magazine's female art director. [Photograph by Jo Deitz]

In 1992, Pennsylvania State University officials removed a reproduction of the celebrated *Nude Maja* by Spanish painter Francisco de Goya from a classroom wall, and banished it from classrooms altogether, following professor Nancy Stumhofer's complaint that it made her and her female students "uncomfortable." In an effort to explain her stance to her faculty colleagues, Stumhofer circulated excerpts from a book that analyzes representations of the female figure as the eternal object of the male gaze. Because the circulated materials included pictures of nude women, two men on campus then filed a sexual harassment complaint against Stumhofer.

[Prado, Madrid, Spain; courtesy Alinari/Art Resource, New York]

(*Opposite*) *Aphrodite* was included in an exhibit of woodcuts by Brazilian artist Zoravia Bettiol, which were on display in the Menlo Park, California, City Hall in 1993 until city officials shut down the exhibit in response to a female employee's complaint that the nude bodies portrayed in some of these works made her feel "violated." Bettiol, who was an outspoken proponent of artistic freedom under Brazil's former military dictatorship, has sued Menlo Park for violating her First Amendment rights.

[Color woodcut, 51 x 81 cm, from Olympic God Series, 80 images by Zoravia Bettiol, 1976]

This image of Veronica Vera in an Indian temple appears in her video *Portrait of a Sexual Evolutionary,* an autobiographical account of her experiences as a porn actress, producer of female-oriented erotic films, and prostitutes' rights activist. This video, among others, was removed from an exhibit at a conference on prostitution at the University of Michigan Law School in 1992. Leading antiporn crusaders Dworkin and MacKinnon played influential roles in this episode. [Photo by Robert Maxwell; courtesy Veronica Vera]

When Attorney General Edwin Meese announced the widely criticized report of his "Pornography Commission" in 1986, he stood in front of an enormous nude female statue of Justice in the U.S. Justice Department. News reporters gleefully snapped the ironic image of Ed Meese denouncing porn beneath the statue's pendulous breasts (from some angles, his head appeared to be nestled in her crotch). *Esquire*'s caption beneath the photo read "Tits and Ass." Both the statue itself, as well as the news photograph, would be "pornographic" under the Dworkin-MacKinnon law. [©GRACE/SYGMA]

This work, *Le Viol,* by the French surrealist René Magritte, would be doubly damned under the model feminist antipornography law: it shows a woman "reduced to" her body parts and it at least suggests sexual violence, since its title means "the rape."

According to legend, the Christian saint and virgin martyr Agatha rejected the love of the Roman governor and was therefore thrown into a brothel and subjected to violent tortures, including the cutting off of her breasts. Any description or depiction of this legend, such as this painting, *The Martyrdom of St. Agatha,* by Sebastiano del Piombo, would fall afoul of the feminist antipornography law. The many other religious works that would also be imperiled include the Bible, which has often been blamed for instigating rapes and sexual abuse. [Palazzo Pitti, Florence, Italy; courtesy Giraudon/Art Resource, New York]

(*Opposite*) Roberta Cohen, whose works explore issues of domestic violence, explains that this drawing, entitled *Confronting Your Fears,* is about "the fact that four thousand U.S. women are beaten to death by their husbands each year." In 1994, in response to a complaint that this work was "pornographic," local officials in Baton Rouge, Louisiana, demanded that it (and another work by Cohen) be removed from an exhibit at a private gallery located on city property; the gallery doors were locked until the artworks were removed. (Cohen and the other artists are being represented by the ACLU's Arts Censorship Project.) [Charcoal, pastel, and chalk on paper; courtesy Roberta Cohen]

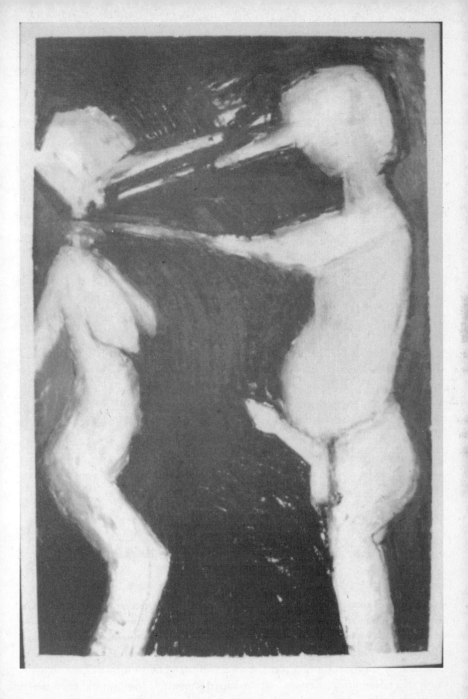

**THE GRANDMOTHER OF LESBIAN FILM: BARBARA HAMMER**

# ON OUR BACKS

ENTERTAINMENT FOR THE ADVENTUROUS LESBIAN

MAY/JUNE 1993  $3.95

A Farewell
Tribute to
Knots Landing

Sneak Peek:
Lesbian & Gay
Film Festival

Penetrating
the Virgin Veil

## Dawn Wan In Flames

This photo of model Dawn Wan, which was her idea, appeared on a 1993 cover of *On Our Backs,* a lesbian erotic magazine; many viewers saw it as countering stereotypes about the passivity of Asian women. But a lesbian feminist antipornography organization, Dykes Against Porn, denounced the image as racist pornography that promoted violence against Asian women, tore the covers off copies of the magazine in bookstores, and demonstrated against and vandalized feminist, lesbian/gay, and other bookstores that sold it.  [Courtesy *On Our Backs,* 526 Castro, San Francisco, CA 94114]

## CHAPTER 8

# Positive Aspects
# of Pornographic Imagery

If pornography is part of your sexuality, then you
have no right to your sexuality.

CATHARINE MACKINNON[1]

I take this personally, the effort to repress material I
enjoy—to tell me how wrong it is for me to enjoy it.
Anti-pornography legislation is directed at me: as a
user, as a writer. Catharine MacKinnon and Andrea
Dworkin . . . are themselves prurient, scurrying after
sex in every corner. They look down on me and
shake a finger: *Bad girl. Mustn't touch.* That branch of
feminism tells me my very thoughts are bad. Pornography tells me the opposite: that *none* of my
thoughts are bad, that anything goes. . . . The message
of pornography . . . is that our sexual selves are real.

SALLIE TISDALE, writer[2]

### Sexual Egalitarianism

Even if words and images could be interpreted literally, we
would still have to reject the pornophobic feminists' simplistic
stance that pornography conveys unrelentingly negative messages about women. Much commercial erotica depicts women
in nonsubordinated roles, and contains images and ideas that
may well be seen as positive for women and feminists.

Although Catharine MacKinnon has described pornography

with characteristic oversimplification as "man's boot on woman's neck,"[3] in many films and photos, the shoe is, literally, on the other foot—rather, the woman's boot is on the man's neck, if not on an even more vulnerable section of his anatomy. The female dominatrix and male slave are familiar characters in sexually explicit materials. Taking issue with the antipornography feminists' views that women are never on top sexually, either in the real world or in erotic materials, Norman Mailer observed with his typical saltiness, "I've seen any number of pornographic films where you have girls sitting on guys' heads."[4] And feminist aficionada of erotica Sallie Tisdale emphatically corroborates this perspective: "Women in modern films are often the initiators of sex; men in such films seem perfectly content for that to be so."[5]

Many sexual materials defy traditional stereotypes of both women and pornography by depicting females as voluntarily, joyfully participating in sexual encounters with men on an equal basis. Procensorship feminists may well view a woman's apparent welcoming of sex with a man as degrading, but this is because of their negative attitudes toward women's ability to make sexual choices. Other viewers are likely to see such a scene as positive and healthy. As feminist lawyer Nan Hunter asked, "What if a woman says to a man, 'fuck me'? Is that begging, or is it demanding? Is she submitting, or is she in control?"[6]

Men's rights activist Jack Kammer notes that "one of men's most enduring 'pornographic' fantasies is . . . about equalizing" sexual control between men and women, in a societal context in which women have often derived power from withholding sex. Accordingly, he notes:

An archetype of male erotica is the woman who participates enthusiastically in sex, who loves male sexuality, who needs not to be cajoled, seduced or promised ulterior rewards. Erotica portraying such joyful, egalitarian sex does not demean women any more than men are denigrated by stories of women and men working cooperatively in an office where men no longer think it is their right to have women fetch them coffee.

Ironically, [MacKinnon's] greatest effect may be only to enhance men's need for what she wants to suppress. The more women accept arguments about the inherent cruelty, selfishness and danger of male sexuality, the more men will need to fantasize, possibly by resorting to pornography, about women who offer egalitarian, joyful, trusting sexual companionship.[7]

## Sexual Opportunities and Options

Even the Meese Commission acknowledged "two areas in which sexually explicit materials have been used for positive ends: the treatment of sexual dysfunctions and the diagnosis and treatment of some paraphilias."[8] (*Webster's Third New International Dictionary* defines "paraphilia" as "a preference for or addiction to unusual sex practices.") Moreover, the Meese Commission recognized that pornography might have other beneficial effects, including providing entertainment, relieving people of the impulse to commit crimes (of course, this contradicts one of the Commission's other contentions, that pornography *causes* crime; see chapter 12 for more on this point), and improving marital relations by teaching about sexual techniques.

Popular sex manuals such as *The Joy of Sex* have recommended erotic pictures and videos as aphrodisiacs, and experts widely believe that it can improve the sex lives of many couples. In a 1992 letter to the Senate Judiciary Committee, opposing the then-pending Pornography Victims' Compensation Act, Patti Britton, Ph.D., wrote:

> As a board-certified clinical sexologist, I can tell you that it is common knowledge in my field that sexually explicit films and videos are often recommended as a mode of treatment for couples or individuals with clinical sexual problems. Such materials are viewed by professionals as helpful, not harmful, assets in the treatment process.[9]

Even for couples and individuals with no "clinical sexual problems," sexually explicit materials can spice up their sex lives,

and hence solidify their relationships. At a conference at
Columbia University, the eminent psychoanalyst Otto
Kernberg said that inhibition too often

> limits a couple to conventional standards that stifle passion.
> Pornography, on the other hand, can stimulate an active fantasy
> life—can be an antidote to stifled passion. A rebellious sex life
> within the bounds of a couple can be the cement of marriage.[10]

To the extent that erotic publications and videos offer an
alternative sexual outlet for people who otherwise would be
driven to engage in psychologically or physically risky sexual
relations, they serve a positive public health function. This
point was trumpeted by a banner that a Manhattan bookstore
recently hung over a display of sexually oriented publications
that had been threatened with censorship: "Enjoy some safe
sex!" In the age of AIDS—to say nothing of the continuing rise
of unwanted teenage pregnancies—sex itself is often fraught
with risks. Yet sexually explicit materials *are* a safe alternative.

In addition, sexually explicit materials may well be the only
source of sexual information or pleasure for many people who,
for a host of reasons, do not have sexual contact with others—shy
or inhibited people, people with mental or physical disabilities,
people with emotional problems, gay people who are confused
about their sexual orientation or are afraid to reveal or express it,
people who are quite young or old, geographically isolated people, unattractive people. Disability rights activists protested
Congress's attempt, in the mid-1980s, to prevent the Library of
Congress from publishing *Playboy* in braille. Noting that this
was "part of a long history of disabled people's sexual oppression,"
Barbara Faye Waxman, an expert in the sexual and reproductive
health of disabled women, wrote, "[T]he last thing I'm going to
do is call for any form of censorship that will inevitably have a
backlash and reinforce the policies and practices that have kept
disabled people sexually disempowered for so long."[11]

Even for individuals who generally have sexual relations with
other people, pornography may well serve as a welcome alternative stimulus and outlet in situations where that is not possible,

such as when travel separates them from their partners. Many hotels all over the United States, including some of the finest, now offer sexually explicit videos for in-room viewing.

Erotic publications and videos serve an egalitarian, pluralistic function beyond providing vicarious sexual experiences. Pornography depicts an enormous range of people and sexual practices, thus helping *all* viewers to explore and affirm their own sexuality, their own sexual practices and preferences, and their potential sexual relationships with all other human beings. As Paula Webster has written, "Pornography implies that we could find all races, genders, ages, and shapes sexually interesting, if only in our minds."[12]

This radically egalitarian premise that sex and sexual expression can break down any other barriers separating people is no doubt one of the reasons that they consistently have been viewed as threatening to established political, as well as moral and cultural, norms.

### Instruction and Inspiration
### for Women's Sexual Pleasure

Contrary to the stereotypes of pornophobic feminists, many other feminists and many women in general say that porn has much to offer them. Let's now consider their views, so often drowned out by antiporn crusaders. Judith Kegan Gardiner, professor of English and Women's Studies at the University of Illinois, has cataloged some of pornography's positive aspects, specifically from a woman's perspective:

> For some women, pornography may actually de-objectify women because they can use it to validate their own desires and pleasures. They can also reinterpret or take control of the fantasy. For example, they may point out that a particular pictured position is not fun, but awkward and uncomfortable. Furthermore, women too can make comparisons between their lovers and the performers, for instance to the male stars' larger organs or more sustained

erections, and they can use the pornography to encourage or instruct their partners how to please them. Pornography may also serve women to defamiliarize and romanticize the relationships in which they are already. For example, in a pornography sequence produced by the women of Femme Productions, a woman dressed in sexy finery is picked up by a man on the street who turns out to be her husband. The woman has left their child with her mother in preparation for their sexy night together.[13]

At the most basic level, porn provides information about women's bodies and techniques for facilitating female sexual pleasure, which is otherwise sadly lacking in our society. Precisely to fill this gap, a growing number of women are becoming producers, as well as consumers, of pornography. In a 1994 interview, erotica author Laurie Sue Brockway explains that she likes to write "really graphic stuff so people know where the thing is and what to do with it," noting:

> A man friend of mine recently said to me, "I feel like I'm just doing figure eights around a woman's clitoris [when giving oral sex]. Am I doing a good job? I don't know how to make her come." And I said, "Suck it." And he said, "*Suck* it?" And this is somebody who is fairly experienced. So, if you have a bunch of different characters in a bunch of different scenes, there's a lot of data in there.[14]

Pornography enhances women's ability to attain sexual pleasure on their own, as well as with men. Recovered MacDworkinite Lisa Palac, noting that many women do not masturbate, wrote that when she began looking at "dirty pictures" and masturbating in response to them, she "became sexually autonomous . . . in complete control of my own erotic destiny."[15] In the same spirit, cartoonist Kris Kovic declared, "The First Amendment is your most effective sex toy."[16]

As noted by Heather Findlay, then editor of the lesbian erotic magazine *On Our Backs:*

> [M]any women have come to appreciate their bodies through porn. . . . Betty Dodson's classic masturbation manifesto, *Sex for*

*One,* tells the delightful story of how Dodson, who thought she'd deformed her pussy by jilling off too much, realized she was normal—and beautiful—by looking at split beavers in men's sex magazines. In 1973, Dodson put together a "cunt positive" slide show . . . took it on the road and inspired hundreds of women to feel proud of their equipment. One audience member, Dodson relates, felt so puffed up by the slide show she demanded a raise from her boss the next morning—and got it. So much for porn degrading women![17]

Back in 1913, Dr. Howard Kelly said in the journal *Medical Gynecology,* "Good women possess no language and no terminology either for their feelings or their anatomy." But Susie Bright, author of the "Cliterati" column in the *San Francisco Review of Books,* says now, "In many years of teaching and talking sex, I have never had a man come up and say, 'I don't know where my penis is, and I've never had an orgasm.' . . . It's feminists who've put the Clitoris on the map."[18] Let's not let pro-censorship feminists take it off again.

## Lesbian and Gay Images and Identity

As law professor Kathleen Sullivan has written, "In a world where sodomy may still be made a crime, gay pornography is the samizdat of the oppressed."[19] In light of the long-standing and ongoing legal and societal discrimination faced by lesbians and gay men, materials depicting and exploring their sexuality are especially important, serving to educate, liberate, and empower. The positive role that lesbian erotica played in her own life was described by the Canadian lesbian feminist writer and activist Chris Bearchell:

My erotica "habit" began when I was coming out in a small Canadian city in the late '60s. It was hard admitting that I was sexually attracted to other women, but it got a lot easier when I saw pictures of women having sex. I squirreled away copies of soft-core men's magazines . . . I was vaguely disappointed by the lack of authenticity in much of what I saw, and by the meagerness of my collection, but I never gave up hope of finding more and better (juicier) images. Eventually, I moved to the big city—Toronto—and grew from a baby dyke into a gay activist and journalist. Then, what seemed to be a miracle happened. . . . [L]esbians began to make and distribute sexual imagery of our own.[20]

Referring to another beneficial aspect of porn from a lesbian and gay perspective, writer Pat Califia has noted that, should the antipornography feminists have their way, "homosexuals and other sexual minorities would lose a vital source of contact—the sex ads."[21]

The paucity of pornography produced specifically by and for lesbians, until recently, has led one lesbian feminist to put an amusing spin on the clichéd "excuse," in our porn-panicked society, for those "caught looking" at such magazines as *Playboy* and *Penthouse*: "I only read it for its articles." Noting that for lesbians who do not have access to lesbian porn, the only source of visual sexual stimulation is in straight-male-oriented magazines, Heather Findlay "confessed" that she occasionally bought them. Seeking to distance herself from what she described as the "male whining" in their texts, *her* defensive explanation, to *her* peers, was: "[B]ut, really, I only buy it for the pictorials!"[22]

If the procensorship feminists had their way, pornography would be equally unattainable for women and men, for gays and straights. Those concerned about the rights of lesbians, gays, and bisexuals should not delude themselves that the feminist antipornography juggernaut would not ride roughshod over their preferred sexual materials along with everyone else's. Such an exemption is available neither in theory nor in practice.

In theory, the feminist antipornography activists have made clear that homosexual, as well as heterosexual, materials are equally subject to censorship. Recall (from chapter 4) that the MacDworkin model law permits the suppression of any sexually oriented expression regardless of the genders (or the sexual orientations) of the individuals depicted. In this respect, the law reflects the procensorship feminists' equally condemnatory attitude toward all pornography—they certainly cannot be accused of discriminating on the basis of gender or sexual orientation!

The late John Preston, a gay activist and writer, illustrated Andrea Dworkin's long-standing antipathy toward *any* expression of male sexuality, including gay male sexuality, by recounting her actions during the early 1970s when he was director of the Gay House, Inc., in Minneapolis:

> Dworkin used to run a lesbian discussion group in the center. One of her favorite antics back then was to deface any poster or other material that promoted male homosexuality. "THIS OPPRESSES WOMEN!" she'd write all over the place. . . . I've come to understand that it's the expression of *any* male sexuality that she feels fuels the oppression of women in our society. That makes gay men not allies, but a big part of the problem.[23]

Further demonstrating her equal-opportunity loathing for all porn, Dworkin has also denounced lesbian pornography as "an expression of self-hatred."[24] This view has been echoed by other antipornography feminists. Norma Ramos, general counsel of Women Against Pornography, said in a 1994 *Ms.* magazine symposium:

> [T]here's no distinction between what lesbian pornographers are doing and what these women who are fronting for the [mainstream] pornography industry are doing. . . . They may package it as art, or say that they are introducing a new vision. But it is sexual exploitation.[25]

Likewise, the organization Dykes Against Porn, which has chapters in cities around the country, has stated that "[i]t was formed because of the need that many saw to fight pornography in the lesbian community, as well as heterosexual male porn."[26] *On Our Backs,* a lesbian erotic magazine published in San Francisco, has been repeatedly attacked by antipornography feminists, including Dykes Against Porn, as in the "Dawn Wan in Flames" incident described in the previous chapter.

Even more significant than the pornophobic feminists'

nondiscriminatory denunciations of homosexual and hetero-sexual porn is the fact that any censorship measure would be enforced by government officials and legal systems that reflect society's pervasive homophobia and heterosexism. Thus, it is not surprising that *in the real world,* as under the first feminist antipornography scheme to go into operation, in Canada, les-bian and gay erotica has borne the brunt of the censorship.

### Unreal Rape

Just as it is vitally important to enforce criminal and societal sanctions against *real* rape—defined by University of Southern California law professor Susan Estrich, in her book of that title, as all intentional nonconsensual sex[27]—it is also vitally impor-tant *not* to enforce sanctions against *unreal* rape—words or images *describing* or *depicting* nonconsensual sex.

The distinction between the imagined and the actual, between fantasy and reality, should be crystal clear. But the fem-inist antipornography movement has blurred it. For example, in her 1993 book, MacKinnon writes, "In pornography, pictures and words are sex"[28] and "[s]exual words and pictures . . . have sex."[29] Indeed, the title of that book, *Only Words,* conveys MacKinnon's sarcastic dismissal of the view that pornographic words are, in fact, only words.

This confusion between expression and action is yet another common bond between feminist censors and other censors. As writer Wendy Kaminer remarked, "[I]f pornography is sex dis-crimination, then an editorial criticizing the President is trea-son."[30] (Indeed, under English common law, it was a crime to "compass"—or imagine—the death of the king;[31] the law would be moving backward toward that long discredited notion were it to adopt the feminist procensorship philosophy.) And Thelma McCormack retorted to the MacDworkinite charge that pornography is rape by comparing it to "the Ayatollah Khomeini saying 'The Satanic Verses' is not a work of art but an act of heresy."[32]

To MacKinnon, there are apparently no distinctions between women who are raped by actual men in real life, and female actresses in erotic productions whose rapes are simulated by male actors. Moreover, MacKinnon apparently concedes no distinction between real-life rape victims and female models who are "raped" by the cameras that simply record their nude or sexual poses. In a 1993 article in *Ms.* magazine, MacKinnon wrote, "Pornography is made from rape in film studios, on sets, in private bedrooms, in basements, in alleys, in prison cells, and in brothels."[33]

Likewise, in *Only Words,* MacKinnon asserts that women are "gang raped," "hurt and penetrated, tied and gagged, undressed and genitally spread," and even "killed . . . to make pornography," and that these violent actions are "essential . . . to make pornography."[34] It should be emphasized that, since Mac-Kinnon defines pornography as including verbal and visual representations—for example, stories and drawings—she is claiming not only that pornography necessitates harm to actual women who serve as models or actresses for photographs or films (this claim is itself inaccurate, as discussed in the following chapter); but further, she is claiming that pornography drawn solely from the writer's or artist's imagination inevitably harms women. Again, MacKinnon conflates imagination, acting, and actuality.

Precisely to dramatize and criticize MacKinnon's equation of words with actions, Carlin Romano—a former philosophy instructor and who in 1994 became president of the National Book Critics Circle—included in his *Nation* magazine review of *Only Words* a fantasized, fictionalized rape of MacKinnon herself.[35] His strategy backfired, though, to the extent that MacKinnon and her allies reacted with all the ire that one would anticipate following a real-life assault. Indeed, MacKinnon declared that the review "was a public rape,"[36] and her publishers attacked *The Nation* for its "use of rape as a tool for the conduct of criticism."[37] Predictably, too, some procensorship feminists denounced the review as pornographic.[38]

In the MacDworkinites' virtual-reality universe, where "virtual rape" is seemingly identical with actual rape, it is hard to understand why their vicious verbal attacks against Romano would not likewise be deemed actual, punishable attacks. Romano's trenchant criticism of MacKinnon's *ideas* could not fairly be construed as "threatening MacKinnon" *herself* "with rape," as charged by Dexter Guerreri of a Brooklyn-based antiporn organization.[39] Ironically, though, as part of their verbal vendetta against Romano, both MacKinnon and her then-fiancé, Jeffrey Masson, made statements that could plausibly be viewed as the kind of "threat" that has long and appropriately been punishable under our legal system—namely, an utterance that is intended to, and does, instill a reasonable fear of impending personal harm. Masson wrote a letter to Romano stating:

> [W]hat you have done to Catharine . . . makes me so mad that I feel my blood start to boil, and I feel that if we were talking about it right now, I could not guarantee that I wouldn't hit you. I have never hit anybody, but I feel this rage rise up in me when I think of you that makes me want to grab you and shake you and hurt you in the same way that you thought of hurting Catharine. . . . I just want you to think for a minute about what you have done. And to recognize that there are so many people, more than you think, who are enraged by it. . . . I am not threatening you, but I want you to know, if there is ever anything I can do to hurt your career, I will do it.[40]

In short, while MacKinnon decrees a fictionalized rape to be an actual rape, Masson decrees an actual threat to be a non-threat! (Consistent with his vow to strive to damage Romano's career, Masson sent this letter not to Romano himself, but rather, to the editor of *The Philadelphia Inquirer,* where Romano is the literary critic.) And MacKinnon herself echoed Masson's threatening words: "I do think Carlin Romano should be held accountable for what he did. There are a lot of people out there and a lot of ways that can be done."[41]

Many women can and do distinguish between real rape and descriptions or depictions of rape. By definition, no one wants to be raped; the very essence of this heinous crime is unwanted sex. That does not mean, though, that the unmitigatedly evil nature of real rape extends as well to unreal rape: rape fantasies, verbal descriptions of fictional rapes, paintings or sculpture depicting rape scenes, or photographs and films showing simulated rapes.

In her latest collection of women's sexual fantasies, the 1993 book *Women on Top,* Nancy Friday writes:

> The most popular guilt-avoiding device [in these fantasies] was the so-called rape fantasy—"so-called" because no rape, bodily harm, or humiliation took place in the fantasy. It simply had to be understood that what went on was against the woman's will. Saying she was "raped" was the most expedient way of getting past the big No to sex that had been imprinted on her mind since early childhood.[42]

And Jean MacKellar writes in her book *Rape: The Bait and the Trap*:

> [Rape fantasies] serve practical and healthy functions in human experience; they add *change*. And they do this without shattering the pattern of reality. This is important, for often a real change is neither desirable nor possible. The most important difference between a fantasy of rape and a desire for the real experience is the element of control. In the fantasy . . . the helpless victim actually controls the acts of the offender. . . . Real terror and uncontrolled pain are not experienced in these fantasies.[43]

Rape scenes in films or writing may also effectively galvanize constructive responses to the problem of actual rape in the real world. Feminists widely praised the gang rape scene in the movie *The Accused* and the attempted rape scene in the film *Thelma and Louise* because they dramatically decried sexual violence against women, despite the fact that, to some viewers, these rape scenes had strong erotic elements. As novelist Anne Rice commented about *Thelma and Louise*:

> I praise that movie because I think it showed how awful rape is. And it's hard to show it without its being sexy because it is sexy.

And rape fantasies are part of our brain. They're part of our genetic heritage, and that's not going to go away if you ban pornography. It's an archetypal fantasy.[44]

Pornography, including pornographic rape scenes, may serve another, intensely political end for women who read or see them: they go against the grain, thus allowing viewers to express rebellion and individuality. In this sense, too, words or images that literally depict a woman's powerlessness may well have an empowering impact on female viewers. As journalist Ellen Willis has written:

> A woman who is raped is a victim; a woman who enjoys pornography (even if that means enjoying a rape fantasy) is in a sense a rebel, insisting on an aspect of her sexuality that has been defined as a male preserve. Insofar as pornography glorifies male supremacy and sexual alienation, it is deeply reactionary. But in rejecting sexual repression and hypocrisy—which have inflicted even more damage on women than on men—it expresses a radical impulse.[45]

### Fantasies for Feminists and Other Freedom Fighters

[I]f social convention, backed by religion and law, confines sexuality to the heterosexual, monogamous, marital, familial, and reproductive, then the ambisexual, promiscuous, adulterous, selfish, and gratification-centered world of pornography is a charter of sexual revolution that is potentially liberating rather than confining for women.

KATHLEEN SULLIVAN
Stanford University law professor[46]

Several anthologies of feminist writings illuminate the range of messages in pornography, specifically from the viewpoints of feminists and women in general.[47] Feminist writer and literature professor Ann Snitow, who coedited one such anthology, *Powers of Desire,* has described some of porn's positive facets:

> Pornography sometimes includes elements of play, as if the fear women feel toward men had evaporated and women were relaxed and willing at last. Such a fantasy—sexual revolution as *fait accompli* . . . can . . . be wishful, eager and utopian.
>
> Porn can depict thrilling (as opposed to threatening) danger. . . . [S]ome of its manic quality . . . seems propelled by fear and joy about breaching the always uncertain boundaries of flesh and personality. . . .
>
> Some pornography is defiant and thumbs a nose at death, at the limitations of the body and nature. . . .
>
> Porn offers . . . a private path to arousal, an arousal that may be all too easily routed by fear or shame. . . .
>
> [P]ornography also flouts authority, which no doubt in part explains its appeal to young boys.[48]

Feminist artist Myrna Kostash theorizes further positive, liberating aspects of pornography: "Until there is a revolution in the institutions that regulate sexual relations—the family, the school, the workplace—perhaps the pornographic fantasy is one of the few ways that women and men, captives together of those institutions, victims alike of their alienating procedures, are permitted connection."[49]

Pornography also contains many elements that are harmonious with feminist values. As the Feminist Anti-Censorship Taskforce brief noted in the Indianapolis case, it "may convey the message that sexuality need not be tied to reproduction, men or domesticity."[50] Feminists Lisa Duggan, Nan Hunter, and Carole Vance have suggested additional profeminist aspects of pornography:

> [P]ornography has served to flout conventional sexual mores, to ridicule sexual hypocrisy and to underscore the importance of sexual needs. Pornography carries many messages other than woman-hating: it advocates sexual adventure, sex outside of marriage, sex for no reason other than pleasure, casual sex,

anonymous sex, group sex, voyeuristic sex, illegal sex, public sex. Some of these ideas appeal to women reading or seeing pornography, who may interpret some images as legitimating their own sense of sexual urgency or desire to be sexually aggressive. Women's experience of pornography is not as universally victimizing as the [MacKinnon-Dworkin] ordinance would have it.[51]

Indeed, as feminist writer and video artist Sara Diamond has noted, "[F]eminism and porn have something in common. Both insist that women are sexual beings. Both have made sex an experience open to public examination and . . . debate."[52]

In response to the charge by procensorship feminists that pornography exploits women, Ann Snitow explains that its subversive quality challenges the entire status quo, including social structures that inhibit women's freedom:

> Though pornography's critics are right—pornography *is* exploitation—it is exploitation of everything. Promiscuity by definition is a breakdown of barriers. . . .
>
> It is a fantasy of an extreme state in which all social constraints are overwhelmed by a flood of sexual energy. Think, for example, of all the pornography about servants fucking mistresses, old men fucking young girls, guardians fucking wards. Class, age, custom—all are deliciously sacrificed, dissolved by sex.[53]

The fact that pornography always has rebelled against conventional constraints is precisely the reason it always has provoked such anxiety among moral traditionalists and political conservatives. Just as sex itself has enormous power to break down individual and social boundaries, so speech about sex threatens all manner of accepted bounds; the more unconventional the sexual expression is, the more revolutionary its social and political implications become.

The essays that were collected in the 1993 book edited by Lynn Hunt, *The Invention of Pornography: Obscenity and the Origins of Pornography, 1500–1800,* show that pornography was closely tied to democratic political movements during the period described.

The essay by Margaret Jacob, for example, points to pornography's historic role in weakening state authority and strengthening democracy by mocking dogmatic religious credos.[54]

Walter Kendrick's 1987 history of pornography in modern culture, *The Secret Museum,* demonstrates that the zeal to restrict sexual expression consistently has reflected political anxiety, as well as moral or religious concern. He described America's leading crusader against sexual expression from the 1870s through the early years of this century, Anthony Comstock (whom we revisit in chapter 11) from this vantage point:

> Comstock represented . . . the urge to limit dissemination of all kinds, to control the availability of representations almost irrespective of their subjects. Like his more sophisticated contemporaries in France and England, Comstock at bottom feared nothing so much as the universal distribution of information. The prospect called up nightmarish images of a world without structure, where all barriers had been breached and all differences leveled. It was appropriate that sex should become the focus of such nightmares, since long before the modern threat arose, sex already stood for loss of control and the scattering of substance.[55]

When the U.S. Commission on Pornography and Obscenity submitted its report to President Nixon in 1970, recommending that all sexual expression be decriminalized for consenting adults, Nixon denounced the report in terms that expressly acknowledged the politically subversive implications of such expression. Nixon declared:

> Pornography is to freedom of expression what anarchy is to liberty; as free men willingly restrain a measure of their freedom to prevent anarchy, so must we draw the line against pornography to protect freedom of expression. Moreover, *if an attitude of permissiveness were to be adopted regarding pornography, this would contribute to an atmosphere condoning anarchy in every other field*—and would increase the threat to our social order as well as to our moral principles.[56] [emphasis added]

As Kendrick commented, "On the surface, pornography threatens nothing but the unleashing of sexuality; but that unleashing, as Nixon said, turns immediately into wantonness of every other kind, including the promiscuous redistribution of property."[57]

Just as *suppressing* sexual speech plays an essential role in *maintaining* the political, social, and economic status quo, conversely, *protecting* sexual speech plays an essential role in *challenging* the status quo. Accordingly, the women's rights cause should naturally be allied with the free speech cause for all expression, including sexual. Once again, the sexual *is* political.

CHAPTER 9

# Posing for Pornography:
# Coercion or Consent?

> [M]any intelligent, self-confident women . . . have
> chosen to work in this lucrative industry. What sort
> of "feminism" is this that tells me I need "reform-
> ing" just because dancing buck naked on stage while
> people throw money at me is my idea of fun? By
> depicting sex workers as either too emotionally crip-
> pled or too stupid to escape a fate which apparently
> any decent woman would find unspeakably degrad-
> ing, they help perpetuate the sorts of patronizing
> stereotypes a true women's liberation movement
> should strive to eradicate.
>
> "KAREN," stage name of a law student
> who works as a nude dancer
> at New York City clubs[1]

Antipornography feminists often seek to justify censorship by
arguing that some women who pose for sexually explicit pictures or films have been forced into doing so, either through
physical violence or through other types of coercion, such as
fraud or duress. It is clearly illegal to coerce anyone into producing a sexual image, just as coercion is illegal in any setting. On
that point, the procensorship and anticensorship feminists are
united.

The two groups are sharply divided, though, on three related points. First, anticensorship feminists stress that the law
already prohibits violence and other forms of coercion, and provides remedies when it occurs.

Second, anticensorship feminists reject the view of their procensorship counterparts that women who pose for sexual images are always and inevitably victims of coercion. Worse yet, the procensorship feminists' view that women cannot consent to pose for sexual pictures or films is antithetical to women's full and equal citizenship, relegating women to the subordinated legal status of children.

Third, anticensorship feminists stress that outlawing the production of any sexually explicit materials will decrease the protections available to women who participate in such productions. Rather than eliminating sexually explicit materials, Dworkin-MacKinnon–style laws would simply drive their production underground, where it would be impossible for models and actresses to invoke legal protections against violence and duress.

Any individuals responsible for physically assaulting women in the process of making sexually oriented materials can be criminally prosecuted as well as sued for damages. The law also provides civil and criminal remedies for fraud or duress. In addition, many states authorize damage actions for privacy-related torts, which could provide further avenues of redress for women who have been physically or psychologically forced into pornographic productions. Such tort actions allow recovery of damages for wrongfully disclosing private facts about someone in public and for wrongfully portraying someone in a false light in public. Another privacy-related tort action, for the wrongful appropriation of a person's image or identity, could also assist women who do not knowingly or voluntarily consent to pose for pornographic materials. Models have recovered damages for emotional distress when sexually oriented magazines wrongfully used nude photographs of them.[2]

Despite the existing panoply of criminal and civil remedies for women who have been physically or psychologically abused in the production of sexual materials, procensorship feminists insist that these measures are insufficient to counter the particular type of coercion that they believe to be inevitable whenever a woman poses for such materials. Procensorship feminists conclude that—at least in the realm of sexuality and sexual expression—women can never make free, voluntary, consensual choices, and that, rather, women are *always* coerced in this context, whether they realize it or not.

But women should not be treated like children or mentally disabled persons and deprived of the right to enter into contracts for the production of sexually explicit materials. That is the end result of the MacDworkin model antipornography law, which provides that a woman's decision to pose for a sexual image should be treated as the product of coercion even under circumstances where a man's decision would be treated as voluntary and consensual. Specifically, the model law provides that proof of any of the following will *not* disprove coercion:

> that the [allegedly coerced] person actually consented to a use of the performance that is changed into pornography; or . . . that the person knew that the purpose of the acts or events in question was to make pornography; or . . . that the person showed no resistance or appeared to cooperate actively in the photographic sessions or in the sexual events that produced pornography; or . . . that the person signed a contract, or made statements affirming a willingness to cooperate in the production of pornography; or . . . that no physical force, threats, or weapons were used in the making of the pornography; or . . . that the person was paid or otherwise compensated.

This provision denies women our freedom of choice; indeed, consistent with the antisex aspect of the procensorship feminist philosophy, it presumes that women are incapable of exercising such freedom, at least as far as sex and sexual expression are concerned.

Even beyond its direct infantilization of women who voluntarily work in the sex business, this provision's "maternalistic" attitude toward women exemplifies the insultingly "matronizing" view that pervades the procensorship feminist critique of pornography. Indeed, Catharine MacKinnon and other supporters of feminist-style antipornography laws have expressly drawn analogies between women and children. MacKinnon has said: "Some of the same reasons children are granted some specific legal avenue for redress . . . also hold true for the social position of women compared to men."[3] Likewise, the proposed Minneapolis antipornography ordinance, drafted by Dworkin and MacKinnon, stated:

> Children are incapable of consenting to engage in pornographic conduct, even absent physical coercion, and therefore require special protection. By the same token, the physical and psychological well-being of women ought to be afforded comparable protection.[4]

### Everyone's Looking at (Just) Linda

Some women who previously modeled or acted for pornographic publications or films have said that they were coerced to perform through physical violence. The most famous example, and one that Dworkin and MacKinnon consistently cite in an attempt to justify suppressing pornography, is Linda Marchiano, who starred in the movie *Deep Throat* under the stage name "Linda Lovelace." In her 1980 book *Ordeal,* Marchiano describes how she was raped and in other ways forced to make the film against her will.[5]

Although Linda Marchiano's *Ordeal* recounts deplorable physical and psychological abuse, which should be punished and prevented under the many existing laws that these acts clearly violated, Marchiano's ordeal provides no support for the conclusion that procensorship feminists repeatedly seek to draw from it—namely, that women who pose for pornographic materials are usually, if not inevitably, brutalized by the producers of such materials. Recently, in interviews published in *Ms.* and *The New York Times Magazine,* Dworkin and MacKinnon, respectively, cited Linda Marchiano as the sole "proof" that pornography is made by assaulting and abusing actual women.[6]

The violence and coercion that Marchiano suffered were

outrageous. Yet her own account does not support the inference that producers of pornography generally inflict such violence and coercion upon the women who pose for them, for two reasons. First, in Marchiano's own case, it was not the participants in the porn industry who raped, beat, and forced her to take part in the movie, but rather, her own husband, Chuck Traynor, who had no other connection to the pornography business. Marchiano's autobiographical writings not only make clear that she experienced no abuse or force at the hands of participants in the porn industry; her writings also show that her career as a "porn star" gave her a welcome, if temporary, refuge from her husband's brutality. In *Ordeal*, Marchiano describes the sense of freedom she felt on the set of *Deep Throat*, and how she enjoyed the company of her costar, Harry Reems. She wrote, "Something was happening to me, something strange. No one was treating me like garbage. . . . We laughed a lot that first day of shooting. . . . And no one was asking me to do anything I didn't want to do."[7] Evidently threatened by Marchiano's enjoyment of her participation in *Deep Throat*, her husband brutally beat her after that first day of shooting, throwing her against the wall and kicking her for hours.

Marchiano's autobiography underscores that her subsequent contacts with the pornography industry, after she had escaped from her abusive husband, were completely voluntary. Recounting the lucrative film offers she later received to reenact the *Deep Throat* sex scenes, Marchiano wrote in her 1986 book *Out of Bondage,* "[I]f I acted in a dirty movie, I would be doing it out of need and greed. . . . I had a choice."[8]

Procensorship feminists have distorted Linda Marchiano's actual experience in the pornography industry, manipulating it to suit their pornophobic agenda. As Dan Greenberg and Thomas H. Tobiason commented in a 1993 law review article:

> MacKinnon's view that women cannot authentically choose to be actors in pornographic films is not even true of the one woman she takes as a paradigm case of a coerced actor: Linda

Lovelace. . . . Lovelace's autobiographical account of her life after the filming of *Deep Throat* unambiguously demonstrates that coercion is the exception, not the rule. . . . Although MacKinnon uses the life of Linda Lovelace to illuminate MacKinnon's reiterations that women who act in pornographic films have no choice but to do so, she does not explain why the experiences of Lovelace, the woman who is at the center of MacKinnon's accounts of coercion, are flatly irreconcilable with her theories.[9]

In the same vein, Leora Tanenbaum writes:

Andrea Dworkin asks in *Ms.* magazine's recent roundtable discussion on pornography: "Why did a woman have to be brutalized to make that film [*Deep Throat*]?" The answer is: she didn't. *Ordeal* makes this clear.

In the years following the publication of *Ordeal,* though, Marchiano has been all too willing to accommodate her antiporn sisters. When she appeared on *Geraldo* in 1988, Marchiano spoke of her experience working on *Deep Throat* in a passive voice, obfuscating the source of her coercion: "I was beaten and I was forced into it, and I had a .45 pointed at me, an M-16 semiautomatic machine gun," she told the audience. . . . Not once did she mention that the abuser was her husband.[10]

The second reason Marchiano's experience does not provide proof of abusive working conditions within the porn industry is that she speaks only for herself. Therefore, even assuming for the sake of argument—directly contrary to what she herself has written—that Marchiano had been abused by members of the pornography industry, that still would provide no basis for concluding that other sex industry workers also suffered such abuse. Nor does the fact that Marchiano's then-husband forced her to perform in *Deep Throat* support the contention that other pornography models or actresses are also performing under duress.

It bears repeating that any instance of any form of physical or psychological abuse is deplorable whenever it occurs, including when it is inflicted to force a woman to pose for pornographic pictures or films (or to do anything else against her will). Instances of such abuse, however, cannot justify the complete prohibition of all posing for pornography. It is as illogical to leap to the conclusion that, because of Marchiano's ordeal, all women should be "protected" against performing in pornographic films, as it would be to conclude that, because numerous Navy women were sexually abused during the 1991 Tailhook convention, all women should be "protected" against joining the Navy.

For every Linda Lovelace who was coerced to perform for a pornographic work, there is a Nina Hartley, who proclaims herself to be an exhibitionist; a Veronica Vera, who celebrates the personal growth she experienced through performing in porn films; a Candida Royalle, who proudly declares that she produces pornography "from a woman's point of view"; and countless others. Royalle, who starred in over a dozen X-rated movies before she became a director, recently commented about the antipornography feminists who want to "protect" her: "I understand their desire to help women, but they are out of touch with women in the industry."[11] Many women who perform for pornography affirm that they do so voluntarily, and that their sister sex workers do likewise. Testifying before the Subcomittee on Juvenile Justice of the Senate Judiciary Committee, Veronica Vera, who has decades of experience with porn films as an actress and director, said that she had "never met a woman who was coerced . . . into participating" in such works.[12] The recent increase of homemade pornographic films, in which unpaid women and men voluntarily perform for others' viewing, is telling. It should not be surprising that some women willingly do for money what others willingly do even for no money.

Women who voluntarily perform for pornography resent the procensorship feminists' attempts to outlaw their chosen occupation. When the MacDworkin law was passed in Indianapolis, deeming the production of pornography a civil rights violation, one actress who appears in porn films protested, "For them to tell me I can't make films about naked men and women making love is a grotesque violation of *my* civil rights."[13] And, underscoring the debilitating impact that antipornography laws would have on *all* women, not just those who choose to work in the pornography business, Veronica Vera said, "I don't think it would help women to beg the government to play Daddy and protect us from ourselves and then at the same time expect equality."[14]

Some sex industry workers affirm their occupational choice in explicitly feminist terms, stressing that they find it empowering as well as enjoyable. For example, Nina Hartley, who has worked in the porn business since 1983 and has hundreds of pornographic films to her credit, explains that the sex industry "provides a surprisingly flexible and supportive arena for me to grow in as a performer, both sexually and nonsexually." Proudly, she declares that "an intelligent, sexual woman could choose a job in the sex industry and not be a victim, but instead emerge even stronger and more self-confident, with a feeling, even, of self-actualization."[15]

Despite the fact that MacKinnon and Marchiano espouse views that many feminists and sex trade workers vehemently reject, both were celebrated by the Meese Commission as if their views and experiences were typical. The Commission unfairly stacked the deck even further by selectively hearing from a disproportionate number of other witnesses who endorsed the MacKinnon-Marchiano perspective. As law professor Edward de Grazia commented in his 1993 book *Girls Lean Back Everywhere: The Law of Obscenity and the Assault on Genius*:

> The Meese Commission trundled out a parade of born-again basket-cases, antisex feminists and fun-hating fundamentalists. Their testimony was sad, misdirected—even pathetic. It was also inflammatory, misinformed scapegoating. In a court of law such witnesses would be dismissed for lack of credibility. Trial by headline—unsupported by evidence, unchallenged by cross-examination or witnesses for the defense—is a far cry from due process. But it was the method of the Meese Commission, with

its fundamentalist foundation, as it had been for Joe McCarthy. This was nothing more nor less than sexual McCarthyism.[16]

One witness who powerfully countered the Meese-MacKinnon-Marchiano stereotypes—namely, the unmitigated evils of sexual materials and the inherent victimization of women who participate in producing those materials—was Dottie Meyer, a former fashion model, *Penthouse* centerfold, and "Pet of the Year," who went on to work at *Penthouse* as a promotion and circulation coordinator. Unlike the parade of self-described pornography victims, Meyer was subjected to scathing, skeptical cross-examination, and her views, along with those of Veronica Vera and other prosex, anticensorship feminists, were completely disregarded in the Commission's report and recommendations. Therefore, it is especially important to pay respect to her words here:

> I was born in Saskatchewan, Canada, 38 years ago. My parents raised me, my brother and sister in a normal, healthy home. . . . I was encouraged to read the Bible and I joined many church organizations.
>
> I consider myself sexually normal and healthy. I enjoy looking at erotic videotapes and reading erotic literature. Both my husband and I feel these sexual aids have enhanced the intimate part of our lives. As a policeman my husband is involved in the constant stress and threats of violence. I believe the fantasy of erotica helps him cope with those situations. We were married . . . before I posed for the centerfold, and for us it was just another modeling assignment. My involvement with *Penthouse* was one of my own choosing. They didn't come to me. I went to them. . . .
>
> The term "Pet" is a term of endearment especially in England where the magazine originated. It is used affectionately. . . . And while I was growing up my mother being English often referred to me as Pet. . . .
>
> In summary, I am a working woman. I work at a job that I like. I go home to my husband and my dog. I cook and clean my own house. . . . It hurts me when righteous so-called do-gooders assume anyone who has been a centerfold is an empty-

headed bubble-brained idiot who's been led down the garden path into a life of moral decadence.[17]

While Dottie Meyer did not feel degraded by her modeling and other work for *Penthouse,* she *did* feel degraded by the questioning she underwent by members of the Meese Commission, including detailed questions about her sexual tastes and practices. She said:

> You know, the Meese Commission complains about erotica being degrading to women, well, the Meese Commission was degrading to me. I walked out of there feeling . . . *horrible.* I think I felt more insulted about the questions they asked me than anything I've ever done in my life. . . . [18]

### "No" Means "No," and "Yes" Means "Yes"

As grown-ups, we have won the right to say "no" and to be believed and taken seriously. As grown-ups, we also have the right to repeat, after Molly Bloom, "Yes I said yes I will Yes."

KAREN DECROW, former president
National Organization for Women[19]

Physically the woman in intercourse is a space invaded, a literal territory occupied literally; occupied even if there has been no resistance; even if the occupied person said, "Yes, please, yes, hurry, yes, more."

ANDREA DWORKIN[20]

The 1992 Canadian Supreme Court decision endorsing the procensorship feminists' analysis in general also specifically adopted their position that a woman's consent to perform for sexually explicit photographs or films cannot prevent the works from being classified as "degrading" or "dehumanizing." To the contrary, in an Orwellian twist, the Court "reasoned" that a woman's consent may well "make the depicted acts even more degrading or dehumanizing."[21]

But what could be more degrading or dehumanizing to women than this view, espoused by the procensorship feminists, that woman are powerless to consent to pose for pornographic depictions, and that if they seek to do so, they are debasing themselves? This argument demeans all women. In accepting the MacDworkin theory that a woman's *consent* to perform for pornography should have no legal importance, the Canadian Supreme Court was showing precisely the same disregard for women's autonomy and dignity that previous courts showed when they ruled that a woman's *nonconsent* to sexual intercourse did not mean that she had been raped. The two views are flip sides of the same devalued coin.

The procensorship feminists' assumption that women cannot meaningfully consent to participate in producing sexual expression is one facet of their even broader, even more debasing, assumption that women cannot meaningfully consent to participate in sexual relations. The antisex aspect of the procensorship philosophy, as demonstrated throughout this book, is an important reason why it is profoundly inconsistent with women's equality.

### Scarlet Collar Workers—Better Off in Pink?

Most people's work choices are constrained at least by economic pressures, and often by other pressures as well, including those exerted by peers or family members and internal psychological factors. All too many people find little self-fulfillment in their work but, to the contrary, find much that is self-abasing. From a corporate manager in a gray flannel suit to a porn star in her birthday suit, most working people do things they probably would not do were they independently wealthy.

Contrary to the claim of pornocentric feminists, though, choices are no more constrained for those who pose for sexually explicit materials than they are for other workers. Given the relatively high pay, many "scarlet collar workers" make an economically rational choice to enter the sex industry rather than to pursue more socially acceptable, but less remunerative, work.

Nor is there any reason to believe that force or violence are endemic in the sex industry, or more prevalent there than in other sectors of our society, including other workplaces and the home. Indeed, citing FBI reports about the prevalence of domestic violence, some experts maintain that "the home is the center of violence in twentieth-century America," in the words of women's rights lawyer Karen DeCrow;[22] Linda Marchiano's brutalization fits squarely into this general pattern.

Candida Royalle has said that she was never subjected to any violence or sexual harassment in the porn industry, but that she did experience both in "straight" jobs, recounting that, while she was working as a receptionist at a New York City health club, her boss sexually assaulted her, and that when she worked at Ticketron, her employer made her kiss him good night every night to keep her job.[23] In a 1994 interview with Leora Tanenbaum in *In These Times,* Royalle said:

> I was never forced to do anything in pornography. The closest I ever came to any attempt at coercion was during a film I made with a very famous director, about a guy who had abused prostitutes, who were now getting back at him. So the director was passing out beers. I was like, What is this? "This is the, uh, urination scene." I was like, Excuse me? I not only refused to do it, I organized all the other women and said, "We're not going to do anything we don't want to do." Four of the women did agree because they had no problem with it, but the rest of us didn't. The director was very angry, and said I would never work for him again, and that was fine.[24]

Although antipornography activists brandish accusations about the alleged prevalence of "snuff" films, in which women are purportedly actually murdered on camera, there is absolutely no evidence that *any* such film has *ever* been produced, let alone that it typifies the pornographic genre. To the contrary, as writer Susie Bright has noted, the original movie entitled *Snuff* "was long ago exposed as a fraud, a low-budget horror F/X [special effects] grossity with a helluva marketing angle."[25] The actress who was supposedly murdered on-screen later stepped forward to demonstrate that she was very much alive.

For many sex industry workers, working conditions are less dangerous and onerous than those experienced by the women who labor in mills and on assembly lines. By some estimates, more than ten thousand workers die each year, or about thirty per day, from on-the-job injuries; about seventy thousand more workers are permanently disabled annually. According to the National Institute for Occupational Safety and Health, one in five poultry workers, who are mostly women, have been seriously injured in the hands, wrists, or shoulders. And job-related illnesses and crippling injuries are on the rise throughout the workforce.[26]

A 1994 Justice Department report reveals that violence is a serious problem in all workplaces: about one out of every six violent crimes happens at work, including 8 percent of all rapes and 16 percent of all assaults. Other data indicate that 4 percent of all homicides occur in the workplace.[27]

These troubling facts should mobilize efforts to make all workplaces safer for all working women and men. When we learn of hazards faced by poultry workers, we do not call for closing down the poultry industry, but rather for requirements that it protect its workers' safety and health; we should do likewise concerning the pornography industry. Censoring pornography, though, would make it impossible to enforce any such requirements.

## Censorship Would Harm, Not Help, Pornography Performers

By driving many pornography businesses out of existence, the censorship regime would deprive women of occupational options that many now affirm they have freely chosen.

Furthermore, as even procensorship feminists recognize, the practical impact of their approach would not be to prevent the production of all pornography, but rather, to drive that production underground. This development would also be devastating to the women who continued to work in the porn business. As observed by federal Court of Appeals Judge Richard Posner, a leading exponent of analyzing legal issues from an economic perspective:

> When an economic activity is placed outside the protection of the law—as we know from Prohibition, prostitution, the campaign against drugs and the employment of illegal immigrants—the participants in that activity will resort to threats and violence in lieu of the contractual and other legal remedies denied them. The pimp is an artifact of the illegality of prostitution, and the exploitation of pornographic actresses and models by their employers is parallel to the exploitation of illegal immigrant labor by their employers. These women would be better off if all pornography were legal.[28]

Improved working terms and conditions for porn models and actresses could be achieved under a noncensorship regime through both private contracts (for either individual women or organized groups) and government regulation. If the sex industries were treated as legitimate businesses, they would be subject to a whole range of laws that would enhance the lives of the women who work in them. Conversely, if pornography were made illegal, the women who performed for pornographic materials would have no protection under a panoply of measures that can promote their welfare, including laws prohibiting coercion or duress, sanitation codes, wage and hour laws, the social security system, insurance and pension laws, laws protecting safety and health, and laws guaranteeing collective bargaining rights.

While MacDworkinite laws would not criminalize pornography, they would subject it to such crippling penalties that it would probably be produced by underworld-type operators, not likely to abide by applicable laws and regulations. As Judge

Posner indicated, scarlet collar workers are already exploited because some sexual expression is now subject to legal sanctions; they would be even more exploited should more sexual expression be subject to legal sanctions.

For the foregoing reasons, it is not surprising that virtually all of the organizations representing sex trade workers have opposed schemes to censor pornography. Sex workers, including pornography models and actresses, have repeatedly lobbied the National Organization for Women to refrain from supporting the antipornography movement. Leonore Tiefer, a psychology professor who specializes in clinical and research work on sexuality, has written, "These women have appealed to feminists for support, not rejection. . . . Sex industry workers, like all women, are striving for economic survival and a decent life, and if feminism means anything it means sisterhood and solidarity with these women."[29]

Here is one such appeal, in the form of a letter written to me in 1993 by a woman who enjoys working in the scarlet collar industry—"Karen" (who is also quoted at the beginning of this chapter):

Dear Ms. Strossen:
After reading your interview in December's issue of *Vogue,* I feel compelled to thank you for your strong stand against antipornography/procensorship "feminists," and your rejection of the condescending images they propagate against women such as myself.

I am a "stripper" in a club here in New York. I am one of those women who consider nude dancing "a perfectly legitimate way to make a living."

I am also a first year law student at one of the top law schools in the country. No one coerced me into the sex industry. I had a good, although not terribly lucrative, job as an assistant editor when I first started dancing. I do not do drugs. I have not been brainwashed. As a student, I find dancing to be a dream job. I work once a week, and make enough money to support myself.

I find it sad and ironic that some of the loudest voices in

feminism today perpetuate outmoded and patronizing stereotypes of women in the sex industry. Many of us are intelligent,
well-educated women. Many of us are feminists, though we
may feel torn and confused about what that means anymore.

Throughout college, I unequivocally considered myself a
feminist, but since I started dancing I have begun to feel that
the feminist "establishment" considers me, at best, an unen-
lightened victim, at worst, the enemy. In the current political
climate, erotic dancing is now doubly stigmatized. Because I am
also pursuing a "legitimate" career in law, my dancing career
must remain my dark secret.

Rather than liberating us, the puritanical wing of contemporary feminism inhibits female sexual awareness and freedom.
By painting all pornography or erotic dancing as a perverse and
dangerous dark monster, inescapably degrading to women and
responsible for violent sex crimes, the women's movement
denies women's own sexuality. Women have sexual fantasies
too—dirty, shocking, kinky fantasies. Many women are sexually
aroused by a wide spectrum of erotic images and writing.
Women rent porno movies; women read dirty books; a few
women even come to watch us dance (much to my delight).
Whereas everything the MacKinnon camp has to say about
erotica implies that only men find erotica arousing. Their
rhetoric is predicated on a false and repressive dichotomy
between "perverse," "predatory" male sexuality and squeaky
clean, politically correct female desire for intimacy. My grandmother's generation of young women was taught that lust was
something only men felt. The 1960s were supposed to have
changed all that.

Today increasing numbers of women direct pornographic
movies, in which women play more interesting and aggressive
roles than in traditional pornography. Their efforts should be
applauded as an important contribution to *true women's liberation*.
Instead, to the extent they are discussed at all by antipornography
feminists (which isn't much), they are denounced as collaborators. As if sexual explicitness must always be exploitive of
women.

Erotic dancing has been tremendously liberating for me. The first time I ever got up on stage and took off my clothes, I was terrified. But at some point I crossed a line after which I left behind forever a lifetime of feeling self-conscious about my naked body, left behind all the baggage of sexual inhibition civilized society had impressed upon me. Women who still cling to that baggage imagine the woman who dances or poses nude as vulnerable and degraded. They don't understand that for the woman who has crossed that line and embraced the taboo, she feels instead the thrill of empowerment.

I hope you will understand if I do not feel comfortable signing my full name. Thank you for taking the time to read my letter.

> Sincerely,
> Karen[30]

## The Woman-as-Male-Pawn Worldview

As noted by writer Cathy Young, cofounder of the Women's Freedom Network, there is a striking parallel between the views of some abortion opponents that no woman could freely choose to have an abortion—or, as they would characterize it, to "kill her baby"—and the views of antipornography activists that no woman can freely choose to perform for sexually explicit materials. Both views presuppose an infantilized or irresponsible woman incapable of deciding what is in her own best interests or of making moral choices and needing the protection of the state, or of other women (or men) who invoke the state's legal apparatus, to make those determinations for her. In this respect, as in so many others, the procensorship feminists' alliance with the radical right is substantive, as well as strategic.

Young reports that Olivia Gans, the head of an organization called American Victims of Abortion, declared on a nationally televised panel discussion, "My child died because of *Roe v. Wade*." When another panelist pointed out that Gans chose to have an abortion and that the Court's historic decision merely gave her the right to make that choice, Gans responded, "It was a choice I was forced to make, because of the pressure of the abortionist."[31]

This woman-as-male-pawn worldview echoes the common procensorship feminist theme that women who choose to pose for, look at, or defend pornography are really the dupes of the men for whom they are fronts. It must be stressed that Gans and others who contend that no woman could truly make a voluntary choice to terminate a pregnancy—some of whom call themselves "feminists for life"—believe they are protecting women's long-range interests in making the "right" decisions about their bodies and their lives. Of course, procensorship feminists share the identical belief. So we are faced with a through-the-looking-glass world in which antiabortion feminists believe that women's right to choose abortions really empowers only abortionists, and in which antiporn feminists believe that women's right to choose sexual expression really empowers only pornographers. Moreover, both groups ignore the fact that the occupations they respectively most despise, abortionist and pornographer, include many women as well as men.

Another unifying theme among Dworkin, Gans, and Mac-Kinnon is that they all invoke the powerful, negative concept of rape to describe what they see as an inevitably involuntary act on the woman's part: Dworkin and MacKinnon analogize all heterosexual intercourse to rape; Gans and her allies describe abortion as "surgical rape."[32] Further reinforcing the commonality of the antiabortion and antiporn views, Dworkin has described childbirth through cesarean section as surgical rape. In her book *Pornography: Men Possessing Women,* Dworkin decries the "pornography of pregnancy" and condemns childbirth through C-section as a "surgical fuck" committed "by the new rapist, the surgeon." To be sure, there is much evidence that C-sections have been overused in the United States, but Dworkin's sensationalized, sexualized demonization of doctors may well redound to the disadvantage of the women at risk, by making it easy for readers to dismiss the serious problem buried beneath her hyperbolic harangue. Here is her horrific description:

Pregnancy is confirmation that the woman has been fucked: it is confirmation that she is a cunt. . . . The display marks her as a whore. . . . Her belly is proof that she has been used. Her belly is his phallic triumph. . . . The pregnancy is punishment for her participation in sex. She will get sick, her body will go wrong in a thousand different ways, she will die. The sexual excitement is in her possible death. . . . And now, the doctors have added more sex—to birth itself. . . . They cut directly into the uterus with a knife—a surgical fuck. She is tied down—literally cuffed and tied, immobilized by bondage. . . . her legs spread; they pour drugs into her to induce labor; their bondage and their drugs cause intense and unbearable pain; . . . she is drugged and sliced into, surgically fucked. The epidemic of cesarean sections in this country is a sexual, not a medical, phenomenon. The doctors save the vagina—the birth canal of old—for the husband; they fuck the uterus directly, with a knife. Modern childbirth . . . comes from the metaphysics of male sexual domination; she is a whore, there to be used, the uterus of the whore entered directly by the new rapist, the surgeon, the vagina saved to serve the husband.[33]

Consistent with the procensorship feminists' view of women's nonagency in the sexual domain, MacKinnon has made statements specifically about abortion rights that are startlingly similar to statements by antiabortion activists. Looking at the world through the eye of her own ubiquitous needle, MacKinnon has even criticized the Supreme Court's landmark 1973 *Roe v. Wade* decision, which held that women have a fundamental constitutional right to choose abortion, for "facilitating women's heterosexual availability" and "freeing male aggression" by removing one of the few "legitimized reasons women had for refusing sex."[34] In fact, although MacKinnon supports a woman's right to an abortion, she says she does so for a reason that is eerily consonant with the antiabortion philosophy—namely, that women should not be forced to carry to term pregnancies that resulted from nonconsensual sex;[35] likewise, many "pro-life" activists are willing to tolerate abortion when a pregnancy results from rape. As Cardozo law professor Jeanne Schroeder has observed, summarizing MacKinnon's views:

> Women need abortion as a remedy because sexuality . . . is thrust upon them. Abortion restores choice by permitting women to reject the *consequences* of heterosexuality. . . . For MacKinnon, whether abortion would be necessary, or even ethically acceptable, in a society where sexual equality existed, cannot be known.[36]

The procensorship feminists' devalued view of women is not only that we can never freely, intelligently consent to pose for pornographic materials. In their worldview, women's bodies are merely the instruments for male sexual aggression and domination. Ironically, then, while a major rallying cry of the reproductive freedom movement has been, "A Woman's Body, A Woman's Choice," an appropriate rallying cry for the procensorship feminists would seem to be, "A Woman's Body, A Man's Choice."

## CHAPTER 10

# Would-Be Censors Subordinate Valuable Works to Their Agenda

My own book, *The Feminine Mystique,* which . . . helped to start the modern women's movement, was suppressed as pornographic in libraries in the Midwest. Why, I don't know. Its only passion was for the personhood of women.

BETTY FRIEDAN, founding President
National Organization for Women[1]

Given the inescapable ambiguity of the central concepts in the feminist antipornography laws—subordinating or degrading descriptions or depictions—and the subjectivity of any interpretation of sexually oriented expression, these laws necessarily arm individual women and government officials with the power to impose on others their views about what forms of sexuality are politically or morally acceptable. All of us would be hostage to the tastes of the individual women who sued under an antipornography law and of the judges and jurors who ruled on their claims. To envision what this would really mean, in this chapter I address first the many types of works that could be construed, by people with various motives, to fit the broad criteria of "subordination" in the Dworkin-MacKinnon model law. I then consider what kinds of works Dworkin and MacKinnon themselves find subordinating, based on their current activism, to provide a glimpse of the law's consequences as contemplated by its designers.

## Who Decides for Women about Images of Women?

> It is no goal of feminism to restrict individual choices or
> stamp out sexual imagery. . . . Women are as varied as any
> citizens of a democracy. . . . It is the right and responsibil-
> ity of each woman to read, view or produce the sexual
> material she chooses without the intervention of the state
> "for her own good." We believe genuine feminism en-
> courages individuals to make these choices for themselves.
> This is the great benefit of being feminists in a free society.
>
> Feminists for Free Expression, opposing the
> Pornography Victims' Compensation Act[2]

As political analyst Ann Lewis has aptly observed, the key slogan of the abortion rights movement—"Who decides?"—
applies equally well to the pornography controversy.[3] In this
context, the fundamental questions are: Who decides which
sexual expression is subordinating and which is liberating?
Which contains negative imagery and which positive? Which
makes the viewer feel unpleasant terror and which makes her
feel pleasurable excitement? Under the procensorship feminists' model law, the government ultimately makes all of these
decisions. Thus, as indicated in the last chapter, the antipornography movement's approach to sexual speech is strik-
ingly similar to the antiabortion movement's approach to
reproduction. In both cases, decisions that have an enormous
impact in the quintessentially personal realm of sexuality are
made not by the individual who is centrally and directly affected, but rather, by the government.

To be sure, under the civil lawsuit enforcement mechanism
that procensorship feminists advocate, individual women (and
men) will initiate any crackdown on particular words or
images—as if it should be any consolation that the challenged
materials are being outlawed in part through the efforts of a cit-
izen vigilante rather than wholly through official government
agents.

This book contains descriptions and illustrations of some of the innumerable, varied materials that would be endangered if procensorship feminists prevailed. These items not only fit within the law's sweeping definition of pornography, but many have already been attacked by procensorship feminists and others, in some cases successfully. They include examples of the following endangered species of sexual speech: celebrated paintings and sculptures by classic masters; photographs by renowned photographers; works by female, feminist artists; family photographs; erotica that is produced by women for women, including for lesbians by lesbians; nonsexual cartoons conveying witty, satirical messages about current political and social controversies; news coverage of female victims of sexual violence; materials conveying vital information about health, sexuality, contraception, and disease control; historical works about women's sexual subordination; works expressing feminist critiques of our patriarchal system and of stereotypical gender roles; and even antipornography protests by advocates of the Dworkin-MacKinnon law.

Although the Dworkin-MacKinnon model statute sets forth eight criteria for assessing whether any challenged expression depicts a woman's subordination, these criteria accentuate rather than mitigate the problems of ambiguity, subjectivity, and the resulting discretionary power handed over to those who enforce the law. These vague criteria (quoted in chapter 3) are merely open-ended invitations for value-laden interpretations. No two people could possibly agree on their precise meanings or on whether they are satisfied by any particular sexual expression.

What does it mean, for example, that "women are presented as sexual objects," a "standard" that is contained in four of the eight criteria? Or that "women are presented in postures of sexual . . . display"? Or that, through the exhibition of their "body parts—including but not limited to vaginas, breasts and buttocks," women "are reduced to those parts"? Surely these all-encompassing criteria would engulf all words or images with any sexual connotation. Indeed, since the last-mentioned criterion would also extend to women being "reduced to" *any* body parts—not just their specifically sexual parts—it would threaten any description or depiction of any portion of the female physiognomy.

Another criterion that expressly extends far beyond sexually oriented materials is the one that proscribes "women . . . shown as filthy . . . bleeding, bruised, or hurt in a context that makes these conditions sexual." This portion of the law would jeopardize news coverage or documentaries that disclose—and hence help to galvanize constructive societal responses to—the very real suffering endured by actual women. For example, this standard would clearly cover MacKinnon's own graphic descriptions of the massive, brutal rapes in the Balkans, especially because she herself argued that these rapes were both caused by, and in turn used for, pornography.[4]

As if this indication of the law's sweeping scope is not scary enough, recall that it is not confined to images of women. Decreeing that "[t]he use of men [or] children in place of women . . . is pornography for purposes of this law," its proponents ensure that virtually no words or pictures would be beyond its reach. Some sense of the law's breathtaking breadth is provided by this excerpt from the ACLU's trial court brief in the *Hudnut* case, successfully challenging the Indianapolis antipornography ordinance:

> [T]he ordinance would deter the distribution of much unabashedly erotic literature of considerable literary or historic value. . . .
>
> [S]cholars could not describe, students could not study, patrons could not purchase, printers could not produce, institutions could not exhibit, and dealers could not purvey an array of visual art and sculpture comprising a principal part of our collective cultural heritage. Not even religious imagery—often sexually explicit—would be immune. . . .
>
> The ordinance would prohibit much clinical sexual literature. . . . Since the sexual subordination of women is a historical reality, the ordinance would be likely to deter much historical or

anthropological work graphically describing such perspectives and practices. Much post-Freudian psychological as well as prominent philosophical literature involves the notion of sexual objectification. . . .

The purely descriptive and academically detached nature of many . . . scholarly depictions would not shield them.

The breadth of the Dworkin-MacKinnon model law cannot be dismissed as just the accidental product of poor draftswomanship. To the contrary, its scope accurately reflects the procensorship feminists' views about the scope of the underlying problem and its appropriate solution. As they emphasize, male domination has deep and pervasive roots in our society, so it is not surprising that our culture is permeated by expression that reflects women's inferior status; if the answer is, as they contend, to suppress such expression, then the sweep of censorship must indeed be expansive. For this reason, the courts that struck down the Indianapolis version of the MacDworkin law concluded that it could not be salvaged through a narrowing construction. As the appellate court said, "No amount of struggle with particular words and phrases in this ordinance can leave anything in effect." This conclusion followed from the court's determination that the law's core feature—and the core conception of the procensorship analysis—is its open-ended definition of pornography, which is "defective root and branch."

### Frightening Feminists

A phallocentric culture is more likely to begin its censorship purges with books on pelvic self-examination for women or books containing lyrical paeans to lesbianism than with *See Him Tear and Kill Her*.

ROBIN MORGAN, writer[7]

As Robin Morgan indicates, one of the images that would fit squarely within the MacDworkin definition of pornography is that of a woman conducting a pelvic self-examination; directly violating one of the law's criteria, the woman would be "presented being penetrated by" an "object"—namely, a speculum. No doubt this is a significant reason that Morgan, who coined the oft-quoted epigram, "Pornography is the theory and rape is the practice," has "urged women not to rely solely on patriarchal law" in challenging pornography.[8]

The classic, popular book on women's health and sexuality, *Our Bodies, Ourselves,* contains many words and images—including those of women conducting pelvic self-examinations—that would subject it to the feminist antipornography law. Not surprisingly, then, the book's publisher, the Boston Women's Health Book Collective, campaigned against the version of the MacKinnon-Dworkin law that was proposed in Cambridge, Massachusetts, in 1985. The book already had been the target of concerted censorship efforts spearheaded by fundamentalists and conservatives, who labeled it "too explicit" and "filthy." In 1977, Phyllis Schlafly's conservative Eagle Forum, apparently angered by the book's increasing availability in small-town libraries, launched a series of local campaigns to ban it, claiming that it encourages masturbation, lesbianism, premarital sex, and abortion. In Helena, Montana, the Eagle Forum succeeded in removing the book from school libraries, until the ACLU forced its reinstatement through a lawsuit. These earlier efforts to suppress *Our Bodies, Ourselves* were unsuccessful because the book clearly does not constitute proscribable obscenity. But it could well fall afoul of the broader, feminist-style antipornography laws.

Many other works that are especially important to women and feminists, which have already been subject to right-wing censorship efforts, would—ironically—also be even more endangered under a MacDworkinite measure. These include *Ms.* magazine, which has been removed from high school libraries for containing information about contraception, lesbianism, and masturbation, and Judy Blume's novels about adolescent sexuality, which are among the most widely censored books in the United States, removed from both school and public libraries all over the country. The American Civil Liberties Union's brief in the Indianapolis case made this salient point:

> Ironically, much overtly feminist scholarly material designed to address the same concerns prompting the [Dworkin-MacKinnon law] would fall within [its] sweeping definition of pornography. Prominent examples include Kate Millett's *The Basement,* a graphic chronicle of sexual torture; Dr. Paul Abramson's *Sarah: A Sexual Biography,* a detailed scholarly case study of vicious sexual abuse; sundry works on rape, wife beating and domestic violence; court testimony and photographic evidence in rape and sexual assault cases; works like [Susan] Brownmiller's *Against Our Will: Men, Women and Rape*; and psychiatric literature describing sexual pathologies and therapeutic modalities. Indeed, *Pornography: Men Possessing Women,* a work by Andrea Dworkin, one of the ordinance's original drafters, contains, by way of illustration, so many far-from-isolated passages graphically depicting the explicit sexual subordination of women that it could easily be pornographic under the ordinance.[9]

As already noted, nine years after the ACLU filed this brief, Andrea Dworkin's book *Pornography* (as well as another book she wrote) was indeed held hostage to Canada's version of the feminist antipornography law, seized by Canadian customs officials. We warned you, Andrea!

Although it is not surprising that Dworkin's antipornography manifestos contain pornographic descriptions of the works she condemns, it is noteworthy that Dworkin's fiction also contains many similar passages, some of which I quoted in chapter 7. Dworkin has acknowledged that her own work would be censored under her model law, but she apparently considers this a price worth paying for the power to censor other works that would also be viewed as pornography.[10] Even assuming that she or other procensorship feminists do take such a position, they certainly do not speak for all feminists on this point. Many may well believe that Dworkin's antipornography tracts, by depicting and deploring violence and discrimination against women, make valuable contributions to redressing those problems. And many may find her novels valuable from an artistic or political perspective. Some readers may find her novels erotically stimulating and pleasurable. The ACLU would certainly oppose any effort to suppress any of Dworkin's writings or statements.

Just as the ACLU brief accurately—alas—predicted that Dworkin's writings would be censored under her model law, the other items on the ACLU's list of endangered feminist works also cannot be dismissed as the mere fevered fears of civil libertarians. To the contrary, procensorship feminists themselves have recognized that some of these materials would be deemed punishable pornography under MacDworkinite laws; in some cases, they have even advocated that outcome.

Examples of expression that MacKinnon has deplored as pornographic, despite their clear benefits for women and feminists, include medical school textbooks[11] and the testimony of female victims of sexual assault and harassment.[12] In *Only Words,* MacKinnon writes, "When words of sexual abuse are in [women's] mouths, that is pornography. . . ."[13] University of Pennsylvania law professor C. Edwin Baker has noted that, by this logic, Anita Hill was pornographic when she repeated the words that she attributed to Clarence Thomas.[14] And writer Judith Levine reminds us, "To be safe from sexual violence, we must be able to publicly describe it in every obscene detail."[15]

Given procensorship feminists' far-reaching views of what constitutes proscribable pornography, I would feel no more comfortable giving them the power to decide what reading or viewing material will be available to me than I would feel giving that power to Phyllis Schlafly, Janet Reno, or any woman or man, whether in government or not. Both Dworkin and MacKinnon recently played key roles in situations involving the suppression of speech by feminist women, on issues of vital importance to women, including reproductive options and female sexuality. These frightening episodes confirm that Big Sister is already watching over us, and should shore up our resolve to beware of giving her even more power to do so.

## Today's Procensorship Tactics, Tomorrow's Censorship Targets

Assuming for the sake of argument that the envisioned law could somehow be enforced only by Dworkin, MacKinnon, and like-minded women, it still would impose irreparable injuries upon expression by, for, and about women. This conclusion is supported by two incidents that took place in fall 1992. Whether or not these incidents involved formal censorship (as Dworkin's and MacKinnon's critics have contended but they have denied), they are nonetheless important in illuminating the formal censorship regime that the MacDworkin law would institute. The works that were targeted in these 1992 situations could all be labeled pornographic, and hence legally suppressed, under that law.

During the fall of 1992, Andrea Dworkin sought to prevent the publication, distribution, and sale of a book about women's reproductive health, written by two respected feminists, because she disagreed with one point they made in two paragraphs of the book. Moreover, although Dworkin complained to the book's (male) publisher and orchestrated a nationwide protest and boycott effort against the book, she refused to speak to the female, feminist authors of the book, or even to answer their letters.

*A Woman's Book of Choices,* a consumer guide to legal abortion and other means for safely ending unwanted pregnancies when legal abortions are not available, was written by Rebecca Chalker and Carol Downer, leaders of the women's health and reproductive freedom movement.[16] Chalker has long worked as an abortion counselor and writer. Downer, who was the founder and longtime director of the Federation of Feminist Women's Health Centers, has been described as a folk heroine of the women's health movement because of her 1972 trial and acquittal on charges of practicing medicine without a license; she had applied yogurt to a vaginal yeast infection.

Issued at a time when abortion rights supporters widely feared that the Supreme Court would overturn *Roe v. Wade, A*

*Woman's Book of Choices* was warmly welcomed by leading feminists. Feminist social critic Barbara Ehrenreich, who wrote the book's foreword, called it "the most important book on reproductive rights ever written";[17] Barbara Seaman, the pioneering feminist author of *The Doctor's Case against the Pill,* lauded it as "perhaps the most important book ever written on women's rights and women's lives";[18] and the Boston Women's Health Book Collective, which publishes *Our Bodies, Ourselves,* also enthusiastically endorsed it. Andrea Dworkin, however, refused to endorse the book; worse yet, because she strenuously disagreed with one passage in it, she did everything she could to prevent it from being published and to deter anyone from buying it.

The passage at issue appears in a section of the book containing stories of women who were forced to take desperate steps to obtain abortions before *Roe v. Wade* made them legal. One of these stories, entitled "Faking Rape," recounts the experiences during the 1950s of a Miami artist named Belinda. A doctor told Belinda that she could give her an abortion if she had been raped. Belinda thereupon filed a fabricated rape complaint, thus securing a police report that served as her license to have an abortion.

After Belinda's story, the book's authors appended this comment: "Today, rape crisis and sexual abuse counseling are pretty thorough and standardized, so trying to fake such situations is not as easy as it used to be. It may require some research, pre-planning and the help of sympathetic counselors."[19] The book then quotes a former rape counselor as "suggesting" that women could make false rape reports more convincing by wearing torn clothes and borrowing semen from a friend or lover to spread on their clothes or bodies.

The authors of *A Woman's Book of Choices* maintain that Belinda's story and their commentary about it simply describe a practice of women under duress, and do not suggest that either women who complain of rape, or rape counselors, are generally lying. But when the book's publisher, Dan Simon of Four Walls Eight Windows, gave Andrea Dworkin galleys of the book shortly before its scheduled publication, seeking her endorsement, Dworkin vociferously objected to this section of the book, contending that it bolstered the already widespread tendency to discount rape victims' complaints.

According to Simon, who had also published Dworkin's most recent book, *Mercy,* Dworkin threatened to (in her own words) "kill" the book if this passage were not removed.[20] Dworkin conveyed her fervent objections to various colleagues in the women's movement, who contacted the publisher to claim that this section was "dangerous" to women and to demand that it be rewritten. The publisher told Dworkin that it was too late in the publishing process to make the demanded changes, and that they would have to be deferred until the second printing.

At that point, still without having contacted the book's authors, Andrea Dworkin and her allies began a public campaign against *A Woman's Book of Choices,* faxing and calling feminists, health educators, and rape crisis counselors across the country, stating that the book encouraged the belief that women lie about being raped. In response, the publisher and authors received numerous protests, as well as threats of boycotts and lawsuits from people who, according to Chalker, had not "even seen a copy of the book, let alone read it."[21] Even worse, some bookstore owners, including owners of feminist bookstores, agreed to boycott the book.

Defending against charges that Dworkin's campaign against *A Woman's Book of Choices* was a form of censorship, Dworkin's agent, Elaine Markson, said:

> Andrea did not try to censor the authors. . . . She meant to protect the authors as well as the rape crisis centers.[22]

Just as many women do not feel "protected" by Dworkin's efforts to shield them from pornography, Rebecca Chalker and Carol Downer did not feel protected by Dworkin's efforts to shield women from their book. As Downer commented, "She's spread poison around the country. We're facing whispers and half-truths everywhere we go."[23]

Nor can Markson's rhetoric about "protection" camouflage

the censorial impact of such coercive tactics as boycotts. Consider the following "reasons why feminists should think twice about boycotting books," suggested by ACLU attorney Marjorie Heins:

> [T]he goal of boycotting a bookseller is to suppress, or censor, some literature, because of its offensive content. . . .
>
> Although censorship by private individuals or groups doesn't raise the same legal questions as government censorship . . . it does raise some of the same moral and political questions. [In both cases,] censorship has the same dangerous purpose: To shrink the expressive landscape. [T]he boycotters hope, through economic coercion, to . . . impose an ideological litmus test on works that [publishers and booksellers] consider for sale or publication. . . .
>
> Because selling books is a relatively precarious trade, publishers and booksellers are highly vulnerable to pressures from both governmental and private groups. Witness the shocking acquiescence of Waldenbooks a few years ago in removing *The Satanic Verses* from its stores after Islamic fundamentalists pronounced a death sentence on Salman Rushdie.[24]

Shortly after Simon had declared that *A Woman's Book of Choices* was too far along to be revised, he discovered that it had been printed but not bound, therefore making revision costly but possible. Accordingly, Chalker and Downer rewrote the controverted paragraph so it read:

> Only in desperate situations—such as women may find themselves in in the future if states ban abortions except for certain reasons such as rape—should women even consider resorting to faking rape. Doing so has the potential to undermine the gains of the movement against violence against women which has worked to overcome the myth used by hostile prosecutors and judges that women who report rape cannot be trusted.[25]

Through her agent, Dworkin said that *A Woman's Book of Choices* was no longer "heinous" after the changes,[26] and indicated that she would cease her active campaign against the book. The authors, though, remained frustrated, because

Dworkin was not as publicly forthcoming with this opinion as she had been with her previous denunciations. Consequently, they continued to face angry rape counselors and threatened boycotts. Worse yet, some major feminist bookstores that Dworkin had contacted refused to carry the book. Chalker says that Dworkin's actions hurt the book's reputation and sales, despite the change. She noted that the New York State branch of the National Organization for Women had been planning to purchase hundreds of copies of the book to distribute to chapters in small towns where it might not otherwise be sold, but "someone stopped it because of this idea it's dangerous for women."[27] As Dan Simon said in a letter to Andrea Dworkin, "[Y]ou have crossed the line from being a helpful critic to attempting to silence an important publication."[28]

Dworkin seems to blink away the historical reality that, in the pre-*Roe* days when virtually all abortions were illegal, women were driven to such desperate measures as faking rape. She also blinks away the continuing reality that, for many women, including poor women, abortion still is not a practical option in all too many instances; for them, alas, faking rape may remain the only way to terminate an unwanted pregnancy. While Congress denies Medicaid funding for virtually all abortions for poor women, for example, one of the few situations in which such funding has been available is when the pregnancy is the result of rape.

But the merits of *A Woman's Book of Choices* are beside the point here. For whether or not one agrees with any or all of the book's ideas, it is indisputable, as the book's title underscores, that Chalker and Downer were trying to expand women's choices. In stark contrast, by seeking to bar women's access to the book, Dworkin was seeking to block women's choice about "choice."

Both MacKinnon and Dworkin played a role in a fall 1992 episode at the University of Michigan Law School, where MacKinnon teaches, in suppressing documentary photography and videos by seven feminist artists, five of whom are female, on the themes of sexuality and prostitution.[29] While MacKinnon has argued that the decision to censor these works was made by law students, she and Dworkin at least influenced the students' decision, as explained below. More important, MacKinnon expressly approved that decision after the fact, stating that the inclusion of pornography in an academic conference constitutes "trafficking in women" and "sets women up for harassment and rape."[30] Moreover, after MacKinnon had subsequently looked at the removed videotapes, she pronounced them to be, indeed, pornographic, and hence to have been properly removed.[31] By ratifying the students' removal of the videotapes, MacKinnon gives us a frightening indication of the works—by, about, and for feminist women—that would be subject to legal sanctions under her and Dworkin's antipornography law.

MacKinnon's and Dworkin's views on prostitution are closely related to their views on pornography. They believe that, just as women cannot voluntarily consent to pose for pornography, they cannot voluntarily consent to work in any aspect of the sex industry, including prostitution. Accordingly, just as they advocate imposing legal sanctions on pornography, they oppose lifting legal sanctions from prostitution.[32]

During the spring of 1992, the student editors of the then-new *Michigan Journal of Gender & Law,* behind which Mac-Kinnon was a "moving force,"[33] were planning a symposium on prostitution for the fall of 1992. In conjunction with this conference, they invited artist Carol Jacobsen to curate an art exhibit on prostitution, including her own work, to present the views and experiences of prostitutes in their own voices. Although the students assured Jacobsen that the symposium would not be dominated by MacKinnon's antipornography, antilegalization-of-prostitution perspective, in fact, the symposium turned out to be exclusively for speakers with that perspective, including Dworkin and MacKinnon themselves.

Shortly before the symposium took place, student organizers admitted to Jacobsen that it had in fact become more a forum for the antipornography movement than for a discussion of prostitution. The invited antipornography, antilegalization-of-prostitution activists, following their familiar tactic, refused to appear if feminists holding different views were also invited. Although Jacobsen found these developments disturbing, they also made her feel that her exhibit would be more important than ever, since it would provide the only dissent from the MacDworkinite view at the two-day conference.

Jacobsen's exhibit included Jacobsen's own *Street Sex* (1989), candid video interviews with Detroit prostitutes who had just been released from jail; *Angelina Foxy* (1986–present), an ongoing photo-text essay by Paula Allen, documenting the life of a Jersey City prostitute; *The Salt Mines* (1990), a critically acclaimed documentary about homeless transvestite hustlers in New York City by Susanna Aikin and Carlos Aparicio; *Outlaw Poverty, Not Prostitutes* (1991), an activist video by Carol Leigh (aka "Scarlot Harlot") chronicling prostitutes' international organizing to improve their working conditions; *Portrait of a Sexual Evolutionary* (1987) by Veronica Vera, an autobiographical account of her experiences as a former porn actress, producer of female-oriented erotic films, and prostitutes' rights activist; and two pieces by Randy Barbato, *Transvestite Prostitutes,* a short, campy view of transvestite street prostitutes with RuPaul in Manhattan, and *My Own Private Seattle,* about rent boys in Seattle.

The exhibit had been on display for only a few hours when a conference speaker, objecting to the sexual imagery it contained, complained to MacKinnon. MacKinnon in turn conveyed this complaint to the student organizers, who promptly removed a composite videotape containing the works of five of the exhibit's seven artists. According to Jacobsen, the student who removed the tape explained to her that she had done so under pressure from MacKinnon, who had received a complaint that the tape was pornographic.[34]

Jacobsen read a statement at the conference deploring the removal of the tape, stressing that she had selected the videos on it specifically because "they focus on prostitutes' and sex workers' own voices." She announced that she had reinstalled the tape and concluded, "If the conference organizers wish to censor or remove any part of the exhibit *again,* they must censor all of it."[35] Shortly after this statement, the student organizers met with MacKinnon, Dworkin, and two other antipornography activists who were speaking at the conference. According to press accounts, during this meeting, MacKinnon warned the students of the dangers of showing pornography, even in an academic context, and Dworkin told them that she had been harassed by men who had viewed pornography.[36] After this discussion, the students decided to tell Jacobsen that the entire exhibit would have to be removed.

As a result of this censorial action, a two-day conference purportedly on "Prostitution: From Academia to Activism," was completely stripped of any expression on behalf of the many sex industry activists who support decriminalization of prostitution. In fact, it included no voices of any current sex industry workers at all. As Veronica Vera wrote in an open letter to the University of Michigan newspaper: "If you were trying to study any other subject, you would study the experts. Carol Jacobsen offered you practical experts."[37] The voices—as well as the choices—of these women, along with the many other feminists who call for decriminalizing prostitution, were silenced by the conference organizers and speakers.

MacKinnon has sought to dissociate herself from this sorry episode by saying that she did not explicitly tell the students to remove the art exhibit. But, regardless of whether MacKinnon expressly urged them to remove the Jacobsen exhibit, a student confided to Jacobsen that she felt pressured by MacKinnon. As observed by ACLU attorney Marjorie Heins, who (along with Robert Carbeck of the Michigan ACLU) represented Jacobsen and the other artists in challenging this suppression of their work, "MacKinnon expressed to the students her already well-known opinions about pornography. . . . The students were practicing what the professor had frequently preached."[38]

Across the country, critics denounced this removal of feminist artworks from a law school–underwritten and –sponsored conference. In response, apologists for the episode asserted that the students were acting to protect the safety and comfort of symposium participants. As student Brian Wells said, "We really didn't think of it as a censorship issue, but as a safety issue, because two of our speakers said that based on their experience at other events, the tape would be a threat to their safety."[39]

Again, the familiar MacDworkinite tactic of eluding the appropriate—and appropriately stigmatizing—term "censorship" simply masks the real impact of the actions they initiate, influence, and endorse. In the Michigan episode, MacKinnon's and Dworkin's views at least influenced others to deprive female, feminist artists and their potential audience of an opportunity to display or view images and to express or hear views on crucially important issues concerning women's equality, women's sexuality, and women's safety. As stated by Leanne Katz, the executive director of the National Coalition Against Censorship, "The . . . suppression of an art exhibit . . . because the ideas expressed in the exhibit were 'wrong' is blatant censorship. There's no other word for it."[40]

This ugly episode demonstrates that the feminist antipornography movement will inevitably suppress not only works that are especially valuable to women and feminists because they deal with the centrally important topics of sex and gender, but also works that have broad-ranging artistic and political value. Important issues examined in the censored tapes included police abuse, prison conditions, poverty, and homelessness. It is nothing short of Orwellian that such works, in many respects as compelling artistically as they were politically, could be peremptorily confiscated as "pornography" that threatened conferees' "safety." That this action happened at a prestigious law school, and was defended by a dean who has written books about the First Amendment,[41] heightens its nightmarish quality. As Carole Vance concluded, "This case . . . shatters the illusion that restricting sexual imagery for feminist purposes is distinguishable from fundamentalist censorship—either in method or consequence."[42]

In light of the actual record of MacDworkinites' disrespect for other female, feminist voices and choices, it should be clear that the "protection" they seek to bestow would hardly be beneficial to all women. Many of us would like to be protected against such protection.

## CHAPTER 11

# Lessons from Enforcement

## WHEN THE POWERFUL GET MORE POWER

> In a male supremacist society the only obscenity law that will not be used against women is no law at all. . . . How long will it take oppressed groups to learn that if we give the state enough rope, it will end up around our necks?
>
> ELLEN WILLIS, writer[1]

> The master's tools will never dismantle the master's house.
>
> AUDRE LORDE, poet[2]

The last chapter showed how much we would have to fear from enforcement of their antipornography scheme by Dworkin and MacKinnon themselves. This chapter shows how much we would have to fear from enforcement of that scheme by any individuals or government officials. Most ominously, the enforcement record in Canada, which in 1992 embraced the procensorship feminists' notion of pornography, has turned anticensorship feminists' fears into realities.

The fundamental premise in the procensorship feminists' philosophy—that our entire societal and legal system is patriarchal, reflecting and perpetuating the subordination of women—itself conclusively refutes their conclusion that we should hand over to that system additional power. The procensorship feminists cannot have it both ways. If, as they contend, governmental power is inevitably used to the particular disadvantage of relatively disempowered groups, such as women, it follows that women's rights advocates should oppose measures that augment that power, including Dworkin-MacKinnon–type laws. As columnist George Will observed: "For someone who so strenuously loathes American society, which she says is defined by pornography, MacKinnon is remarkably eager to vest in this society's representative government vast powers to regulate expression."[3]

## The Conspicuous Absence
## of Sexual Speech in Repressive Regimes

Under patriarchy, no woman is safe to live her life, or to love, or to mother children. Under patriarchy, every woman is a victim, past, present, and future. Under patriarchy, every woman's daughter is a victim, past, present, and future. Under patriarchy, every woman's son is her potential betrayer and also the inevitable rapist or exploiter of another woman.

ANDREA DWORKIN[4]

[I]t is the state—not free speech—that has been the oppressor of women. It was the state, not pornography, that burned women as witches. It was 18th and 19th century law, not pornography, that defined women as chattel. . . . 20th century laws refuse to recognize rape within marriage. . . . It is the state, not pornography, that has raised barriers against women. It is censorship, not freedom, that will keep the walls intact.

WENDY MCELROY, writer[5]

Sexual expression is an integral aspect of human freedom. Throughout history, down to the present day, the suppression of sexually explicit speech has characterized regimes that repress both free speech and human rights in general. Measures to suppress sexual expression consistently have targeted views that challenge the prevailing political, religious, cultural, or social orthodoxy.

Sexually explicit speech has been banned by the most repressive regimes, including Communism in the former Soviet Union, Eastern bloc countries, and China; apartheid in South Africa; and fascist or clerical dictatorships in Chile, Iran, and Iraq. Conversely, recent studies of Russia have correlated improvements in human rights, including women's rights, with the rise of free sexual expression. Writer Pete Hamill explains the connection:

> Recent history teaches us that most tyrannies have a puritanical nature. The sexual restrictions of Stalin's Soviet Union, Hitler's Germany and Mao's China would have gladdened the hearts of those Americans who fear sexual images and literature. Their ironfisted puritanism wasn't motivated by a need to erase inequality. They wanted to smother the personal chaos that can accompany sexual freedom and subordinate it to the granite face of the state. Every tyrant knows that if he can control human sexuality, he can control life.[6]

In places where real pornography is conspicuously absent, tellingly, works of political dissent are labeled as such. Laws banning obscene or pornographic expression have been used to suppress all kinds of expression, and the pejorative terms "obscene" and "pornographic" have been used to condemn a wide range of views, far beyond the legal or dictionary definitions of those terms, and even altogether outside the realm of sexuality. The Communist government of the former Soviet Union denounced dissenting political views as pornographic and obscene, and suppressed political dissidents under obscenity laws. In August 1987, when the Chinese Communist government dramatically increased its censorship of books and magazines with Western political and literary messages, it condemned them as "obscene," "pornographic," and "bawdy." The white supremacist South African government banned black writing as "pornographically immoral." In Nazi Germany and the former Soviet Union, Jewish writings were reviled as "pornographic," as were any works that criticized the Nazi or Communist party, respectively.[7]

Even in societies that generally respect human rights, including free speech, as we have seen, the term "pornography" tends to be used as an epithet to stigmatize expression that is politically or socially unpopular. Accordingly, the freedom to produce or consume anything called "pornography" is an essential aspect of the freedom to defy prevailing political and social mores. Pornography is not just the samizdat of individuals who are oppressed or dissident sexually, to paraphrase Stanford law professor Kathleen Sullivan; it is also the samizdat of those who are oppressed or dissident in any respect.

Legal scholar Kenneth L. Karst provides intriguing insights into the link between sexual freedom, including free sexual expression, and freedom from discrimination:

> The suppression of Unreason is rooted in the same fears that produce group subordination: men's fear of the feminine, whites' fear of blackness, heterosexuals' anxiety about sexual orientation. Historically, all these fears have been closely connected with the fear of sexuality. It is no accident that the 1960s, a period of sexual "revolution," also saw the acceleration of three movements that sought major redefinitions of America's social boundaries: the civil rights movement, the gay liberation movement, and the women's movement.[8]

Like all groups who seek equal rights and freedoms, women and feminists have an especially important stake in securing free speech. Throughout history, free speech consistently has been the greatest ally of those seeking equal rights for groups that have been subject to discrimination. Correspondingly, censorship measures have consistently been used to the particular detriment of the relatively unpopular and powerless.

## Hating Speech

The pattern of disempowered groups being disproportionately targeted under censorship schemes extends even to censorship schemes that are allegedly designed for their benefit. This phenomenon is vividly illustrated by the enforcement record of laws against "hate speech"—speech that expresses racial, sexist, religious, and other forms of invidious discrimination. I addressed the First Amendment flaws of hate speech laws in chapter 3; since feminist-style antipornography laws are simply a specific kind of anti–hate speech law, it is important also to examine such laws' historical enforcement record. This record demonstrates, once again, that procensorship feminists posit a false choice between free speech and equality values. As Justice Hugo Black noted in dissenting from a 1952 Supreme Court decision upholding a hate speech law (which has been implicitly overturned by subsequent decisions),[9] "If there be minority groups who hail this holding as their victory, they might consider the possible relevancy of this ancient remark: 'Another such victory and I am undone.' "[10]

The first individuals prosecuted under the British Race Relations Act of 1965, which criminalized the incitement of racial hatred, were black power leaders. Their overtly racist messages undoubtedly expressed legitimate anger at real discrimination, yet the statute drew no such fine lines, nor could any similar law possibly do so. Rather than curbing speech offensive to minorities, this British law instead has been used regularly to curb the speech of blacks, trade unionists, and antinuclear activists. Perhaps the ultimate irony of this law, intended to restrain the National Front, a neo-Nazi group, is that it instead has barred expression by the Anti-Nazi League.

The British experience is typical. None of the anti-Semites who were responsible for arousing France against Captain Alfred Dreyfus was ever prosecuted for group libel. But Emile Zola was prosecuted for libeling the French clergy and military in his classic letter "J'Accuse," and he had to flee to England to escape punishment.

Similarly, University of Michigan Law School professor Eric Stein has documented that although the German Criminal Code of 1871 punished offenses against personal honor, "The German Supreme Court . . . consistently refused to apply this article to insults against Jews as a group—although it gave the benefit of its protection to such groups as Germans living in Prussian provinces, large landowners, all Christian clerics, German officers, and Prussian troops who fought in Belgium and Northern France."[11]

That the foregoing examples simply illustrate a long-standing global pattern was documented in a 1992 book published by Article XIX, the London-based International Centre Against Censorship (which takes its name from the free speech guarantee in the Universal Declaration of Human Rights) and the Human Rights Centre at the University of Essex in Great Britain, which draws upon contemporary analyses of the situations in fourteen different countries with various laws punishing racist and other hate speech. According to Sandra Coliver, Article XIX's legal director:

> The flagrant abuse of laws which restrict hate speech by the authorities . . . provides the most troubling indictment of such laws. Thus, the laws in Sri Lanka and South Africa have been used almost exclusively against the oppressed and politically weakest communities. . . . Selective or lax enforcement by the authorities, including in the UK, Israel and the former Soviet Union, allows governments to compromise the right of dissent and inevitably leads to disaffection and feelings of alienation among minority groups.[12]

The international pattern also holds true in specific, localized contexts—namely, on university and college campuses, where, as we have seen, antipornography feminists have made some headway. Again, the British experience is instructive. In 1974, in a move aimed at the National Front, the British National Union of Students (NUS) adopted a resolution that representatives of "openly racist and fascist organizations" were to be prevented from speaking on college campuses "by whatever means necessary (including disruption of the meeting)."[13]

The rule had been designed in large part to stem an increase in campus anti-Semitism. But following the United Nations' cue, some British students deemed Zionism a form of racism beyond the bounds of permitted discussion, and in 1975 British students invoked the NUS resolution to disrupt speeches by Israelis and Zionists, including the Israeli ambassador to Great Britain. The intended target of the NUS resolution, the National Front, applauded this result. The NUS itself, in contrast, became disenchanted by this and other unintended consequences of its resolution and repealed it in 1977.

The British experience parallels what has happened in the United States, judging from the campus hate speech codes for which enforcement information is available.[14] One such code was in effect at the University of Michigan from April 1988 until October 1989. Because the American Civil Liberties Union brought a lawsuit to challenge the code (which resulted in a ruling that the code was unconstitutional),[15] the university was forced to disclose information that otherwise would have been unavailable to the public about how it had been enforced. This enforcement record, while not surprising to anyone familiar with the consistent history of censorship measures, should come as a rude awakening to any who believe that anti-hate speech laws will protect or benefit racial minorities, women, or any other group that has traditionally suffered discrimination.

During the year and a half that the University of Michigan rule was in effect, there were more than twenty cases of whites charging blacks with racist speech. More importantly, the only two instances in which the rule was invoked to sanction racist speech (as opposed to other forms of hate speech) involved the punishment of speech by or on behalf of black students. The only student who was subjected to a full-fledged disciplinary hearing under the Michigan rule was an African-American student accused of homophobic and sexist expression. In seeking clemency from the punishment that was imposed on him after this hearing, the student asserted that he had been singled out because of his race and his political views.

Others who were punished at Michigan included several

Jewish students accused of engaging in anti-Semitic expression (they wrote graffiti, including a swastika, on a classroom blackboard; they said they intended it as a practical joke) and an Asian-American student accused of making an antiblack comment (his allegedly "hateful" remark was to ask why black people feel discriminated against; he said he raised this question because the black students in his dormitory tended to socialize together, making him feel isolated). Likewise, the student who in 1989 challenged the University of Connecticut's hate speech policy, under which she had been penalized for an allegedly homophobic remark, was Asian-American. She claimed that other students had engaged in similar expression, but that she had been singled out for punishment because of her ethnic background. (Representing this student, the ACLU persuaded the university to drop the challenged policy.)[16] And the first complaint filed under Trinity College's then-new policy prohibiting racial harassment, in 1989, was against an African-American speaker who had been sponsored by a black student organization, Black-Power Serves Itself.

The hate speech lesson from enforcement? Watch what you say about others, depending on not only who those others are, but also who you are. If you are a member of a group that has traditionally suffered discrimination, including women, restrictions on hate speech are especially likely to be wielded against your speech. In fact, as we now shall see, all forms of censorship have consistently been used to suppress speech of and for women.

### Women in the Wake of Censorship

Censorship has been, throughout history, the single most widely used patriarchal tool for "protecting" women—from birth control, abortion, sexual satisfaction and non-heterosexual relationships. Without free speech we can have no feminist movement.

> National Organization for Women
> of New York State[17]

> I believe that censorship only springs back against the givers
> of culture—against authors, artists, and feminists, against
> anybody who wants to change society. Should censorship be
> imposed . . . feminists would be the first to suffer.
>
> ERICA JONG, writer[18]

Although we "babes" have "come a long way," as the saying goes, could we have come further, faster without the "help" of censors? Here, the lesson from enforcement is that women should go slow on censorship, because censorship consistently has been used to slow our search for equal status.

Until recently, the "gag rule," in effect from 1988 until 1993, banned the dissemination of information about abortion at federally funded family planning clinics. (In the fall of 1994, more than three hundred Republican congressional candidates pledged to reinstate the gag rule as part of the Contract with America.) As columnist Anna Quindlen observed, "What the gag rule has taught us is that reproductive freedom is not possible without free speech."[19] Indeed, that lesson should have been learned from the steady use of censorship, throughout our history, to fetter women's reproductive freedom.

Of particular note, laws permitting the suppression of sexually oriented information have often been used to suppress information that is essential not only for women's reproductive rights, but also for other aspects of the women's rights cause. Antiobscenity laws consistently have been used to suppress information about contraception. Dr. Charles Knowlton, author of the first known medical work about contraception in the United States, *Fruits of Philosophy; or, The Private Companion of Young Married People,* was prosecuted in 1839 under the Massachusetts antiobscenity law.

Likewise, the first federal antiobscenity statute, passed in 1873, criminalized the interstate mailing of both sexually oriented material and material related to contraception or abortion. This statute, which is generally known as the "Comstock" law, in honor of the leading antiobscenity crusader Anthony Comstock, who had lobbied for it, provided:

No obscene, lewd, or lascivious book, pamphlet, picture, paper, print, or other publication of an indecent character, or any article or thing designed or intended for the prevention of conception or procuring of abortion, nor any article or thing intended or adapted for any indecent or immoral use or nature . . . shall be carried in the mail.[20]

Each violation of the law could be punished with a fine of up to five thousand dollars or imprisonment at hard labor for one to ten years. Twenty-four states enacted legislation that was modeled on this federal law, prohibiting not only the intrastate transportation of obscene materials, contraceptives, and abortifacients, but also their advertisement or publications about them. Moreover, fourteen state antiobscenity statutes also enjoined speech about contraception and abortion.

Armed with this legislation, Comstock, the longtime director of the Society for the Suppression of Vice, as well as his successor, John Sumner, zealously prosecuted feminists and pioneering birth control advocates who tried to distribute information about women's sexuality and reproduction. Among those Comstock persecuted, at least fifteen women committed suicide, including Ida Craddock, who was imprisoned in 1902 for writing advice manuals on conjugal relations.

In her 1992 biography of Margaret Sanger, the leading early birth control champion, Ellen Chesler noted that the Comstock-inspired antiobscenity laws all but banned any discussion of contraception, even between doctors and patients and within the medical community.[21] Because these laws suppressed much scientific, accurate information about contraception and abortion, the only "information" readily available was in underground publications by quacks and charlatans.[22]

Sanger was persecuted under the antiobscenity laws throughout her career. Her campaign to convey accurate sexual information began in 1912 with two articles in a New York City newspaper. The first, entitled "What Every Mother Should Know," ran without incident, but the U.S. Post Office barred the second, "What Every Girl Should Know." The article contained no information on birth control, but postal officials were offended by Sanger's explanation of venereal disease and her use of words such as "gonorrhea" and "syphilis." Consequently, the newspaper's next issue contained the following announcement: "What Every Girl Should Know: 'NOTHING!' By order of the Post Office."[23]

In 1913, Anthony Comstock prosecuted Sanger for her writings on sexuality and birth control. She was criminally prosecuted again in 1917 and served thirty days in a workhouse for having operated a birth control clinic in Brooklyn. Sanger also served time in jail in Portland, Oregon, for distributing information about birth control. In 1929, she was "banned in Boston"—prohibited from speaking there.

Margaret Sanger had the dubious distinction of being one of the first victims of a new form of censorship that was applied to a then-new medium early in this century. The Supreme Court had ruled in 1915 that movies were not protected "speech" under the First Amendment,[24] and one of the first films banned under that decision was *Birth Control,* a 1917 picture produced by and featuring Margaret Sanger. The New York Court of Appeals held that this movie, a dramatization of Sanger's family planning work, could be censored "in the interest of morality, decency, and public safety and welfare."[25]

This episode underscores several significant themes explored in this book: the close connections between sex and politics, and between sexual and political repression; and the bad tendencies of the former "bad tendency" rationale for suppressing speech (that speech may be censored because it might tend to bring about some future harm), which procensorship feminists are seeking to revive. The court stressed that the film "tends to ridicule the public authorities and the provisions of . . . the Penal Law forbidding the dissemination of contraceptive knowledge," and therefore held that it could be barred, even for adult-only audiences, because it "may engender a desire to obtain" birth control information, and thus might "lead to violations of the law."

The banning of films concerning birth control and other sexual-political subjects of particular interest to women and feminists continued into the second half of this century. In support of his argument that "women who are claiming their equal citizenship should think twice about pressing the argument that pornography is not protected speech," UCLA law professor Kenneth Karst noted that, until the 1950s, New York censors routinely banned films that treated themes of particular concern to women's rights advocates: pregnancy, venereal disease, birth control, abortion, illegitimacy, prostitution, miscegenation, and divorce.[26]

From 1873, when the Comstock Act was passed, through the 1930s, other feminists and health experts who tried to present information about women's sexuality and reproductive options were also plagued by obscenity laws. Charges were brought against Emma Goldman for giving information about birth control during a lecture in New York. Mary Ware Dennett was convicted and sentenced to pay a three hundred dollar fine for her book *The Sex Side of Life: An Explanation for Young People*,[27] which she had written for the education of her adolescent sons. Marie Stopes's *Married Love,* which offered basic anatomical information and health advice to newly married couples, was prosecuted under American antiobscenity laws, even though it was an established bestseller in Europe and had already been expurgated for the American market.[28] (The ACLU represented Dennett and Stopes, and on appeal succeeded in overturning Dennett's conviction and the U.S. Customs Service's ban on both their books.)

Edward Bliss Foote, a popular health writer, was convicted in a prosecution brought by Comstock and forced to eliminate all information about contraception from his published writings. Comstock also successfully prosecuted Ezra Heywood, who had distributed a journal that advertised contraceptives. *A Marriage Manual,* by Hannah and Abraham Stone, was subjected to censorship efforts when it was first published in 1935.

The gag has been loosened or tightened at various times, but never removed. In 1990 Janet Benshoof, director of the ACLU's Reproductive Freedom Project, was charged with the misdemeanor of "soliciting abortion" under the strict antiabortion law that Guam had just passed. Her alleged crime? Benshoof said, during a speech at the Guam Press Club, that Guamanian women could still get legal, low-cost abortions in Hawaii, despite Guam's law criminalizing virtually all abortions, and she gave Guamanian women the address and phone number of Planned Parenthood in Hawaii.[29] This was eighty years after Margaret Sanger, Planned Parenthood's founding mother, was first prosecuted for providing similar information.

We women must go forward. The past is not as different from the present as the future must be. In Anna Quindlen's words:

> In the fight to keep women free it is important to remember this: freedom of speech is the bedrock of it all. Silence is what kept us in our place for too long. If we now silence others, our liberty is false. No more gag rules—that should be our goal. In clinics, in colleges, in lecture halls. Anywhere.[30]

### *Butler* Did It: "Big Surprise" in Canada

Thanks to the Canadian Supreme Court's February 1992 decision in *Butler v. The Queen,* we have been able to observe the MacDworkinite regime in operation. As far as Canada is concerned, Erica Jong's prediction quoted earlier—that "feminists would be the first to suffer" under any newly imposed censorship—is, alas, now a description.

Andrea Dworkin has said, "The *Butler* decision is probably the best articulation of how pornography, and what kinds of pornography, hurt the civil status and civil rights of women,"[31] and Catharine MacKinnon has enthused, "[The *Butler* decision] is a stunning victory for women. This is of world historic importance. This makes Canada the first place in the world that says what is obscene is what harms women, not what offends our values."[32] Others, though they may agree about the decision's "world historic importance," offer dramatically different assessments:

You presented a brief to the Supreme Court that has us in the shits right now. . . . [Y]ou handed them post-modern language. . . . the language that they had been looking for to come back after us, and now they are busting our bookstores.

Elaine Carol, performance artist, addressing feminist lawyer whose arguments were adopted in *Butler*, 1993[33]

This law isn't protecting us; it's silencing us.

Liz Czach, member of feminist caucus of the Ontario Coalition Against Film and Video Censorship[34]

Andrea Dworkin has done more damage to women's culture in her tenure as darling of the media than anyone who is a leader of the right wing. She is morally responsible for what is happening to women's literature in Canada.

Pat Califia, feminist writer, 1993[35]

*Butler* is just about morality. It's morality in the guise of protecting women and children. And who needs the protection of the male patriarchy anyway, of the state?

Ellen Flanders, feminist writer[36]

The *Butler* decision has been a potent weapon to suppress free speech for all, as well as the equality rights of various disempowered groups, including the very women whose rights it was supposed to enhance. As a 1993 article in *The Nation* commented, "This epidemic of censorship shows how 'progressive' controls on expression are bound to backfire." It concluded, "If Canada's border fiasco gives pause to MacKinnonites in other countries—the lobby for the Pornography Victims' Compensation Act in the United States, for example—maybe it will have been worth the absurdities."[37]

Because Canada's experience under *Butler* provides the only record of the actual impact of a Dworkin-MacKinnon–style law in operation, it is important to examine that record in detail. At the very least, the Canadian experience imposes a heavy burden of proof on antipornography advocates to show that the enforcement trends in Canada would not be replicated here. That burden of proof seems to be insurmountable, though, since the Canadian enforcement trends result from two factors that transcend the U.S.-Canada border: the inherently vague concept of "subordinating" or "degrading" material that is at the heart of all MacDworkinite laws; and the homophobic, antifeminist orientation that many Canadian officials share not only with their U.S. counterparts, but also with many private citizens in both countries.

Indeed, in two important respects, the Canadian version of the feminist antipornography law is less sweeping than the original Dworkin-MacKinnon model. First, notwithstanding *Butler*'s incorporation of the MacDworkinite concept of pornography into the Canadian antiobscenity law, that law continues to provide that no material will be deemed obscene if it has an artistic purpose or is part of the serious treatment of a sexual theme. This is similar to the provision in the U.S. Supreme Court's definition of obscenity that excludes any material with serious literary, artistic, political, or scientific value. The Dworkin-MacKinnon model law, though, contains no comparable limitation.

Second, and relatedly, the Canadian obscenity law, again parallel to American obscenity law, applies only to works considered as a whole. Therefore, a work cannot be suppressed just because isolated passages meet the obscenity definition. Under the Dworkin-MacKinnon law, in contrast, even an isolated sexually explicit, subordinating depiction would warrant suppressing an entire work, regardless of its overall value.

The spring 1993 issue of *Feminist Bookstore News,* a Canadian publication, contained the following description of Canada's first year of experience with the antipornography definition that was supposed to be such a boon to feminists: "The *Butler* decision has been used . . . only to seize lesbian, gay and feminist material."[38] Within the first two and a half years after the *Butler* decision, well over half of all Canadian feminist bookstores had had materials confiscated or detained by customs. From Quebec to Victoria, Canadian bookstore managers had the same comment: that *Butler* increased censorship in Canada by customs, police, and lower courts, and that the predominant targets have been gay, lesbian, and women's literature.

Even those Canadian feminists who championed the *Butler* decision—working through the Women's Legal Education and Action Fund (LEAF), which MacKinnon cofounded—have been forced to acknowledge that it has become an engine for oppressing feminist, gay, and lesbian expression. Karen Busby, a lawyer who worked on the LEAF brief, made the following confession at a symposium in Toronto during the fall of 1993:

> Before the ink was dry on *Butler* . . . the Toronto police raided Glad Day Bookshop, a lesbian and gay bookstore, and confiscated *Bad Attitude,* a lesbian erotic magazine. . . . It was a shocking raid. Police ignored representations made by men of women in most cities across Canada, including . . . Toronto . . . and yet the one thing that they raid is this one magazine that sells about forty copies every two months in Canada when it comes out. It's hardly a threat to women's equality and yet that's the magazine that they chose.[39]

To add insult to injury, while Glad Day's owner and manager were arrested for selling *Bad Attitude,* a nearby mainstream bookstore that also sold it was left alone.

*Bad Attitude* is a magazine published by and for women—specifically, lesbian women. Its editor has explained that the magazine "is called *Bad Attitude* because that's what women who take their sexuality into their own hands (so to speak) are told they have."[40] Nonetheless, the judge who ruled in the Glad Day case found that this feminist, lesbian publication harmed women, and he therefore convicted the Glad Day principals. His ruling was based on a story (told just in words, with no photographs or illustrations) in the magazine about a sex fantasy, entitled "Wunna My Fantasies," by San Francisco writer Trish Thomas. The story is about a woman who surprises another woman in a shower, grabbing her, tying her, slapping her, and pulling her hair. While the showering woman initially resists her assailant's sexual advances, she ultimately succumbs, and they both end up enjoying their sexual encounter. Thomas has said that when she does public readings of her stories about this kind of lesbian fantasy, with some sadomasochistic elements, she is "amazed" by "not just the numbers of women that come up to me . . . to tell me that they've had these fantasies, but the diversity of women—very conservative women too."[41]

Despite the fact that women enjoy the type of fantasy described in "Wunna My Fantasies," the male judge who found it "degrading" and "demeaning," Claude Paris, explained that its fatal flaw was that it described "enjoyable sex after subordination by bondage and physical abuse at the hands of a total stranger." He dismissed the fact that the fantasy's aggressor is female as "irrelevant." Taking his cue from the Canadian Supreme Court in *Butler*, Judge Paris ruled that the ultimately consensual nature of the sex the story describes is not enough to absolve it of the criminalizing "degrading" label. He stated: "The consent . . . far from redeeming the material, makes it degrading and dehumanizing."[42]

A second lower court decision enforcing *Butler* also resulted from seizures of homosexual erotica from Glad Day Bookshop and also held homosexual expression to be "degrading." This decision, issued by Judge F. C. Hayes, held all thirteen of the confiscated gay publications to be "degrading and dehumanizing," explaining only that they showed sexual encounters "without any real, meaningful human relationship."[43] As Karen Busby of LEAF acknowledged, "Judge Hayes' decision [is] clearly homophobic. . . . He said that sex between men in and of itself was degrading and dehumanizing."[44] Chris Bearchell, a lesbian feminist journalist in Canada, commented:

> Before Hayes's ruling, some people no doubt hoped that the Butler decision might bring more enlightened obscenity rulings, because of the court's declaration that its role was to protect women and children from harm. . . . Now they are probably wondering just what pictures and descriptions of consenting men having sex with each other have to do with violence against women and children.[45]

Despite the boasting of Dworkin, MacKinnon, and (at least initially) their LEAF allies that *Butler* ushered in a brave new era of profeminist censorship, Judge Hayes's ruling makes clear instead that *Butler* simply allows censorship on traditional moralistic grounds. Indeed, precisely that interpretation of *Butler* has been made by "Project P," the antiobscenity squad of the Ontario Provincial Police. According to a spokesman, Project P interprets *Butler* to permit explicit sexual expression only if it includes romance and a story line.[46] This prompted Susan Ditta, former curator of the National Gallery of Canada and now the media arts officer at the Canada Council, to comment, "As someone who's spent a great deal of time writing about the deconstruction of narrative in contemporary video art practice, I got really worried about there having to be a story line."[47]

The fact that *Butler* merely provides a new gloss on an old notion of obscenity is underscored by its lack of any impact on the detailed regulations that Canadian Customs officials had previously followed in enforcing the obscenity law at the border. After *Butler,* government lawyers reviewed those regulations and concluded that not one word needed to be changed. As stated by Jacques Boivin, a Canadian artist, this "just goes to show that the reputedly 'feminist' definition of 'degradation' is not a departure but . . . a further reformulation of paternalistic control. Same old baloney with a recycled label."[48] Lawyer Brenda Cossman, who teaches at Canada's York University, calls the new label "sexual morality in drag."[49]

Another aspect of the Glad Day case, the singling out of publications, publishers, distributors, and stores that are relatively small and powerless, also heralded what has been a continuing enforcement pattern under *Butler.* Inland Books, a New York–based small-press book distribution company and the largest U.S. exporter of lesbian and gay literature to Canada, had 73 percent of its shipments to Canada detained during 1993. In one of the biggest book detentions in its history, Canadian Customs detained a 1993 shipment of hundreds of titles from Inland to thirty-six Canadian stores, including university bookstores, literary bookshops, and even a religious bookstore. The distributors that serve lesbian and gay bookstores often carry political publications other than those targeted specifically for the lesbian and gay audience. Because it was part of such a shipment, a September 1993 issue of *The Nation* was detained by Canadian Customs officials.

The *Butler* decision has been used preponderantly against publications with a feminist or lesbian/gay orientation. More mainstream-oriented materials that tend to be sold in mainstream establishments have been undisturbed, benefiting from an apparent double standard in the enforcement of *Butler*. A prominent example is Madonna's *Sex*, which was published by a major commercial house and was sold in large, chain bookstores. (The book's sexually explicit contents, including scenes of rape and bestiality, were deemed sufficiently degrading by MacDworkinites that they publicly ripped it to shreds at the previously discussed 1992 feminist procensorship conference at the University of Chicago Law School.) Likewise, since *Butler*, Canadian authorities have not interfered with the importation or sale of Bret Easton Ellis's *American Psycho*, which contains extremely violent, sexually graphic accounts of the mutilation of women.

*The Toronto Star* has reported that, in many further instances, books destined for nonmainstream bookstores have been seized and banned by customs while the big chain stores are allowed to sell the very same books. Small bookstores are thus suffering substantial economic hardships. The Toronto-based *Globe and Mail* estimated that 75 percent of shipments to Glad Day and similar stores are "opened, delayed, lost, forgotten and occasionally sent back without more than a handful of Canadian citizens knowing about it."[50] According to *The Toronto Star*, "Books dealing with homosexual activities are seized regularly and often held for months, quite literally in an attempt to close down the offending stores."[51] Notes Bruce Walsh, a spokesperson for the Canadian anticensorship coalition CENSORSTOP, "[E]very gay bookseller in this country has attempted to sell their bookstores, but nobody wants to buy them."[52]

One lesbian bookstore has fought back against the Canadian government's selective suppression of lesbian sexual expression. The Little Sisters Book and Art Emporium in Vancouver brought a lawsuit claiming that it had been subjected to government harassment. After the lawsuit was instituted—and, some critics charge, specifically to blunt its allegations—Canadian officials broadened their enforcement efforts to include feminist bookstores, university bookstores, and radical bookstores.

CENSORSTOP has charged that the officials who are implementing *Butler* are "really interested in controlling radical dissent."[53] When Le Dernier Mot (LDM) bookstore published and sold transcripts of a telephone conversation that was politically embarrassing to the Canadian government, and that the government had attempted to ban from publication, customs authorities immediately began to seize books that were being shipped to LDM as allegedly violating the *Butler* obscenity standard. Prior to this incident, no LDM books had ever been seized. Likewise, just one week after Pages Bookstore in Toronto had installed a provocative anticensorship display, customs seized allegedly obscene books that were being shipped to it.

Whether or not Canadian officials have actually exercised their discretionary authority under *Butler* to target political dissent, it is indisputable that the Canadian Supreme Court's adoption of the Dworkin-MacKinnon antipornography standard has given officials a powerful weapon that they could easily aim at dissent, should they wish to do so.

Recalling that *Butler*'s supposed rationale is to protect women from works that harm them, it is hard to understand how the feminist writings that have been seized under *Butler* would harm women. Indeed, some material has been suppressed under *Butler* on the ground that it is allegedly degrading and harmful not to women, but to men. For example, Canadian Customs has seized a book entitled *Weenie-Toons! Women Artists Mock Cocks* because of its alleged "degradation of the male penis."[54] Similarly, customs' banned list includes a lesbian feminist magazine entitled *Hothead Paisan,* even though it portrays no sexual activity, because it is purportedly "sexually degrading to men."[55] This comic book–style magazine depicts the adventures of a lesbian terrorist who won't take any guff from men, and who makes those who give her trouble disappear.

In one of the condemned *Hothead Paisan* strips, a white man wearing a business suit chains himself to a statue of Christopher Columbus (on which is engraved, "I found it, it's mine, kill those people") and declares, "Women will have the right to choose over my dead body!" In response, the magazine's heroine, the lesbian avenger "Hothead," springs into action. Crying "Now that's an engraved invitation!" she beats this antichoice demonstrator into the ground.[56] In addition to turning the tables on the incapacitating woman-as-victim stereotype, this strip conveys messages about other political issues, including colonialism and reproductive freedom. What a travesty that it has been suppressed in the name of feminism, under a feminist-advocated law!

And of course two books written by Andrea Dworkin herself, *Pornography: Men Possessing Women* and *Woman Hating*, were seized at the U.S.-Canada border. According to customs, they "illegally eroticized pain and bondage."[57] Dworkin's graphic, sexually explicit descriptions of men committing violent and degrading acts against women are presumably provided for purposes of persuading society to mobilize against misogynistic violence and discrimination. But neither the *Butler* decision nor any other version of the Dworkin-MacKinnon antipornography law contains any exception for subordinating sexually explicit depictions that are part of a feminist presentation. Nor could any such exception possibly be added without compounding the law's already overwhelming subjectivity. (In my view, this book—the one you are reading—is a feminist work, but would Andrea Dworkin or Catharine MacKinnon agree?)

At least one other book that described sexual violence expressly for the purpose of condemning it and aiding people to resist it was also, ironically, among the first targets of *Butler*'s censorial regime. It was a novel by Robert Lally, a retired Canadian psychologist who had worked with child molesters. He wrote the book to mobilize the public to take serious action against pedophiles. Its main character, based on a composite of Lally's patients, was designed to show laypeople how pedophiles think and operate. In Lally's words, the book "was supposed to disgust people and frighten the hell out of them, so they would say, 'Let's do something about pedophiles.'" Lally sent one copy of his manuscript to a literary agent in the United States. When she returned it to him, Canadian Customs officials intercepted the manuscript pursuant to the *Butler* ruling. As Mary Williams Walsh wrote in the *Los Angeles Times*:

> Lally's project would . . . appear to be just the sort of undertaking the antipornography lobby would applaud: In his own way, he wanted to protect society from sex crimes. But the plan back-fired. Under *Butler,* Lally's opus itself was found to be obscene. Three Mounties and a Customs officer raided his house and seized his only other copy of the manuscript. Then they clapped their alleged porn kingpin into the back seat of their squad car.[58]

It is quite possible that Canadian Customs confiscated Dworkin's *Woman Hating* purely on the basis of its title. And just as Ohio law enforcement officials went after Debbie Reynolds's exercise video *Doing It Debbie's Way* because of its "provocative" title (see chapter 4), Canadian Customs recently confiscated *Hot, Hotter, Hottest,*[59] apparently for the same reason; if you look beyond the title page, you will see that this volume is a cookbook containing recipes for spicy cuisine! Laughable as these incidents may be, they illustrate the frightening force of the feminist antipornography law to suppress a limitless range of materials that are valued by diverse audiences.

Although the primary targets of Canada's post-*Butler* enforcement efforts have been feminist, lesbian, and gay materials, *Butler* also has emboldened customs officials to seize other works, including serious mainstream books. Canadian Customs seized thirty copies of Marguerite Duras's novella *The Man Sitting in the Corridor* that had been ordered by Trent University. This novella by the respected writer was detained because it includes several scenes in which a woman is beaten after passionate sex; in the last such scene, she dies. Canadian Customs also has seized books by critically acclaimed authors such as Kathy Acker, Ambrose Bierce, Langston Hughes, Zora Neale Hurston, David Leavitt, Audre

Lorde, Anne Rice, Gertrude Stein, and Oscar Wilde. It has barred *Weird Smut Comics,* a publication dealing with the evils of censorship; the political journal *Lies of Our Times;* and the illustrated collection of essays published by the Feminist Anti-Censorship Taskforce, *Caught Looking.*

In 1993, customs detained a shipment of fifteen hundred copies of *Black Looks: Race and Representations,* by black feminist academic bell hooks, that were en route to several Canadian universities. Although all of the other books were seized pursuant to *Butler, Black Looks* was detained under a Canadian law prohibiting hate speech more generally, which the procensorship feminists also support.

Canadian authorities have not enforced *Butler* against the type of violent, misogynistic heterosexual materials that its advocates had hoped they would proscribe. Indeed, Catharine MacKinnon appeared to concede that enforcement of the decision had not advanced women's interests, in a telephone conversation she had with Leanne Katz, executive director of the National Coalition Against Censorship, in September 1993. MacKinnon noted that the Canadian government authorities were not going after the kind of violent, heterosexual materials that had been involved in the *Butler* case itself, to which Leanne Katz replied, "Big surprise." MacKinnon echoed, "Big surprise."[60]

### And an Even Bigger Chill

As if the direct government censorship of allegedly degrading sexually oriented materials under *Butler* were not damaging enough to free speech and equality values, *Butler* has also spurred two indirect, even more expansive forms of censorship. Like all censorial schemes, it has led to self-censorship, and it also has created a "slippery slope," encouraging the adoption of additional censorship measures.

The massive self-censorship among Canadians, triggered by *Butler,* was described in a February 1994 report by the Free Expression Project of Human Rights Watch:

The indirect effect of daily customs seizures and police raids is self-censorship by the bookstores, video stores and private citizens who for financial reasons cannot afford to mount legal challenges. Oxford University Press refused to distribute *Gay Ideas: Outing and Other Controversies,* a Beacon Press book by Canadian philosopher Richard Mohr, rather than incur the wrath of Customs. Many publishers send page proofs to the Prohibited Importations Unit in Ottawa prior to printing their Canadian editions. The Unit's staff go through the various magazines, whiting out text and replacing offending photos with black dots. Customs has even deleted safe-sex information in U.S. publications imported for Canadian gay men.[61]

The second spillover effect of *Butler* has been that Canadian government officials have been emboldened to pass other measures that suppress an even broader range of expression. As a September 1993 *Los Angeles Times* article noted, *Butler* led the Canadian House of Commons and provincial legislatures to write sweeping new laws against controversial expression, including a prohibition on serial killer trading cards and a law making it a crime to make, print, publish, import, distribute, or sell—and in some cases even possess—any depiction of a sexual act by anyone under eighteen years old, even in fiction or art,[62] and even though Canadian law recognizes that people as young as twelve may legally engage in sexual acts.[63]

The first prosecution under the draconian, *Butler*-inspired law barring sexual depictions of young people illustrates its dangerous overbreadth. Charged in the case was a twenty-six-year-old Toronto artist, Eli Langer, whose paintings and drawings were seized from the Mercer Union, one of Toronto's most respected artist-run galleries. The works portray both children and adults engaging in sexual behavior. Langer says his works were made not from models, but from his imagination. Moreover, these paintings explore the impact of child sexual abuse.

In response to pressure from the arts community, the government decided not to prosecute Langer. However, prosecutors still sought judicial permission to destroy Langer's seized paintings, and to establish a precedent for prosecuting future cases.

Although the law banning sexual depictions of young people contains an exemption for works with artistic merit (as well as educational, scientific, or medical value), it puts the burden of proof on the accused. In light of the ten-year prison sentence and fines that could be imposed following a conviction, no doubt many serious artists, scientists, and others will avoid all sexual descriptions or depictions of people under eighteen. One wonders whether Shakespeare would have written *Romeo and Juliet* or whether Nabokov would have written *Lolita* had they faced such a law. And what of Judy Blume's novels about and for adolescents? (The law contains no special provision that would exempt any of these authors—or, in the case of deceased writers, anyone who continues to circulate their works—from its general terms.)

### *Unavailing Apologetics*

The Canadian government's use of *Butler*'s feminist antipornography analysis in a discriminatory and harassing fashion has been so blatant and persistent that even LEAF (the Women's Legal Education and Action Fund), which had worked with MacKinnon to promote that analysis, has been forced to recognize the great damage it has done. In June 1993, a group of LEAF leaders and anticensorship activists met and issued a joint news release that "unanimously condemned the use of the *Butler* decision to justify the discriminatory use of law to harass and intimidate lesbians and gays and sex trade workers." The LEAF signatories further conceded that "[s]ince . . . *Butler* . . . Canada Customs, some police forces . . . and some government funders have exploited obscenity law to harass bookstores, artists, and AIDS organizations, sex trade workers, and safe sex educators."[64]

In light of the abysmal experience with Canada's version of the feminist antipornography law, the law's feminist defenders have been unable to explain away its devastating impact on free speech and equality, on women and on lesbians and gay men. As Leanne Katz remarked, "Nearly ten percent of *Only Words* is devoted to a rhapsodic analysis of *Butler*'s acceptance of her ideology. Yet MacKinnon's book says not a word about the real life consequences of her Pyrrhic victory. Only words, indeed."[65]

When (in October 1993) I debated Kathleen Mahoney, the law professor who coauthored the LEAF brief in *Butler* (in collaboration with Catharine MacKinnon) and who argued LEAF's position in the Canadian Supreme Court, she conceded that *Butler* has been used discriminatorily to harass lesbian and gay publications, but maintained that this fact was no basis for criticizing the ruling. Specifically, Mahoney argued that the post-*Butler* enforcement record simply reflected the preexisting homophobia on the part of Canadian law enforcement authorities. She said: "We have as many homophobic police officers, I'm sure, as you do, maybe even more, as well as customs officials. . . . [P]olice activity against gays . . . has always been going on."[66]

Of course. And it always will as long as they—or their feminist allies—keep coming up with new tools to play with.

Rather than condemning the Canadian attacks on feminist and lesbian publications, Dworkin and MacKinnon apparently condone at least some of them. Referring to the conviction of Glad Day Bookshop based on the short story in *Bad Attitude,* Dworkin declared: "Lesbian porn is an expression of self-hatred. . . . When it is trafficked in the world, it becomes a social reality, and the hatred that it spreads then is not [*sic*] longer a hatred only of self, but becomes a hatred of the group."[67] Likewise, in a 1994 letter to *The New York Times,* MacKinnon wrote that "maybe the publications" that had been targeted under *Butler* "do harm on the basis of sex. . . . [T]he *Bad Attitude* publication . . . contained sex between a young girl and a nurse-caretaker."[68]

Aside from apologizing for some of the Canadian censorship under *Butler,* Dworkin and MacKinnon have made three arguments in an effort to distinguish the Canadian experience from what we could expect if their antipornography law were to be enforced in the United States. First, they sound their familiar and wrongheaded argument that the Canadian law that *Butler* interpreted is significantly different from their model law because it is criminal, rather than civil. Second, they note that some of the seizures by Canadian Customs have involved temporary detentions, rather than permanent confiscations. Third, they contend that the customs officials are following different standards from those laid down in *Butler*.[69] All three arguments are unsound. I have already discussed the "distinction without a difference" between criminal prosecutions and civil lawsuits (in chapter 3).

Dworkin and MacKinnon's observation that some customs detentions of materials have "only" been temporary shows a similar failure to come to grips with reality. For all practical purposes, just as "justice delayed is justice denied,"[70] so too, delivery delayed is delivery denied, especially when the materials in question are periodicals. The Canadian press has reported that, under *Butler,* customs officials have seized and held magazines for weeks or months, often rendering them out-of-date and unsalable. In addition, books as well as magazines that have been detained by customs may well be made unsalable because they are returned in damaged condition. According to the Canadian anticensorship organization CENSORSTOP, "Customs destructively treats materials seized, ranging from minor damages to 'accidental loss.' "[71]

Damaging as even a temporary customs detention may be, it is important to realize that many such "detentions" are in fact permanent, and thus amount to outright confiscations. Although detention decisions may be appealed, the rulings are seldom reversed unless there is a rash of adverse publicity—as there was, for example, concerning the seizures of Dworkin's books. The only alternative is court action, which is both expensive and slow. Since many booksellers cannot afford to mount such challenges, the ostensibly temporary detention, imposed by the importations bureaucracy, becomes a permanent ban.

Yet another reason why customs detentions have devastating consequences, unacknowledged by Dworkin and MacKinnon, is that these detentions have led to more self-censorship by

Canadian booksellers. As reported by the Free Expression Project of Human Rights Watch:

> A bureaucratic appeals process often deters even the most committed challengers. Rather than face costly delay and interference, retailers censor their own orders of books and videos, limiting anything remotely suspect. In doing so they limit their consumers' access to alternative viewpoints. . . . Even though magazines are supposed to be reviewed on an issue-by-issue basis, [bookstores] no longer buy the magazines that have been the subject of litigation or publicity. "*Bad Attitude* and *On Our Backs* [lesbian erotic magazines] have effectively been banned in Canada," said Janine Fuller [bookbuyer for Little Sisters bookstore]. Insidiously, *Butler* has also affected the number of titles bookstores order. "Where I used to buy thirty-six copies by a famous lesbian author," said Fuller, "I now order maybe two."[72]

Dworkin and MacKinnon similarly ignore reality when they assert that the customs seizures are carried out under an independent legal authority, not the *Butler* decision. The customs legislation on obscenity incorporates Canadian Criminal Code obscenity provisions, as interpreted by the Canadian courts. As I have explained, after the *Butler* decision, Canadian government lawyers reviewed existing customs regulations to bring them into conformity with *Butler,* and found that the regulations did not need to be revised. Customs now has renewed carte blanche, not a new carte blanche.

### What Have We Learned?

The enforcement record of the MacDworkinite antipornography law in Canada, and the consistent enforcement record of other censorial measures, teaches a clear lesson: *women should beware of any such measure.*

Throughout this book, we have seen that any scheme for censoring pornography would undermine women's rights and interests in many ways: it would suppress many works that are valuable to women and feminists; it would be enforced in a way that discriminates against the least popular, least powerful groups in our society, including feminists and lesbians; it would perpetuate demeaning stereotypes about women, including that sex is bad for us; it would perpetuate the disempowering notion that women are essentially victims; it would distract us from constructive approaches to countering discrimination and violence against women; it would harm women who voluntarily work in the sex industry; it would harm women's efforts to develop their own sexuality; it would reinforce the political power of factions with a patriarchal agenda; by undermining free speech, censorship would deprive feminists of a powerful tool for advancing women's equality; and since sexual freedom and freedom for sexually explicit expression are essential aspects of human freedom, censoring such expression would undermine human rights more broadly.

In contrast to these significant costs that any pornography censorship scheme would impose on feminist goals, procensorship feminists rely on only one asserted benefit of such a scheme: that it would reduce violence and discrimination against women. As we see in the next chapter, this purported benefit is at best merely speculative. Thus, from a feminist perspective, the substantial negative effects of censoring pornography are not offset by any substantial benefits.

Because reducing misogynistic discrimination and violence is so important, some feminists might be tempted to conclude that censorship would be justified by even the possibility that it might advance this goal. Such a conclusion would be unwarranted, however, because it would ignore censorship's countervailing adverse impact on the same goal.

This point is highlighted by considering some other factors, aside from pornography, that are alleged to contribute to misogynistic discrimination and violence; these include women's improving legal and economic status, women's expanding sexual options, and the associated rise of the women's movement. Susan Faludi's 1991 book, *Backlash: The Undeclared War Against American Women*, cites evidence that one of the causes of the

1980s backlash against the women's rights movement was women's increased employment outside the home, which has led to anxiety, depression, and loss of self-esteem among men.[73] Likewise, some research indicates that advances in women's rights may cause some male sexual aggression against women.[74] Furthermore, some feminist theorists and other scholars maintain that sexual assaults (as well as the consumption of pornography) have increased as a result of the women's movement and the misogynistic reactions that some men have to that movement. Andrea Dworkin herself has asserted this causal connection.[75]

Presumably, Dworkin, as well as most other feminists, would resist any effort to curb advances in women's rights, even if that effort were premised on the rationale that advances in women's rights contribute to anti-female violence. This would be a clear case of cutting off one's nose to spite one's face. As we have seen, the same is true of censoring pornography.

In an apparent nod to the dearth of evidence that pornography causes the harm she ascribes to it, Catharine MacKinnon has attempted to bolster her censorial crusade by declaring, "There is no evidence that pornography does no harm."[76] In light of the appalling Canadian experience with MacKinnon's censorship scheme, and the other enforcement lessons we have learned in this chapter, her own phrase should be recast: "There is substantial evidence that censoring pornography does substantial harm."

# Why Censoring Pornography Would Not Reduce Discrimination or Violence against Women

> The only thing pornography is known to cause directly is the solitary act of masturbation. As for corruption, the only immediate victim is English prose.
>
> GORE VIDAL, writer[1]

Most of this book has aimed to illuminate the legal flaws and misconceptions of MacKinnon-Dworkin–style antipornography laws, to show how any such law undermines rather than advances important women's rights and human rights causes, and to paint a picture of the suppressed society that this type of law would produce when put in practice. Especially given recently renewed interest in MacDworkinite laws, they—and their chilling consequences—are my immediate concern. I have accordingly exposed the overwhelming problems that are inherent in all such laws. But, for the sake of argument, let's make the purely hypothetical assumption that we could fix those problems: let's pretend we could wave a magic wand that would miraculously make the laws do what they are supposed to without trampling on rights that are vital to everyone, and without stifling speech that serves women.

Even in this "Never-Never Land," where we could neutralize its negative side effects, would censorship "cure"—or at least reduce—the discrimination and violence against women allegedly caused by pornography? That is the assumption that underlies the feminist procensorship position, fueling the argument that we should trade in our free speech rights to promote women's safety and equality rights. In fact, though, the hoped-for benefits of censorship are as hypothetical as our exercise in wishing away the evils of censorship. I will show this by examining the largely unexamined assumption that censorship would reduce sexism and violence against women. This assumption rests, in turn, on three others:

- that exposure to sexist, violent imagery leads to sexist, violent behavior;
- that the effective suppression of pornography would significantly reduce exposure to sexist, violent imagery; and
- that censorship would effectively suppress pornography.

To justify censoring pornography on the rationale that it would reduce violence or discrimination against women, one would have to provide actual support for all three of these assumptions. Each presupposes the others. Yet the only one of them that has received substantial attention is the first—that exposure to sexist, violent imagery leads to sexist, violent behavior—and, as I show later in this chapter, there is no credible evidence to bear it out. Even feminist advocates of censoring pornography have acknowledged that this asserted causal connection cannot be proven, and therefore fall back on the argument that it should be accepted "on faith." Catharine MacKinnon has well captured this fallback position through her defensive double negative with which I closed the previous chapter: "There is no evidence that pornography does no harm."

Of course, given the impossibility of proving that there is *no* evidence of *no* harm, we would have no free speech, and indeed no freedom of any kind, were such a burden of proof actually to be imposed on those seeking to enjoy their liberties. To appreciate this, just substitute for the word "pornography" in MacKinnon's pronouncement any other type of expression or any other human right. We would have to acknowledge that "there is no evidence" that television does no harm, or that editorials criticizing government officials do no harm, or that religious sermons do no harm, and so forth. There certainly is no evidence that feminist writing in general, or MacKinnon's in particular, does no harm.

In its 1992 *Butler* decision, accepting the antipornography feminist position, the Canadian Supreme Court also accepted this dangerous intuitive approach to limiting sexual expression, stating:

> It might be suggested that proof of actual harm should be required. . . [I]t is sufficient . . . for Parliament to have a reasonable basis for concluding that harm will result and this requirement does not demand actual proof of harm.[2]

Even if we were willing to follow the Canadian Supreme Court and procensorship feminists in believing, without evidence, that exposure to sexist, violent imagery does lead to sexist, violent behavior, we still should not accept their calls for censorship. Even if we assumed that *seeing* pornography leads to committing sexist and violent actions, it still would not follow that *censoring* pornography would reduce sexism or violence, due to flaws in the remaining two assumptions: we still would have to prove that pornography has a corner on the sexism and violence market, and that pornography is in fact entirely suppressible.

Even if pornography could be completely suppressed, the sexist, violent imagery that pervades the mainstream media would remain untouched. Therefore, if exposure to such materials caused violence and sexism, these problems would still remain with us. But no censorship regime could completely suppress pornography. It would continue to exist underground. In this respect, censorship would bring us the worst of both worlds. On one hand, as we have just seen from examining the Canadian situation, suppressive laws make it difficult to obtain a wide range of sexually oriented materials, so that most people would not have access to those materials. On the other hand, though, some such materials would continue to be produced and consumed no matter what. Every governmental effort to prohibit any allegedly harmful material has always caused this kind of "double trouble." Witness the infamous "Prohibition" of alcohol earlier in this century, for example.

Let's now examine in more detail the fallacies in each of the three assumptions underlying the feminist procensorship stance. And let's start with the single assumption that has been the focus of discussion—the alleged causal relationship between exposure to sexist, violent imagery and sexist, violent behavior.

### Monkey See, Monkey Do?

Aside from the mere fear that sexual expression might cause discrimination or violence against women, advocates of censorship attempt to rely on four types of evidence concerning this alleged causal link: laboratory research data concerning the attitudinal effects of showing various types of sexually explicit materials to volunteer subjects, who are usually male college students; correlational data concerning availability of sexually oriented materials and anti-female discrimination or violence; anecdotal data consisting of accounts by sex offenders and their victims concerning any role that pornography may have played in the offenses; and studies of sex offenders, assessing factors that may have led to their crimes.

As even some leading procensorship feminists have acknowledged, along with the Canadian Supreme Court in *Butler,* none of these types of "evidence" prove that pornography harms women. Rather than retracing the previous works that have reviewed this evidence and reaffirmed its failure to substantiate the alleged causal connection, I will simply summarize their conclusions.

### *Laboratory Experiments*

The most comprehensive recent review of the social science data is contained in Marcia Pally's 1994 book *Sex and Sensibility: Reflections on Forbidden Mirrors and the Will to Censor.*[3] It exhaustively canvasses laboratory studies that have evaluated the impact of exposing experimental subjects to sexually explicit expression of many varieties, and concludes that no credible evidence substantiates a clear causal connection between any type of sexually explicit material and any sexist or violent behavior. The book also draws the same conclusion from its thorough review of field and correlational studies, as well as sociological surveys, in the U.S., Canada, Europe, and Asia.

Numerous academic and governmental surveys of the social science studies have similarly rejected the purported link between sexual expression and aggression. The National Research Council's Panel on Understanding and Preventing Violence concluded, in 1993: "Demonstrated empirical links between pornography and sex crimes in general are weak or absent."[4]

Given the overwhelming consensus that laboratory studies do not demonstrate a causal tie between exposure to sexually explicit imagery and violent behavior, the Meese Pornography Commission Report's contrary conclusion, not surprisingly, has been the subject of heated criticism, including criticism by dissenting commissioners and by the very social scientists on whose research the report purportedly relied.

The many grounds on which the Commission's report was widely repudiated include that: six of the Commission's eleven members already were committed antipornography crusaders when they were appointed to it; the Commission was poorly funded and undertook no research; its hearings were slanted toward preconceived antipornography conclusions in terms of the witnesses invited to testify and the questions they were asked; and, in assessing the alleged harmful effects of pornography, the Commission's report relied essentially upon morality, expressly noting at several points that its conclusions were based on "common sense," "personal insight," and "intuition."

Two of the Meese Commission's harshest critics were, interestingly, two female members of that very Commission, Judith Becker and Ellen Levine. Becker is a psychiatrist and psychologist whose entire extensive career has been devoted to studying sexual violence and abuse, from both research and clinical perspectives. Levine is a journalist who has focused on women's issues, and who edits a popular women's magazine. In their formal dissent from the Commission's report, they concluded:

> [T]he social science research has not been designed to evaluate the relationship between exposure to pornography and the commission of sexual crimes; therefore efforts to tease the current data into proof of a casual [*sic*] link between these acts simply cannot be accepted.[5]

Three of the foremost researchers concerned with the alleged causal relationship between sexually explicit materials and sexual violence, Edward Donnerstein, Daniel Linz, and Steven Penrod, also have sharply disputed the Meese Commission's findings about a purported causal relationship.[6]

Since the feminist censorship proposals aim at sexually explicit material that allegedly is "degrading" to women, it is especially noteworthy that research data show no link between exposure to "degrading" sexually explicit material and sexual aggression.

Even two research literature surveys that were conducted for the Meese Commission, one by University of Calgary professor Edna Einseidel and the other by then–Surgeon General C. Everett Koop, also failed to find any link between "degrading" pornography and sex crimes or aggression. Surgeon General Koop's survey concluded that only two reliable generalizations could be made about the impact of exposure to "degrading" sexual material on its viewers: it caused them to think that a variety of sexual practices were more common than they had previously believed, and it caused them to more accurately estimate the prevalence of varied sexual practices.[7]

Experiments also fail to establish any link between women's exposure to such materials and their development of negative self-images. Carol Krafka found that, in comparison with other women, women who were exposed to sexually "degrading" materials did not engage in more sex-role stereotyping; nor did they experience lower self-esteem, have less satisfaction with their body image, accept more anti-woman myths about rape, or show greater acceptance of violence against women.[8] Similar conclusions have been reached by Donnerstein, Linz, and Penrod.[9]

### Correlational Data

Both the Meese Commission and procensorship feminists have attempted to rely on studies that allegedly show a correlation between the availability of sexually explicit materials and sexual offense rates. Of course, though, a positive correlation between two phenomena does not prove that one causes the other. Accordingly, even if the studies did consistently show a positive correlation between the prevalence of sexual materials and sexual offenses—which they do not—they still would not establish that exposure to the materials *caused* the rise in offenses. The same correlation could also reflect the opposite causal chain—if, for example, rapists relived their violent acts by purchasing sexually violent magazines or videotapes.

Any correlation between the availability of sexual materials and the rate of sex offenses could also reflect an independent factor that causes increases in both. Cynthia Gentry's correlational studies have identified just such an independent variable in geographical areas that have high rates of both the circulation of sexually explicit magazines and sexual violence: namely, a high population of men between the ages of eighteen and thirty-four.[10] Similarly, Larry Baron and Murray Straus have noted that areas where both sexual materials and sexual aggression are prevalent are characterized by a "hypermasculated or macho culture pattern," which may well be the underlying causal agent.[11] Accordingly, Joseph Scott and Loretta Schwalm found that communities with higher rape rates experienced stronger sales not only of porn magazines, but also of *all* male-oriented magazines, including *Field and Stream*.[12]

Even more damning to the attempt to rest the "porn-causes-rape-or-discrimination" theory on alleged correlations is that there simply are no consistent correlations. While the asserted correlation would not be *sufficient* to prove the claimed causal connection, it is *necessary* to prove that connection. Therefore, the existence of the alleged causal relationship is conclusively refuted by the fact that levels of violence and discrimination against women are often *inversely* related to the availability of sexually explicit materials, including violent sexually explicit materials. This inverse relationship appears in various kinds of comparisons: between different states within the United States; between different countries; and between different periods within the same country.

Within the United States, the Baron and Straus research has shown no consistent pattern between the availability of sexual materials and the number of rapes from state to state. Utah is the lowest-ranking state in the availability of sexual materials but twenty-fifth in the number of rapes, whereas New Hampshire ranks ninth highest in the availability of sexual materials but only forty-fourth in the number of rapes.

The lack of a consistent correlation between pornography consumption and violence against women is underscored by one claim of the procensorship feminists themselves: they maintain that the availability and consumption of pornography, including violent pornography, have been increasing throughout the United States. At the same time, though, the rates of sex crimes have been decreasing or remaining steady. The Bureau of Justice Statistics reports that between 1973 and 1987, the national rape rate remained steady and the attempted rape rate decreased. Since these data were gathered from household surveys rather than from police records, they are considered to be the most accurate measures of the incidence of crimes. These data also cover the period during which feminists helped to create a social, political, and legal climate that should have encouraged higher percentages of rape victims to report their assaults. Thus, the fact that rapes reported to the Bureau of Justice Statistics have not increased provokes serious questions about the procensorship feminists' theories of pornography-induced harm.[13] Similar questions are raised by data showing a decrease in wife battery between 1975 and 1985, again despite changes that should have encouraged the increased reporting of this chronically underreported crime.[14]

Noting that "[t]he mass-market pornography . . . industr[y] took off after World War II," Marcia Pally has commented:

> In the decades since the 1950s, with the marketing of sexual material . . . , the country has seen the greatest advances in sensitivity to violence against women and children. Before the . . . mass publication of sexual images, no rape or incest hot lines and battered women's shelters existed; date and marital rape were not yet phrases in the language. Should one conclude that the presence of pornography . . . has inspired public outrage at sexual crimes?[15]

Pally's rhetorical question underscores the illogicality of presuming that just because two phenomena happen to coexist, they therefore are causally linked. I have already shown that any correlation that might exist between the increased availability of pornography and *increased* misogynistic discrimination or violence could well be explained by other factors. The same is true for any correlation that might exist between the increased availability of pornography and *decreased* misogynistic discrimination or violence.

In a comparative state-by-state analysis, Larry Baron and Murray Straus have found a positive correlation between the circulation of pornographic magazines and the state's "index of gender equality," a composite of twenty-four indicators of economic, political, and legal equality.[16] As the researchers have observed, these findings may suggest that both sexually explicit material and gender equality flourish in tolerant climates with fewer restrictions on speech.

The absence of any consistent correlation between the availability of sexual materials and sexual violence is also clear in international comparisons. On the one hand, violence and discrimination against women are common in countries where sexually oriented material is almost completely unavailable, including Saudi Arabia, Iran, and China (where the sale and distribution of erotica is now a capital offense). On the other hand, violence against women is uncommon in countries where such material is readily available, including Denmark, Germany, and Japan.

Furthermore, patterns in other countries over time show no

correlation between the increased availability of sexually explicit materials and increased violence against women. The 1991 analysis by University of Copenhagen professor Berl Kutchinsky revealed that, while nonsexual violent crime had increased up to 300 percent in Denmark, Sweden, and West Germany from 1964 to 1984, all three countries' rape rates either declined or remained constant during this same period, despite their lifting of restrictions on sexual materials. Kutchinsky's studies further show that sex crimes against girls dropped from 30 per 100,000 to 5 per 100,000 between 1965, when Denmark liberalized its obscenity laws, and 1982.

In the decade 1964–1974, there was a much greater increase in rape rates in Singapore, which tightly restricts sexually oriented expression, than in Sweden, which had liberalized its obscenity laws during that period. In Japan, where sexually explicit materials are easily accessible and stress themes of bondage, rape, and violence, rape rates decreased 45 percent during the same decade. Moreover, Japan reports a rape rate of 2.4 per 100,000 people, compared with 34.5 in the United States, although violent erotica is more prevalent in Japan.[17]

### Anecdotes and Suspicions

As Seventh Circuit Court of Appeals Judge Richard Posner observed about MacKinnon's book *Only Words*:

> MacKinnon's treatment of the central issue of pornography as she herself poses it—the harm that pornography does to women—is shockingly casual. Much of her evidence is anecdotal, and in a nation of 260 million people, anecdotes are a weak form of evidence.[18]

Many procensorship advocates attempt to rest their case on self-serving "porn-made-me-do-it" claims by sexual offenders, as well as on statements by victims or police officers that sexual offenders had sexually explicit materials in their possession at the time they committed their crimes.

The logical fallacy of relying on anecdotes to establish a general causal connection between exposure to sexual materials and violence against women was aptly noted by journalist Ellen Willis: "Anti-porn activists cite cases of sexual killers who were also users of pornography, but this is no more logical than arguing that marriage causes rape because some rapists are married."[19]

Even assuming that sexual materials really were the triggering factors behind some specific crimes, that could not justify restrictions on such materials. As former Supreme Court justice William O. Douglas wrote: "The First Amendment demands more than a horrible example or two of the perpetrator of a crime of sexual violence, in whose pocket is found a pornographic book, before it allows the Nation to be saddled with a regime of censorship."[20] If we attempted to ban all words or images that had ever been blamed for inspiring or instigating particular crimes by some aberrant or antisocial individual, we would end up with little left to read or view. Throughout history and around the world, criminals have regularly blamed their conduct on a sweeping array of words and images in books, movies, and television.

As noted by the 1979 report of the British Committee on Obscenity and Film Censorship, "For those who are susceptible to them, the stimuli to aggressive behavior are all around us."[21] To illustrate the innumerable crimes that have been incited by words or images, the Committee cited a young man who attempted to kill his parents with a meat cleaver after watching a dramatized version of Dostoyevsky's *The Brothers Karamazov,* and a Jamaican man of African descent in London who raped a white woman, saying that the televised showing of Alex Haley's *Roots* had "inspired" him to treat her as white men had treated black women. Additional examples cited by Ohio State University law professor Earl Finbar Murphy underscore that word blaming and image blaming extend to many religious works, too:

Heinrich Pommerenke, who was a rapist, abuser, and mass slayer of women in Germany, was prompted to his series of ghastly deeds by Cecil B. DeMille's *The Ten Commandments.*

During the scene of the Jewish women dancing about the Golden Calf, all the doubts of his life became clear: Women were the source of the world's troubles and it was his mission to both punish them for this and to execute them. Leaving the theater, he slew the first victim in a park nearby. John George Haigh, the British vampire who sucked his victims' blood through soda straws and dissolved their drained bodies in acid baths, first had his murder-inciting dreams and vampire longings from watching the "voluptuous" procedure of—an Anglican High Church Service.[22]

Were we to ban words or images on the grounds that they had incited some susceptible individuals to commit crimes, the Bible would be in great jeopardy. No other work has more often been blamed for more heinous crimes by the perpetrators of such crimes. The Bible has been named as the instigating or justifying factor for many individual and mass crimes, ranging from the religious wars, inquisitions, witch burnings, and pogroms of earlier eras to systematic child abuse and ritual murders today.

Marcia Pally's *Sex and Sensibility* contains a lengthy litany of some of the multitudinous, horrific bad acts that have been blamed on the "Good Book." She also cites some of the many passages depicting the "graphic, sexually explicit subordination of women" that would allow the entire Bible to be banned under the procensorship feminists' antipornography law. Pally writes:

> [T]he Bible has unbeatable worldwide sales and includes detailed justification of child abuse, wife battery, rape, and the daily humiliation of women. Short stories running through the text serve as models for sexual assault and the mauling of children. The entire set of books is available to children, who are encouraged or required to read it. It is printed and distributed by some of the world's most powerful organizations. . . .
>
> With refreshing frankness, the Bible tells men it is their rightful place to rule women. . . . [It] specifies exactly how many shekels less than men women are worth. Genesis 19:1–8

tells one of many tales about fathers setting up their daughters to be gang raped. Even more prevalent are . . . glamorized war stories in which the fruits of victory are the local girls. . . . [P]erhaps most gruesome is the snuff story about the guy who set his maid up to be gang raped and, after her death from the assault, cut her body up into little pieces. . . . Unlike movies and television programs, these tales are generally taken to be true, not simulated, accounts.[23]

In 1992, Gene Kasmar petitioned the Brooklyn Center, Minnesota, school board to ban the Bible from school classrooms and libraries on the ground that it is lewd, indecent, obscene, offensive, violent, and dangerous to women and children. He specifically complained about biblical references to concubines, explicit sex, child abuse, incest, nakedness, and mistreatment of women—all subjects, significantly, that would trigger the feminist-style antipornography laws.

In response, the chief counsel of Pat Robertson's American Center for Law and Justice in Virginia, Jay Sekulow, flew to Minnesota and argued that the Bible "is worthy of study for its literary and historic qualities."[24] While the Brooklyn Center School Board apparently agreed with this assessment, voting unanimously to reject Kasmar's petition, it must be recalled that Sekulow's argument would be unavailing under Dworkin-MacKinnon–type antipornography laws. Under the MacDworkin model law, any work could be banned on the basis of even one isolated passage that meets the definition of pornography, and the work could not be saved by any serious literary, historic, or other value it might offer. Consequently, the feminist antipornography law could be used by Kasmar and others to ban the Bible not only from public schools, but also from public libraries, bookstores, and all other venues.

The countless expressive works that have been blamed for crimes include many that convey profeminist messages. Therefore, an anecdotal, image-blaming rationale for censorship would condemn many feminist works. For example, the television movie *The Burning Bed,* which told the true story of a battered wife who set fire to her sleeping husband, was blamed for some "copycat" crimes, as well as for some acts of violence by men against women. The argument that such incidents would justify suppression would mark the end of any films or other works depicting—and deploring—the real violence that plagues the lives of too many actual women.

Under a censorship regime that permits anecdotal, book-blaming "evidence," all other feminist materials would be equally endangered, not "just" works that depict the violence that has been inflicted on women. That is because, as feminist writings themselves have observed, some sexual assaults are committed by men who feel threatened by the women's movement. Should feminist works therefore be banned on the theory that they might well motivate a man to act out his misogynistic aggression?

### Studies of Sex Offenders

The scientists who have investigated the impact of exposure to sexual materials in real life have not found that either sexual materials or attitudes toward women play any significant role in prompting actual violence. In general, these studies show that sex offenders had less exposure to sexually explicit materials than most men, that they first saw such materials at a later age than nonoffenders, that they were overwhelmingly more likely to have been punished for looking at them as teenagers, and that they often find sexual images more distressing than arousing.[25]

While no evidence substantiates that viewing pornography leads to violence and discrimination against women, some evidence indicates that, if anything, there may well be an inverse causal relationship between exposure to sexually explicit materials and misogynistic violence or discrimination. One of the leading researchers in this area, Edward Donnerstein of the University of California at Santa Barbara, has written: "A good amount of research strongly supports the position that exposure to erotica can reduce aggressive responses in people who are predisposed to aggress."[26] Similarly, John Money, of Johns Hopkins Medical School, a leading expert on sexual violence, has noted that most people with criminal sexualities were raised with strict, antisexual, repressive attitudes. He predicts that the "current repressive attitudes toward sex will breed an ever-widening epidemic of aberrant sexual behavior."[27]

In one 1989 experiment, males who had been exposed to pornography were more willing to come to the aid of a female subject who appeared to be hurt than were men who had been exposed to other stimuli.[28] Laboratory studies further indicate that there may well be an inverse causal relationship between exposure to violent sexually explicit material and sexual arousal. For example, in 1991, Howard Barbaree and William Marshall, of Queen's College in Ontario, found:

> For most men, hearing a description of an encounter where the man is forcing the woman to have sex, and the woman is in distress or pain, dampens the arousal by about 50 percent compared to arousal levels using a scene of consenting lovemaking. . . . Ordinarily violence inhibits sexual arousal in men. A blood flow loss of 50 percent means a man would not be able to penetrate a woman.[29]

The foregoing research findings are certainly more consistent with what many feminist scholars have been writing about rape than is the procensorship feminists' pornocentric analysis: namely, rape is not a crime about sex, but rather, about violence.[30]

### See No Pornography, See No Sexist and Violent Imagery?

Pornography constitutes only a small subset of the sexist or violent imagery that pervades our culture and media. New York Law School professor Carlin Meyer recently conducted a comprehensive survey of the views of women's sexuality, status, and gender roles that are purveyed in nonpornographic media:

Today, mainstream television, film, advertising, music, art, and popular (including religious) literature are the primary propagators of Western views of sexuality and sex roles. Not only do we read, see and experience their language and imagery more often and at earlier ages than we do most explicit sexual representation, but precisely because mainstream imagery is ordinary and everyday, it more powerfully convinces us that it depicts the world as it is or ought to be.[31]

Other cultural and media analysts have likewise concluded that more-damaging sexist imagery is more broadly purveyed through mainstream, nonsexual representations. Thelma McCormack, director of York University's Feminist Studies Centre, has concluded that "the enemy of women's equality is our mainstream culture with its images of women as family-centered," rather than imagery of women as sexual. According to McCormack:

Surveys and public opinion studies confirm the connection between gender-role traditionalism and an acceptance or belief in the normality of a stratified social system. The more traditional a person's views are about women, the more likely he or she is to accept inequality as inevitable, functional, natural, desirable and immutable. In short, if any image of woman can be said to influence our thinking about gender equality, it is the domestic woman not the Dionysian one.[32]

Social science researchers have found that acceptance of the rape myth and other misogynistic attitudes concerning women and violence are just as likely to result from exposure to many types of mass media—from soap operas to popular commercial films—as from even intense exposure to violent, misogynistic sexually explicit materials.[33] Accordingly, if we really wanted to purge all sexist, violent representations from our culture, we would have to cast the net far beyond pornography, notwithstanding how comprehensive and elastic that category is. Would even procensorship feminists want to deal such a death-blow to First Amendment freedoms?

## Censor Pornography, See No Pornography?

Procensorship feminists themselves have acknowledged that censorship would probably just drive pornography underground. Indeed, as recently as 1987, Catharine MacKinnon recognized that "pornography cannot be reformed or suppressed or banned."[34]

The assumption that censorship would substantially reduce the availability or impact of pornography also overlooks evidence that censorship makes some viewers more desirous of pornography and more receptive to its imagery. This "forbidden fruits" effect has been corroborated by historical experience and social science research. All recent studies of the suppression of sexual expression, including Walter Kendrick's 1987 book *The Secret Museum: Pornography in Modern Culture* and Edward de Grazia's 1992 book *Girls Lean Back Everywhere: The Law of Obscenity and the Assault on Genius,* demonstrate that any censorship effort simply increases the attention that a targeted work receives. Social scientific studies that were included in the report of the 1970 President's Commission on Obscenity and Pornography suggested that censorship of sexually explicit materials may increase their desirability and impact, and also that a viewer's awareness that sexually oriented parts of a film have been censored may lead to frustration and subsequent aggressive behavior.[35]

The foregoing data about the impact of censoring pornography are consistent with broader research findings: the evidence suggests that censorship of *any* material increases an audience's desire to obtain the material and disposes the audience to be more receptive to it.[36] Critical viewing skills, and the ability to regard media images skeptically and analytically, atrophy under a censorial regime. A public that learns to question everything it sees or hears is better equipped to reject culturally propagated values than is one that assumes the media have been purged of all "incorrect" perspectives.

Even assuming for the sake of argument that there were a causal link between pornography and anti-female discrimination and violence, the insignificant contribution that censorship might make to reducing them would not outweigh the substantial damage that censorship would do to feminist goals. From the lack of actual evidence to substantiate the alleged causal link, the conclusion follows even more inescapably: *Censoring pornography would do women more harm than good.*

# Toward Constructive Approaches to Reducing Discrimination and Violence against Women

> I deplore that even a very few feminists have been diverted by the issue of pornography from the basic protection of all our rights. Now, I urge all women to have their eyes opened to the dangers to our basic rights by the pushing of antipornography legislation.
>
> BETTY FRIEDAN, founding President
> National Organization for Women[1]

> In my part of the country, the problems women suffer from images that degrade them are not real high on the list. Where I am, poverty and violence are women's most serious problems, and it always kind of amazes me to find people spending their time worrying about how women are depicted.
>
> MOLLY IVINS, writer[2]

Like all censorship schemes, the feminist proposal to censor sexual expression diverts attention and resources from constructive, meaningful steps to address the societal problem at which the censorship is aimed. Feminist advocates of censoring sexual materials, along with feminist opponents of such censorship, are appropriately concerned about the very real, urgent problems of discrimination and violence against women. But the MacDworkinites' pornocentrism diverts attention both from the root causes of such discrimination and violence—of which violent, misogynistic sexual depictions of women are merely one symptom—and from actual acts of discrimination and violence. In the words of Canadian feminist Varda Burstyn:

> Feminists who oppose censorship . . . do not have another slogan, another quick solution, another panacea to offer in its place. We do have a comprehensive list of tasks we must carry out to bring sexism and violence to an end. Working on any one of these is more helpful—immediately, not in the distant future—than supporting censorship of any kind today, for these tasks get at the structural basis of sexism and violence, and thus insure that we will have a future.[3]

The procensorship feminists' focus on pornography is at best myopic, and at worst blinding. As law professor Carlin Meyer observes, based on her comprehensive survey of gender stereotyping throughout our culture:

> It seems implausible, to say the least, that pornography is more centrally responsible either for rendering erotic or for making possible the actualization of male violence against women than are the ideologies and practices of religion, law, and science. These institutions far more deeply and pervasively undergird male domination of women.

Furthermore, she notes, the procensorship feminists' focus on sexual speech as a central cause of sexism and violence also underemphasizes such institutions and practices as sports and militarism, which foster "male bonding in physically aggressive pursuits."[4]

### Focusing on the Real Causes . . . *Of Discrimination*

By asserting that pornography is a central cause—or even *the* central cause—of sex discrimination, procensorship feminists deflect energy and attention from the factors that feminist scholars and the U.S. Commission on Civil Rights have found to be the most significant causes of such discrimination: sex-segregated labor markets; systematic devaluation of work traditionally done by women; sexist concepts of marriage and family; inadequate income-maintenance programs for women unable to find wage work; lack of day care services and the premise that child care is an exclusively or largely female responsibility; barriers to reproductive freedom; and discrimination and segregation in education.[5]

Feminist sociologist Thelma McCormack has strongly denounced "the uninformed claim that pornography is in any way a factor in" causing gender inequality. She derides this view as "an insult to social scientists and the broader intellectual community for whom structural equality is the crux of social justice and [who] have laboured to develop the knowledge that would clarify and deepen our understanding of it."

McCormack urges those who want to advance women's equality to fight not the "degradation" but the *devaluation* of women that permeates our mainstream culture. She explains:

> Devaluation means that if, by some strange set of circumstances, we could eliminate all forms of pornography . . . [women] would still be under-represented politically, and would still be culturally marginalized. The prohibition of obscenity . . . accomplishes nothing in the struggle for equality because it confuses symbolic degradation with instrumental devaluation.[6]

The pressing work that needs to be done to eliminate women's second-class status in our society, from which the pornocentric feminists have been distracting us with their more sensational agenda, was outlined in a briefing book that the American Civil Liberties Union submitted to the Clinton Administration's transition team in 1992:

> In the late 20th century, women in the United States are still second-class citizens in virtually all aspects of economic and public life. To . . . reach the ultimate goal of complete elimination of all barriers to women's full . . . equality, requires our society's total commitment. . . .

All forms of employment discrimination against women must be eliminated, including pervasive wage discrimination, widespread occupational segregation, the "glass ceiling" on advancement, discrimination on the basis of pregnancy and childbearing capacity, rampant sexual harassment and all other forms of discrimination against women in the workplace.

All forms of discrimination against girls and young women in education must be eradicated at all levels. Women, especially poor women, must have equal access to affordable housing, food, health care, education, job training, child care, child support enforcement and other essential services.[7]

### . . . And of Violence

The pornocentric feminists also avoid facing the real and complex causes of and solutions for anti-female violence. Marcia Pally's comprehensive 1991 analysis of the literature on this issue, in *Sense and Censorship: The Vanity of Bonfires,* concluded:

> Leading feminists and the U.S. Commission on Civil Rights suggest that violence against women begins with educational and economic discrimination. . . . Men learn to consider women burdens, stiflers and drags on their freedom. Women, in turn, do not have the economic independence and access to day care that would enable them to leave abusive settings. Feminists also suggest that violence begins with the infantilization of women so that men hold them in contempt and see them as easily dismissed or lampooned and ready targets for anger.[8]

In arguing that exposure to pornography causes violent crimes against women, procensorship feminists dilute the accountability of men who commit these crimes by displacing some of it onto words and images, or onto those who create or distribute them. In contrast, as the ACLU has advocated, we should focus on the individual men who actually use violence or duress against women, through "[e]nforcement of criminal laws regarding assault, coerced sex, kidnapping, and trespassing; strengthening of rape laws, including elimination of the 'spousal rape' exception, under which husbands may not be prosecuted for raping their wives; [and] enforcement of . . . sex discrimination laws."[9]

The "porn-made-me-do-it" concept (anecdotes about which were discussed in the previous chapter as flawed evidence that pornography leads to violence against women) would severely set back the women's movement's efforts to ensure that our criminal justice system vigorously enforces laws criminalizing sexual assaults. The Senate Judiciary Committee members who opposed the Pornography Victims' Compensation Act (discussed in chapter 3) emphasized that suppressing pornography exonerates actual rapists and others who assault women. Their minority report explained that "the bill sends the wrong message to sex offenders. . . . Criminal defendants could use [this] to assert impaired or diminished capacity, available in many states as a defense to specific intent crimes such as rape."[10] For this reason, feminist law professor Nan Hunter observed that, to convey its actual impact, the Act should be renamed the "Rapists' Exculpation Act." Hunter further warns that to single out pornography as women's archenemy is to

> repeat the mistake of some of our foremothers, the leaders of the women's temperance movement who sought to ban alcohol. Those women believed that alcohol caused much of men's violence against women, particularly domestic violence. But we have learned from the work of anti-violence groups that alcohol is not the *cause* of violence against women; it is the excuse for it. The same is true of pornography.[11]

To hold pornography, and those who produce or distribute it, responsible for crimes it allegedly prompted others to commit is fundamentally inconsistent with notions of accountability that are central to our criminal justice system. If we should accept the "logic" of this approach by holding pornographers responsible for rape, then the same "logic" would require us to hold countless other third parties responsible for rape and other crimes committed by individuals whom they allegedly influenced. Such an inverted "justice" system was effectively pilloried by Teller, of the comedy-magic duo Penn & Teller:

> Of course, there are insane people who see something as innocuous as a cereal commercial and then go machine-gun shoppers at a mall. But when these nuts assert that the cereal box commanded them to kill, we lock them up. We do not accuse the corn flake maker of murder. So why blame pornographers for a rapist's actions? We do not punish his parents—though most rapists were sexually abused by their parents in childhood. We do not punish the peers who teased him at work or the employer who fired him the afternoon before the rape. We punish the rapist, and that is as it should be.[12]

Criminal defendants already have sought to reduce their punishments by relying on the procensorship feminist analysis of pornography. One such defendant was Thomas Schiro. He was convicted and sentenced to death for committing a horrific, brutal rape and murder in Indiana in 1981. Having repeatedly raped and tortured his victim, Schiro then beat her on the head with a vodka bottle until the bottle broke, beat her with an iron, and, when she resisted, finally strangled her to death. Schiro followed all these atrocities with still more: he sexually assaulted and bit into his victim's corpse. (These grisly details, set forth in the court decisions in the case, would make such decisions sanctionable pornography under the Dworkin-MacKinnon model law).

On appeal, seeking to overturn the death penalty for what the court called his "gruesome, sadistic acts, including necrophilia," Schiro claimed that he had viewed violent pornography, and that this should be deemed a "mitigating factor," reducing his culpability and hence the harshness of his punishment. Schiro argued that his viewing of these sexual materials should be given the same legal treatment as intoxication, or mental disease or defect, which are deemed to make defendants unable to appreciate the criminality of their conduct and hence less blameworthy.

In rejecting this contention, the U.S. Court of Appeals for the Seventh Circuit stressed that, if it accepted Schiro's claim, it would have to excuse him not only from the death penalty, but also from any criminal punishment whatsoever. "Under Schiro's theory," the court said, "pornography would constitute a legal excuse to [*sic*] violence against women."[13] As it would under the procensorship feminists' scheme.

Those who agree with the Seventh Circuit's ruling should note that Catharine MacKinnon has argued that Schiro should indeed have been exonerated under the applicable criminal laws. Fundamental to all our criminal laws is the concept that, to be culpable, a defendant must have acted intentionally, and therefore must be capable of appreciating the wrongfulness of his actions. In *Only Words,* MacKinnon argued that pornography had destroyed Schiro's ability to understand the wrongfulness of his grotesque crimes, and therefore that he should have been let off the hook.[14]

And if this conclusion isn't problematic enough, Mac-Kinnon's proposed "remedy" for the problem, as she sees it, is at least as problematic: she wants to dispense with the intentionality requirement for criminal culpability, so that we could pin legal blame on both pornography and the rapists who are subject to its purported power to simultaneously incapacitate and incite.[15] As law professor C. Edwin Baker observes, this proposal reflects MacKinnon's "lack of concern with the moral relevance of human agency" (also reflected in her denial of agency on the part of women who choose to perform for pornography, discussed in chapter 9).[16]

Short of the revolutionary change in our criminal law that MacKinnon recommends, to dispense with the central requirement of intentional conduct, there is no way to escape the logical result of procensorship feminists' theories about pornography's potent effects—namely, the exoneration of all the future Thomas Schiros. Indeed, the adverse consequences could well be even more counterproductive, in terms of the critically important effort to hold rapists and murderers accountable for their crimes, as indicated by another actual case.

In an even more extreme example of the "porn-made-me-do-it" defense than the one made by Thomas Schiro—and seconded by Catharine MacKinnon—Steven P. Mignogna argued that he should not be held fully responsible for raping and killing two young girls, aged twelve and thirteen, in Pennsylvania in 1988 because he had become emotionally unstable as a result of being exposed to pornography at a store he had visited two or three times. Attempting to extend the purported "porn defense" still one step further than Schiro had sought to do, Mignogna did not even show that he had bought or looked at the sexually explicit materials in question. For that reason, the court rejected Mignogna's proffered defense. Thus, the court left open the possibility that, if Mignogna *could* have demonstrated that he had seen these materials, he could have relied on them to reduce his own criminal culpability.[17]

If the procensorship feminists' theories about pornography's powerful push toward sexual violence were accepted, defenses such as Mignogna's would have to be taken seriously. In their joint book *Pornography and Civil Rights,* Dworkin and MacKinnon wrote, "Pornography makes it impossible for [men] to tell when sex is forced, that women are human, and that rape is rape."[18] MacKinnon makes the same point more dramatically in *Only Words* by drawing an analogy between showing pornography to a man and saying "Kill!" to a trained guard dog.[19] Surely we would not blame or punish the dog who responded to the command by attacking; if MacKinnon's comparison is accepted, the man who responded in kind would likewise be innocent.

Need I point out to certain women on behalf of all men that the latter are not dogs—that men have knowledge and attitudes, which presumably mediate their behavior? I say "presumably" because the relationships among knowledge, attitudes, and behavior have not yet been clearly mapped out. Until they are, we cannot know if or when one leads to another, but we can hope that if one can be changed, so can another.

In widely cited laboratory studies by Edward Donnerstein and other researchers, college men appeared to be quite capable of changing their attitudes toward women, notwithstanding massive exposure to violent, sexually explicit, misogynistic films depicting women as welcoming rape. These experiments thus belie procensorship feminists' belief that seeing pornography reduces men to the mental or moral equivalent of trained animals. The increased negative attitudes about women that some of the men displayed after seeing the violent pornography were more than offset by their subsequent exposure to information about women and violence. If "porn made them think it," the facts made them rethink it. The net impact of their exposure to the full range of materials was striking: the college men had more positive, less discriminatory, and less stereotyped attitudes toward women than they had before the experiment. What's more, the combined exposure to misogynistic and feminist materials reduced negative attitudes even more effectively than exposure to the latter alone.[20]

Other studies have corroborated the finding that counter-speech can overcome any temporary negative impact that massive exposure to violent pornography may have on some viewers' attitudes toward women. As the Surgeon General's report to the Meese Pornography Commission summarized, "Several studies have shown that presentations outlining the ways that violent sexual material can foster or reinforce incorrect beliefs or negative attitudes have been able to prevent the expected results of exposure."[21] Capsulizing the policy implications of the social science research, Donnerstein said, "Censorship is not the solution. Education, however, is a viable alternative."[22]

More speech about sex—education, information, and the development of critical viewing skills—not less, is the answer. As the procensorship feminists themselves have demonstrated, pornography can serve as an important tool to galvanize public concern about the ongoing problems of anti-female discrimination and violence. To the extent that censorship would make such images less visible, the protest against sexism would be weakened.

### Digging Out the Roots . . .

Those who are committed to assisting victims of misogynistic violence—rather than to treating their assailants as victims of pornography—and those who are committed to addressing the root causes of such violence, advocate constructive alternative measures, not the continued demonization of pornography. One prominent example is Judith Becker, a professor of psychiatry and psychology, quoted in the previous chapter, who has extensive research and clinical experience in studying sexual abuse and sexual assault. Becker has consistently opposed efforts to restrict pornography, including in her capacity as a dissenting member of the Meese Pornography Commission. Instead, she advocates government funding for services for the victims of sexual assault and abuse, as well as funding of research into the causes of, and means for preventing, sexual violence.[23]

Likewise, Shirley Feldman-Summers, a psychologist who has taught and conducted research on human sexuality, sexual victimization, and sex-role stereotypes, has suggested some of the potentially more productive strategies for reducing sexual violence, from which pornocentric feminists have diverted attention:

[C]hildren who are raised in violent homes are likely to be violence-prone. . . . How can children who are being groomed for a violent adulthood be detected at an early age, and how can intervention best be accomplished? There is also reason to believe that a significant proportion of sex offenders had a sexually repressed upbringing. . . . To what extent can sex education in our schools reduce or counteract a sexually repressive upbringing? . . . According to [social scientists], the extremely low incidence of reported rape in Japan (notwithstanding the ready availability of violent sexual materials) may be attributed to a culturally-induced sense of shame, for which one cannot make amends. In contrast, in the United States, the usual method of internal constraint is by guilt, which can be reduced by making amends. . . . Would it be effective to publicly ridicule and humiliate persons convicted of sexual assault, so as to associate shame with such acts?[24]

Another factor that contributes to male sexual violence against women is no doubt ignored by procensorship feminists not only because of their obsession with pornography, but also because of their "women-as-victims" orientation. Blinded by their victim-centric view of women, the antipornography feminists overlook the fact that most rape victims are men—and the fact that some substantial number of these male victims are likely in turn to attack women. According to conservative estimates, more than 290,000 men are sexually assaulted in jails and prisons every year, while the Bureau of Justice Statistics estimates that 135,000 women are raped annually. Even if the latter number is understated, as some critics charge, it is indisputable that there is an epidemic of male prison rape—an epidemic that preys not only on men behind bars, but also on women in the outside world. Consequently, according to Stephen Donaldson, president of Stop Prisoner Rape, "The fight against rape in our communities is doomed to failure . . . as long as it ignores the network of training grounds for rapists: our prisons, jails and reform schools." In the view of psychologists and rape counselors, he explains, the brutal, often daily, sexual assaults that many prisoners experience lead to a "pent-up rage," which

> can cause victims . . . to erupt in violence once they return to their communities. Some will become rapists, seeking to "regain their manhood" through the same violent means by which they believe it was lost.[25]

Information compiled by the Bureau of Justice Statistics indicates that 23 percent of all *convicted* rapists had prior felony convictions.[26] Additionally, it seems likely that a substantial number of men who commit, but are not convicted of, rapes also served time in prison before assaulting their victims. Thus, those of us who seek to protect potential rape victims in the outside world—as well as potential rape victims in prisons—should heed Donaldson's warning.

### . . . by Digging in Our Heels

The MacDworkinite idea that pornography is violence against women insults the many women who experience actual, brutal, three-dimensional violence in their real lives. Consequently, many women who are dedicating their lives to helping other women who are victims of violence have little patience for discussions of pornography as an alleged threat to women's safety.[27] I'd like you to consider the eloquent plea of one of them, whose many constructive efforts show what can and must be done to *really* help brutalized women.

Colleen Cobel, executive director of the Missouri Coalition Against Domestic Violence, was instrumental in beginning shelter service programs for battered women throughout Missouri, and for setting up the state's first toll-free hotline for victims of domestic and sexual violence. As a lobbyist, she played a key role in the passage of important legislation benefiting battered and raped women, including a domestic violence arrest statute, laws criminalizing marital rape and stalking, laws providing funding for services and shelters for battered women, and a state statute mandating the collection of law enforcement data on domestic violence crimes.

I met Colleen Cobel in 1993 when we both participated in a panel discussion about whether pornography should be censored in the name of feminism, at Washington University in St. Louis, Missouri. After listening to the other speakers, Cobel sought to shift the focus from images to human beings:

> [I]f I can do honor to those women whose lives are consumed with the harsh realities of violence, it is to [address] what they experience daily. . . . Women don't come into shelters saying, "This is pornography that is doing this to me." They don't call rape crisis lines saying, "If he just wouldn't have read that magazine, I don't think I would have been assaulted on my date." . . . I put the word around the state to all of the different shelters and sexual assault programs that I'm privileged enough to work with. And none of the women were in a safe enough place to distill these issues in their own personal life. To be able to name the role that the cultural violence against women through magazines, through film, through commercials, they couldn't name that as being a cause. . . . [T]hey might have got-

ten raped last night because the wrong team won in Monday night football. They might have been assaulted because they served the wrong kind of food, because the kids were too noisy.

When the women come into programs seeking the tools they need to become survivors of violence, they have a long list of things that are more paramount. It is that the judge doesn't know the law and he gave my batterer my kids. It's that the Section 8 housing assistance list is so long that they won't even take names for three years, and I don't have a place to live. It's that I don't have any job skills and since I'm a rural woman it took days to find a place to go. It's that my two-year-old thinks that the way you get a hold of Mom's attention is you hit her in the face.

So I guess I have to expand the parameters of our discussion today in honor of those women whose lives are being affected today by violence and don't have the luxury of this room to sit and discuss the implications of pornography.

When the discussion later returned to antipornography proposals, Cobel interjected along the same lines:

I want to bring us back down to the ground here. When we talk about pornography as the injury, I don't care what causes the injury a lot of days, all I know is that the injury is real and nobody is responding. . . . Our system does not work for the real life injuries and harms to women. When today ends four women are dead and they died at the hands of their partner, every day, every day, every day. I know our discussion is to be in the theoretical, but it is very difficult for me to stay there because I know that the real life devastation can come from any number of causes. . . . And I just feel compelled to again and again say the real injury is the real injury and the real death is the real death. They come from a host of different places, different parts of society but they remain my greatest concern and my greatest focus.[28]

The pornocentric view that sexual abuse and violence stem from sexually explicit images has been disputed not only by activists who work with adult women who are actual victims of abuse, but also by activists who work with sexually abused children. Martin Morse Wooster has written that, consistent with the Meese Commission's preconceptions about the adverse impact of sexual expression, its investigators scoured Los Angeles organizations that help teenage runaways and prostitutes, in an ultimately futile quest to "see teenagers who started turning tricks after their fathers showed them *Playboy* and *Penthouse*." As a staff member at one of these organizations noted, though, "*none* of our kids got started turning tricks because their fathers started using pornography. None. Even if you got rid of all the pornography in the world, you couldn't get rid of abusive or drunk fathers."[29]

It is important to note that the procensorship feminists' "blame-the-book" attitude closely parallels the "blame-the-victim" attitude that often characterized perceptions of female sexual assault victims, and that until recently was enshrined in American law. If a woman's skirt was "too short," or her sweater was "too tight," then it was her fault she was raped. As Marcia Pally has written, "[A]ccording to antipornography logic, it is still the woman's fault—if not the woman in the room, then the woman on the screen, calendar or wall."[30]

What "blaming the book" and "blaming the victim" have in common is the creation of a scapegoat. The many close connections between the traditional right wing and pornophobic feminists include this image-blaming approach to societal violence. In the spring of 1992, Vice President Dan Quayle criticized the title character of the television show *Murphy Brown* for choosing to become a single mother. He said the character had contributed to an erosion of "family values," which he blamed for the rioting that had occurred in Los Angeles in the wake of the acquittal of the police officers who had beaten Rodney King. Liberals promptly and savagely derided Quayle's female-image blaming. Yet as novelist Anne Rice has noted, too many liberals take a very different stance toward the same female-image-blaming strategy on the part of Dworkin and MacKinnon.

In 1992 Rice denounced the Pornography Victims' Compensation Act as "the most evil piece of legislation I have ever heard of." She astutely noted that if you give a rape victim "the right to sue and say that a magazine was the cause of the rape, there's only one step from that for the man to say, 'Yes, it was the magazine that made me do it, and it was also the way she was dressed.' Why can't he sue her?"[31]

As writer Pete Hamill has pointed out, the implications of an image- and word-blaming approach are limitless, and would surely engulf feminist writings and pictures: "Someone could claim that his family was destroyed as the result of published feminist theories attacking the family, and that feminist writers and their publishers must pay for the damage."[32]

The appeal of any censorship movement, including the one directed at pornography, is understandable insofar as it appears to offer a simple, inexpensive solution to complex, troubling societal problems. In contrast, measures that are designed to redress the root causes of these problems are less dramatic, more cumbersome, and more costly than censorship. As aptly expressed by one anticensorship feminist, Lisa Steele, "Censorship is the cheapest item on the shopping list of the women's movement."[33]

I certainly would like nothing better than to find a simple, fast route to equality and safety for women. But censoring sexual speech is really a detour or, worse, a dead end. For without free speech, where can we go but backward along our hard-forged path?

# Notes

Note: The model antipornography law drafted by Andrea Dworkin and Catharine MacKinnon is quoted and referred to throughout this book. It can be found in Andrea Dworkin, "Against the Male Flood: Censorship, Pornography, and Equality," *Harvard Women's Law Journal* 8 (1985).

## INTRODUCTION

1. Catharine A. MacKinnon, "Not a Moral Issue," *Yale Law & Policy Review* 2 (1984): 321–45, at 325.
2. Ad Hoc Committee of Feminists for Free Expression, letter to the members of the Senate Judiciary Committee, 14 February 1992. Reprinted in Nadine Strossen, "A Feminist Critique of 'the' Feminist Critique of Pornography," *Virginia Law Review* 79 (August 1993): 1099–1190, at 1188–90.
3. Henry Louis Gates, Jr., "To Deprave and Corrupt," review of *Girls Lean Back Everywhere: The Law of Obscenity and the Assault on Genius* by Edward de Grazia, *The Nation*, 29 June 1992, pp. 898–903, at p. 898.
4. Department of Justice, *Attorney General's Commission on Pornography, Final Report* (Washington, D.C.: Government Printing Office, 1986).
5. Alex Comfort, *The Joy of Sex* (New York: Simon & Schuster, 1972).
6. I first heard this phrase from Marcia Pally, founder of Feminists for Free Expression.
7. For this analysis by Andrea Dworkin, see: *Pornography: Men Possessing Women* (New York: E. P. Dutton, 1979); "Against the Male Flood: Censorship, Pornography, and Equality," *Harvard Women's Law Journal* 8 (1985); "Pornography's 'Exquisite Volunteers,'" *Ms.*, March 1981; "Pornography: The New Terrorism," *New York University Review of Law and Social Change* 8 (1978-79); "Pornography's Part in Sexual Violence," *Los Angeles Times*, 26 May 1981. For similar analysis by Catharine MacKinnon, see: *Only Words* (Cambridge, Mass.: Harvard University Press, 1993); "Not a Moral Issue"; "Pornography, Civil Rights, and Free Speech," *Harvard Civil Rights–Civil Liberties Law Review* 20 (Winter 1985): 1-70.
8. Cathy Crosson letter to Nadine Strossen, 6 October 1994.
9. Carole S. Vance, quoted in interviews by Sally Chew, "Pornography: Does Women's Equality Depend on What We Do about It?" *Ms.*, January/February 1994, pp. 42–45.
10. *Olmstead v. United States*, 277 U.S. 438, 479 (1928).

## CHAPTER 1
### The Sex Panic and the Feminist Split

1. Maureen Dezell, "Porn Wars," *Boston Phoenix,* 2–8 July 1993.
2. Leanne Katz, introduction to *New York Law School Law Review Symposium: The Sex Panic,* a special issue of the *Review* based on speeches at its same-titled 1992 symposium (forthcoming).
3. Marjorie Heins, "A Public University's Response to Students' Removal of an Art Exhibit" (speech given at the University of Michigan Law School, Ann Arbor, Mich., 16 October 1993).
4. *Webster's Third New International Dictionary of the English Language,* unabridged, Philip Babcock Gove, ed. (Springfield, Mass.: Merriam-Webster, 1986), p. 1767.
5. Walter Kendrick, *The Secret Museum: Pornography in Modern Culture* (New York: Viking, 1987), p. 239.
6. Andrea Dworkin, "Against the Male Flood: Censorship, Pornography, and Equality," *Harvard Women's Law Journal* 8 (1985): 1–29, at 25.
7. *Butler v. the Queen,* 1 S. C. R. 452 (1992, Canada).
8. Gayle Rubin, "Thinking Sex: Notes for a Radical Theory of the Politics of Sexuality," in *Pleasure and Danger: Exploring Female Sexuality,* ed. Carole S. Vance (Boston: Routledge & Kegan Paul, 1984), pp. 267–319, at p. 278.
9. Arts Censorship Project, *Year End Report* (New York: American Civil Liberties Union, 1992), p. 13.
10. Bernard Weinraub, "Despite Clinton, Hollywood Is Still Trading in Violence," *New York Times,* 28 December 1993.
11. Quoted in Dave Gram, "Columbus Mural Brings Charges of Harassment," Associated Press, 29 May 1992.
12. Chris Bentley, "Mall Nixes Artwork as Shocking," Springfield (Mo.) *News-Leader,* 5 March 1992.
13. Nat Hentoff, "Sexual Harassment by Francisco Goya," *Washington Post,* 27 December 1991.
14. Nancy C. Stumhofer, "Goya's 'Naked Maja' and the Classroom Climate," *Democratic Culture,* 3, no. 1 (1994): 18–22, at 19.
15. Hentoff, "Sexual Harassment by Francisco Goya."
16. Ntozake Shange, in "Where Do We Stand on Pornography?" (Roundtable), *Ms.,* January/February 1994, pp. 32–41, at p. 34.
17. Joyce Price, "Breast Fetish Brouhaha Rocks Staid Vanderbilt," *Washington Times,* 6 March 1993.
18. Liza Mundy, "The New Critics," *Lingua Franca,* September/October 1993, pp. 26–33, at p. 27
19. Syracuse University, *Responding to Sexual Harassment at Syracuse University,* 8 October 1993, p. 1.
20. "75% of Female Doctors in Survey Cite Harassment by Patients," *New York Times,* 23 December 1993.
21. Ibid.
22. Joyce Price, "Art Professor Escapes Discipline: Vanderbilt Says He Must Warn Classes," *Washington Times,* 21 March 1993.
23. Ibid.

24. Malcolm Johnes, "In Defense of the Freedom to Read," *St. Petersburg Times,* 13 September 1987.
25. Price, "Breast Fetish Brouhaha."
26. Courtney Leatherman, "Dealing with Sexual Images in Iowa Classrooms," *Chronicle of Higher Education,* 8 December 1993.
27. "Free Expression Debate Had Other Flash Points," *New York Times,* 29 December 1993.
28. Dirk Johnson, "A Sexual Harassment Case to Test Academic Freedom," *New York Times,* 11 May 1994.
29. Morton M. Kondracke, "Sex, Drugs, and Pornography, Government Style," *Roll Call,* 17 January 1994.
30. Thelma McCormack, letter to the editor, *Chicago Tribune,* 28 September 1993.
31. Catharine MacKinnon, *Only Words* (Cambridge, Mass.: Harvard University Press, 1993), p. 71.
32. Indianapolis-Mercer County, Indiana, General Ordinances Nos. 24 and 25 (1984), amendments to Code of Indianapolis and Marion County, Chapter 16, "Human Relations and Equal Opportunity."
33. Brief of the American Civil Liberties Union, Indiana Civil Liberties Union, and the American Civil Liberties Union of Illinois, amici curiae, *Hudnut v. American Booksellers Association* (filed in 7th Cir. 1985), p. 28.
34. *Butler v. the Queen,* 1 S. C. R. 452 (1992, Canada).
35. Catharine MacKinnon, "Not a Moral Issue," *Yale Law and Policy Review* 2 (1984): 321–345, at 325.
36. Catharine MacKinnon, "'More Than Simply a Magazine': *Playboy*'s Money," in *Feminism Unmodified* (Cambridge, Mass.: Harvard University Press, 1987), p. 145.
37. Catharine MacKinnon, quoted in Pete Hamill, "Women on the Verge of a Legal Breakdown," *Playboy,* January 1993, p. 186.
38. Andrea Dworkin, "Pornography: The New Terrorism," *New York University Review of Law and Social Change* 8 (1978-79): 218.
39. Leanne Katz, "In the Realm of the Censors," *In These Times,* 7 March 1994, pp. 24–25.
40. Quoted in Patrick Cooke, "Defending the L-Word," *Vogue,* December 1992, pp. 156–160, at p. 158.
41. Marcia Pally, letter to the editor under heading "Feminist Addenda," *Vogue,* February 1993, p. 58.
42. Kathleen Peratis, letter to Nadine Strossen, 29 November 1993.

### CHAPTER 2
#### Sexual Speech and the Law

1. Madonna, "Rock the Vote Video," MTV Networks, 1992.
2. Susan Sontag, "The Pornographic Imagination," in *Styles of Radical Will* (New York: Anchor Books, 1969), pp. 35–73, at p. 46.
3. Garrison Keillor, statement to the Senate Subcommittee on Education, 29 March 1990. (Testimony on NEA Grant Funding and Restrictions.)
4. Sontag, "Pornographic Imagination," p. 46.
5. Catharine MacKinnon, *Only Words* (Cambridge, Mass.: Harvard Uni-

versity Press, 1993), pp. 45–110; Andrea Dworkin and Catharine Mac-
Kinnon, *Pornography and Civil Rights: A New Day for Women's Equality*
(Minneapolis: Organizing Against Pornography, 1988), p. 85.

6. *United States v. Schwimmer,* 279 U.S. 644, 654-55 (1929) (dissenting).
7. *Texas v. Johnson,* 491 U.S. 397, 414 (1989).
8. Ibid; *U.S. v. Eichman,* 496 U.S. 310 (1990).
9. *R.A.V. v. City of St. Paul,* 112 S. Ct. 2538 (1992). The Court recognized
   that this symbolic expression could be constitutionally prohibited under
   many laws, such as those prohibiting arson, vandalism, and trespass; it
   stressed, though, that this expression could not be prohibited under a law
   that focused on the ideas it conveyed—namely, a city ordinance that prohibited expression that "arouses anger, alarm or resentment . . . on the
   basis of race, color, creed, religion or gender."
10. *Schenck v. United States,* 249 U.S. 47, 52 (1919).
11. *Gitlow v. New York,* 268 U.S. 652, 673 (1925) (dissenting).
12. *American Booksellers Association v. Hudnut,* 771 F. 2d 323, 329-30 (1985).
13. *Butler v. the Queen,* 1 S.C.R. 452, 505 (1992, Canada) (stating that "[i]t
    might be suggested that proof of actual harm should be required. . . . [I]t
    is sufficient . . . for Parliament to have a reasonable basis for concluding
    that harm will result and this requirement does not demand actual proof
    of harm").
14. *Brandenburg v. Ohio,* 395 U.S. 444 (1969).
15. *National Association for the Advancement of Colored People (NAACP) v.
    Claiborne Hardware Co.,* 458 U.S. 886, 928 (1982).
16. *Abrams v. United States,* 250 U.S. 616, 630–31 (1919) (dissenting).
17. *Whitney v. California,* 274 U.S. 357, 375–77 (1927) (concurring).
18. Susie Bright, "I Hate to Break This to You Kitty, But . . . ," *San Diego
    Reader,* 18 November 1993, pp. 1–2.
19. Sontag, "Pornographic Imagination," p. 47.
20. *Webster's Third New International Dictionary of the English Language,* un-
    abridged, Philip Babcock Gove, ed. (Springfield, Mass.: Merriam-Webster,
    1986), p. 1767.
21. *Winters v. New York,* 338 U.S. 507, 510, 528 (1948).
22. President's Commission on Obscenity and Pornography, *Report* (New
    York: Bantam, 1970).
23. *Roe v. Wade,* 410 U.S. 179 (1973).
24. *Miller v. California,* 413 U.S. 15 (1973).
25. *Paris Adult Theatre I v. Slaton,* 413 U.S. 49 (1973).
26. *Memoirs v. Massachusetts,* 383 U.S. 413, 419–20 (1966).
27. *Miller v. California,* 24.
28. *Paris Adult Theatre I v. Slaton,* 60.
29. *Jacobellis v. Ohio,* 378 U.S. 184, 197 (1964) (concurring).
30. *Miller v. California,* 24.
31. *Brockett v. Spokane Arcades,* 472 U.S. 492, 498 (1985).
32. Quoted in Jeff Rosen, "*Miller* Time," *New Republic,* 1 October 1990, p. 17.
33. Quoted in Edward de Grazia, *Girls Lean Back Everywhere: The Law of
    Obscenity and the Assault on Genius* (New York: Vintage Books, 1992), p.
    622.

34. *R.A.V. v. City of St. Paul* (cross); *U.S. v. Eichman* (flag); *Texas v. Johnson* (flag).

35. *Roth v. United States,* 354 U.S. 476, 487 (1957).

36. Laurence H. Tribe, *American Constitutional Law,* 2d ed. (Mineola, N.Y.: The Foundation Press, 1988), p. 905.

37. Marjorie Heins, *Sex, Sin, and Blasphemy* (New York: The New Press, 1993), p. 34.

38. *Pope v. Illinois,* 481 U.S. 497, 507 (1987) (dissenting).

39. Ibid., 504–5 (concurring).

40. *State v. Henry,* 302 Ore. 510, 732 P. 2d 9 (1987); *State v. Kam,* 69 Haw. 483, 748 P. 2d 372 (1988).

41. United States Department of Justice, *Attorney General's Commission on Pornography, Final Report* (Washington, D.C.: U.S. Government Printing Office, 1986), p. 251.

42. Tribe, *American Constitutional Law,* p. 919.

## CHAPTER 3
### The Fatally Flawed Feminist Antipornography Laws

1. Andrea Dworkin, *Letters from a War Zone* (New York: E. P. Dutton, 1988), pp. 256-61; Catharine MacKinnon, *Only Words* (Cambridge, Mass.: Harvard University Press, 1993), pp. 87-89.

2. *New York v. Ferber,* 458 U.S. 747 (1982); *Osborne v. Ohio,* 495 U.S. 103 (1990).

3. Andrea Dworkin, "Against the Male Flood: Censorship, Pornography, and Equality," *Harvard Women's Law Journal* 8 (1985): 25.

4. *R.A.V. v. City of St. Paul,* 112 S. Ct. 2538, 2550 (1992).

5. *Dambrot v. Central Michigan University,* 839 F. Supp. 477 (E.D. Mich. 1993); *U.W.M. Post, Inc. v. Board of Regents of the University of Wisconsin System,* 774 F. Supp. 1163 (E.D. Wis. 1991); *Doe v. University of Michigan,* 721 F. Supp. 852 (E.D. Mich. 1989).

6. Richard Bernstein, *Dictatorship of Virtue: Multiculturalism and the Battle for America's Future* (New York: Knopf, 1994).

7. Catharine A. MacKinnon, *Toward a Feminist Theory of the State* (Cambridge, Mass.: Harvard University Press, 1989), p. 202.

8. *United States v. Levine,* 183 F. 2d 156, 157 (2d Cir. 1936). The earlier, repudiated doctrine was set forth in an 1868 British case, *Regina v. Hicklin,* L.R. 3 Q.B. 360, 368, which American courts had widely adopted. It held that the "test of obscenity" was "whether the tendency of the matter . . . is to deprave and corrupt those whose minds are open to such immoral influences. . . ."

9. *Pornography Victims' Compensation Act of 1991,* 102d Congress, 1st sess., S.R. 1521.

10. Catharine A. MacKinnon, letter to *New York Times* opinion page editor Mitchel Levitas, 1 January 1994.

11. Andrea Dworkin, in "Where Do We Stand on Pornography?" (Round-table), *Ms.,* January/February 1994, pp. 32–41, at p. 37.

12. *New York Times v. Sullivan,* 376 U.S. 254, 277 (1964).

13. *American Booksellers Association v. Hudnut,* 598 F. Supp. 1316, 1340-41 (D. Ind. 1984).

14. *New York Times Co. v. United States,* 403 U.S. 713 (1971).

15. *New York Times v. Sullivan,* 277.

16. Molly Ivins, "Havin' Fun Fightin' for Freedom," in *New York Law School Law Review Symposium: The Sex Panic* (forthcoming).

17. *New York Times v. Sullivan,* 376 U.S. 254 (1964).

18. Joyce Meskis, president of the American Booksellers Association, testifying on behalf of the association before the Senate Judiciary Committee, 23 July 1991.

19. See *Kovacs v. Cooper,* 336 U.S. 77, 87 (1949).

20. *Consolidated Edison Company v. Public Service Commission,* 447 U.S. 530, 542 (1980).

21. *Rowan v. United States Post Office Department,* 397 U.S. 728, 737 (1970).

22. *Bolger v. Youngs Drug Products,* 463 U.S. 60 (1983).

23. *American Booksellers Association v. Hudnut,* 771 F. 2d 323, 333 (7th Cir. 1985).

24. *Erznoznik v. City of Jacksonville,* 422 U.S. 205 (1975).

25. "Policy No. 3: Private Pressure Groups," *Policy Guide of the American Civil Liberties Union.* Adopted 1981.

26. Kate Ellis, Beth Jaker, Nan D. Hunter, Barbara O'Dair, and Abby Tallmer, eds., *Caught Looking: Feminism, Pornography, and Censorship* (East Haven, Conn.: Long River Books, 1986).

27. Carole Vance, in *Ideas—Feminism and Censorship,* transcript from the Canadian Broadcasting Company (Toronto: CBC Radio Works, 1993), p. 14.

28. Marcia Pally, "X-Rated Feminism: Ban Sexism, Not Pornography," *The Nation,* 29 June 1985, pp. 794-96.

29. Andrea Dworkin and Catharine MacKinnon, *Pornography and Civil Rights: A New Day for Women's Equality* (Minneapolis: Organizing Against Pornography, 1988), pp. 138–42.

30. Some versions of the MacDworkin law include a ninth criterion, that "women are presented as whores by nature." See *Caught Looking,* p. 88, quoting Minneapolis version of the Dworkin-MacKinnon model law at p. vii.

31. MacKinnon letter to Mitchel Levitas.

32. Susan J. Berkson, "Minneapolis Saw Early that Porn Causes Harm, But '84 Vetoes Stopped Ordinance from Taking Effect," *Star Tribune,* 20 February 1994.

33. Kathleen Currie and Art Levine, "Whip Me, Beat Me, and While You're at It Cancel My NOW Membership: Feminists War against Each Other over Pornography," *Washington Monthly,* June 1987, p. 17.

34. Quoted in Lisa Duggan, "Censorship in the Name of Feminism," in *Caught Looking,* p. 65. (Reprinted from *Village Voice,* 16 October 1986, pp. 11–12, 16–17, 42.)

35. Quoted in ibid., p. 65.

36. Quoted in ibid.

37. *American Booksellers Association v. Hudnut,* 598 F. Supp. 1316 (D. Ind. 1984), *aff'd.,* 771 F. 2d 323 (7th Cir. 1985), *aff'd. mem.,* 475 U.S. 1001 (1986).

38. *American Booksellers Association v. Hudnut,* 771 F. 2d 323, 325 (7th Cir. 1985).

39. *American Booksellers Association v. Hudnut,* 598 F. Supp. 1316, 1317 (D. Ind. 1984).

40. Catharine MacKinnon, "Sexual Politics of the First Amendment," in *Feminism Unmodified* (Cambridge, Mass.: Harvard University Press, 1987), p. 213.

41. *Dred Scott v. Sandford,* 60 U.S. 393 (1856).

42. *Brown v. Board of Education,* 347 U.S. 483 (1954).

43. *Village Books et al. v. City of Bellingham,* C88-1470D (W.D. Wash.). This decision is not officially reported.

44. *Dworkin v. Hustler Magazine,* 867 F. 2d 1188, 1199 (9th Cir. 1989). Interestingly, the opinion was written by a female judge, Cynthia Holcomb Hall.

45. Quoted in Karen Winkler, "Research on Pornography Gains Respectability," *Chronicle of Higher Education,* 14 June 1989.

46. *Roe v. Wade,* 410 U.S. 179 (1973).

47. For a discussion of these rulings, see Nadine Strossen, "A Feminist Critique of 'the' Feminist Critique of Pornography," *Virginia Law Review* 79 (1993): 1099–1190, at 1120-22.

48. Fred Strebeigh, "Defining Law on the Feminist Frontier," *New York Times Magazine,* 6 October 1991.

## CHAPTER 4
### *The Growing Suppression of "Sexpression"*

1. Marcia Pally, "The Soothing Appeal of Censorship," *Writer's Yearbook* (1993): 80.

2. Quoted in Digby Diehl, "Anne Rice: The *Playboy* Interview," *Playboy,* March 1993, pp. 53–64, at p. 56.

3. Isabel Wilkerson, "Foes of Pornography and Bigotry Join Forces," *New York Times,* 12 March 1993.

4. Alice Echols, "Sex and the Single-Minded," *Voice Literary Supplement,* March 1994, pp. 13, 17.

5. James R. Petersen, "Catharine MacKinnon: Again," *Playboy,* August 1992, pp. 37, 39.

6. Quoted in David Margolick, "At the Bar" (column), *New York Times,* 5 November 1993.

7. Anthony Lewis, "The First Amendment, Under Fire from the Left," *New York Times Magazine,* 13 March 1994.

8. Margolick, "At the Bar."

9. Ibid.

10. Ibid.

11. Catharine MacKinnon, "Linda's Life and Andrea's Work," in *Feminism Unmodified,* p. 133.

12. Leanne Katz, in *New York Law School Law Review Symposium: The Sex Panic* (forthcoming).

13. Wilkerson, "Foes of Pornography and Bigotry Join Forces."

14. Madonna, *Sex* (New York: Warner Books, 1992).

15. Quoted in Catherine Siemann, memo to Nadine Strossen regarding Chicago conference, 12 March 1993.

16. Maureen Dezell, "Woman's Choices," *Boston Phoenix,* 5 February 1993.

17. To correct this imbalance, the *New York Law School Law Review* is publishing a special two-issue collection of articles and essays, *The Sex Panic,* which presents feminist anticensorship perspectives on pornography, scheduled for publication in 1994.

18. Susie Bright, "Better the Devil You Know," *San Francisco Review of Books,* May/June 1993.

19. Jean Bethke Elshtain, "The New Porn Wars," *New Republic,* 25 June 1984, p. 15.

20. "Enough Is Enough" campaign, advertising a kit for creating an anti-pornography billboard.

21. Carole S. Vance, in *New York Law School Law Review Symposium: The Sex Panic* (forthcoming).

22. Carole S. Vance, "Feminist Fundamentalism: Women against Images," *Art in America,* September 1993, pp. 35–39, at p. 36.

23. Judith R. Walkowitz, *Prostitution and Victorian Society: Women, Class, and the State* (New York: Cambridge University Press, 1980), p. 256.

24. ACLU Arts Censorship Project, *Above the Law: The Justice Department's War against the First Amendment* (New York: American Civil Liberties Union, 1991).

25. Deposition of Robert Marinaro in *PHE, Inc. v. U.S. Department of Justice,* 743 F. Supp. 15, 69–70 (D.D.C. 1990) 24 May 1991.

26. Chuck Philips, "A War on Many Fronts," *Los Angeles Times,* 26 December 1990.

27. *Jacobson v. United States,* 112 S. Ct. 1535 (1992).

28. Lawrence A. Stanley, "The Child Porn Myth," *Cardozo Arts & Entertainment Law Journal* 7 (1989): 295–358.

29. *United States v. Mitchell,* 915 F. 2d 521, 524 (9th Cir. 1990).

30. *Washington Revised Code,* annotated (West 1992) 9:68.050-.070, .090.

31. Susan McClary, "Getting Down Off the Beanstalk: The Presence of Woman's Voice in Janika Vandervelde's *Genesis 11,*" *Minnesota Composers' Forum Newsletter* (January 1987), cited in Christina Hoff Sommers, *Who Stole Feminism? How Women Have Betrayed Women* (New York: Simon & Schuster, 1994), p. 28. According to Sommers, "McClary also directs us to be alert to themes of male masturbation in the music of Richard Strauss and Gustav Mahler."

32. Marjorie Heins, *Sex, Sin, and Blasphemy* (New York: The New Press, 1993), pp. 61–63.

33. Ibid., p. 64.

34. Nikki Finke, "All Sides Get Worked Up over Study of Aerobics Video," *Los Angeles Times,* 12 November 1987; see also Margaret Morse, "Artemis Aging: Exercise and the Female Body on Video," *Discourse* 11 (1987-88): 20–53.

35. For example, the ACLU successfully challenged Washington's erotic-lyrics law. See *Soundgarden v. Eikenberry,* 123 Wash. 2d 750, 871 P. 2d 1050 (1994).

36. 750 ILCS 5/12-18.1.

37. *An Act to Protect the Civil Rights of Women and Children,* Massachusetts 177th General Court—1992 Regular Session House Bill 5194.

38. Memorandum to Working Group, Interested Others from Leanne Katz, executive director, National Coalition Against Censorship, 11 August 1994.

39. *Finley v. National Endowment for the Arts,* 795 F. Supp. 1457 (C.D. Cal. 1992); *Bella Lewitsky Dance Foundation v. Frohnmayer,* 754 F. Supp. 774 (C.D. Cal. 1991); *New School for Social Research v. Frohnmayer,* No. 90 Civ. 3510 (LLS), Southern District of New York, February 19, 1991 (settled by stipulation).

40. Holly Hughes, quoted in interviews by Sally Chew in "Pornography: Does Women's Equality Depend on What We Do about It?" *Ms.,* January/February 1994, pp. 42–45.

41. Paul Goldberger, "Clinton Arts Dinner Whetted Appetites Still Unsatisfied," *New York Times,* 23 March 1994.

42. William Grimes, "House Votes a Cut in Arts Endowment's Budget," *New York Times,* 24 June 1994.

43. Paul Goldberger, "Clinton Arts Dinner Whetted Appetites."

44. William Grimes, "For Endowment, One Performer Means Trouble," *New York Times,* 7 July 1994; "Senate Passes 5% Arts Cut," *New York Times,* 27 July 1994.

45. Grimes, "House Votes a Cut in Arts Endowment's Budget."

46. *Finley v. National Endowment for the Arts,* 1475.

47. Barbara Isenberg and Ronald J. Ostrow, "Appeal in NEA Case Criticized," *Los Angeles Times,* 8 April 1993.

48. Quoted in Edward de Grazia, *Girls Lean Back Everywhere: The Law of Obscenity and the Assault on Genius* (New York: Vintage Books, 1992), p. 666.

49. Quoted in ibid., p. 685.

50. Judy Blume, "Is Puberty a Dirty Word?" in *New York Law School Law Review Symposium: The Sex Panic* (forthcoming).

51. Robert Brustein, "The War on the Arts," *New Republic,* 7 September 1992, p. 35.

52. Marilyn French, *The War against Women* (New York: Simon & Schuster, 1992), p. 163.

53. *Finley v. National Endowment for the Arts,* 1461.

54. Quoted in letter from Jeremiah Gutman, Jo List Levinson, and Leanne Katz to Cincinnati prosecutor Terrence Robert Cosgrove, 27 July 1994, p. 2.

55. Ibid., p. 3.

56. Andrea Dworkin, *Pornography: Men Possessing Women* (New York: E. P. Dutton, 1979), p. 23.

## CHAPTER 5
*Revealing Views of Women, Men, and Sex*

1. Andrea Dworkin, *Woman Hating* (New York: E.P. Dutton, 1984), p. 184.

2. Lisa Duggan, Nan D. Hunter, and Carole S. Vance, "False Promises: Feminist Anti-Pornography Legislation," in *Caught Looking: Feminism, Pornography, and Censorship,* ed. Kate Ellis et al. (East Haven, Conn.: Long River Books, 1986), pp. 72–85, at p. 80.

3. Dworkin, *Woman Hating,* p. 184.

4. Quoted in Christina Hoff Sommers, "Hard-Line Feminists Guilty of Ms.-Representation," *Wall Street Journal,* 7 November 1991.

5. Carlin Meyer, "Decriminalizing Prostitution: Liberation or Dehumanization?" *Cardozo Women's Law Journal* 1 (1993): 105–20, at 117.

6. In Charles Bufe, ed., *The Heretic's Handbook of Quotations* (San Francisco: Sharp Press, 1988), p. 63.

7. Jeanne L. Schroeder, "Catharine's Wheel: MacKinnon's Pornography Analysis as a Return to Traditional Christian Sexual Theory," in *New York Law School Law Review Symposium: The Sex Panic* (forthcoming).

8. Andrea Dworkin, *Intercourse* (New York: Free Press, 1987), p. 137.

9. Ibid., pp. 42–43.

10. Andrea Dworkin, *Pornography: Men Possessing Women* (New York: E. P. Dutton, 1979), p. 23

11. Andrea Dworkin, *Letters from a War Zone* (New York: E. P. Dutton, 1988), pp. 176 and 119.

12. Andrea Dworkin, *Ice and Fire* (New York: Weidenfeld and Nicholson, 1987), p. 108.

13. Quoted in Pete Hamill, "Women on the Verge of a Legal Breakdown," *Playboy,* January 1993, p. 187.

14. Catharine MacKinnon, "Feminism, Marxism, Method, and the State: Towards Feminist Jurisprudence," *Signs: Journal of Women in Culture and Society* 8 (1983): 635–58, at 646.

15. Quoted in James R. Petersen, "Catharine MacKinnon: Again," *Playboy,* August 1992, pp. 37–39.

16. Ibid.

17. Ibid.

18. Ibid.

19. Catharine MacKinnon, "Not a Moral Issue," *Yale Law & Policy Review* 2 (1984): 334.

20. Catharine MacKinnon, "Linda's Life and Andrea's Work," in *Feminism Unmodified* (Cambridge, Mass.: Harvard University Press, 1987), pp. 127–33, at p. 130.

21. Catharine A. MacKinnon, *Toward a Feminist Theory of the State* (Cambridge, Mass.: Harvard University Press, 1989), p. 113.

22. Catharine MacKinnon, "Reflections of Sex Equality under Law," *Yale Law Journal* 100 (1991): 1281–1328, at 1302-3.

23. Catharine MacKinnon, "Francis Biddle's Sister," in *Feminism Unmodified,* pp. 163–97, at p. 171.

24. Ibid., p. 172.

25. J. Miller, "Civil Right, Not Censorship," *Village Voice,* 6 November 1994.

26. MacKinnon, "Francis Biddle's Sister," at p. 171.

27. Quoted in Tad Friend, "Yes: Feminist Women Who Like Sex," *Esquire,* February 1994, pp. 48–56, at p. 54.

28. MacKinnon, *Toward a Feminist Theory of the State,* p. 125.

29. Quoted in Petersen, "Catharine MacKinnon: Again," p. 39.

30. Quoted in Friend, "Yes: Feminist Women Who Like Sex," at p. 50.

31. Dorchen Leidholdt, "When Women Defend Pornography," in *The Sexual Liberals and the Attack on Feminism,* ed. Dorchen Leidholdt and Janice G. Raymond (New York: Pergamon Press, 1990), pp. 125-31, at p. 131.

32. Meyer, "Decriminalizing Prostitution," 117.

33. Sally Cline, *Women, Passion, and Celibacy* (New York: Carol Southern Books, 1993), p. 150, p. 1.

34. Catharine MacKinnon, *Only Words* (Cambridge, Mass.: Harvard University Press, 1993), p. 12.

35. Katie Roiphe, *The Morning After: Sex, Fear, and Feminism on Campus* (New York: Little, Brown, 1993), p. 99.

36. Dworkin, *Pornography: Men Possessing Women,* p. 55.

37. Dworkin, *Letters from a War Zone,* p. 309.

38. MacKinnon, *Toward a Feminist Theory of the State,* p. 138.

39. Brief of the American Civil Liberties Union, Indiana Civil Liberties Union, and the American Civil Liberties Union of Illinois, amici curiae, *Hudnut v. American Booksellers Association* (filed in 7th Cir. 1985), p. 28.

40. Germaine Greer, *The Female Eunuch* (New York: McGraw-Hill, 1971), p. 59.

41. Ann Snitow, "Retrenchment versus Transformation: The Politics of the Antipornography Movement," in *Women against Censorship,* ed. Varda Burstyn (Vancouver: Douglas and McIntyre, 1985), pp. 107, 120.

42. Jeanne L. Schroeder, "Feminism Historicized: Medieval Misogynist Stereotypes in Contemporary Feminist Jurisprudence," *Iowa Law Review* 75 (1980): 1135–1217, at 1136.

43. Ibid.

44. Marcia Pally, "The Soothing Appeal of Censorship," *Writer's Yearbook* (1993): 80.

45. Cathy Young, "Victimhood Is Powerful," *Reason,* October 1992, pp. 18–23, at p. 18.

46. Naomi Wolf, *Fire with Fire: The New Female Power and How It Will Change the 21st Century* (New York: Random House, 1993), p. xvii.

47. Ibid., p. 224.

## CHAPTER 6
*Defining Sexual Harassment: Sexuality Does Not Equal Sexism*

1. Catharine A. MacKinnon, *Sexual Harassment of Working Women: A Case of Sex Discrimination* (New Haven, Conn.: Yale University Press, 1979).

2. *Meritor Savings Bank v. Vinson,* 477 U.S. 57 (1986).

3. See, for example, Catharine MacKinnon, "Not a Moral Issue," *Yale Law & Policy Review* 2 (1984): 325. ("Pornography . . . is . . . an institution of gender inequality.")

4. Katie Roiphe, *The Morning After: Sex, Fear, and Feminism on Campus* (New York: Little, Brown, 1993), p. 154.

5. Brief of Feminists for Free Expression, amicus curiae, *Johnson v. County of Los Angeles Fire Department* (filed in C.D. Cal. 1994), p. 16.

6. *Meritor Savings Bank v. Vinson,* 65.

7. Equal Employment Opportunity Commission Guidelines on Discrimination because of Sex, 29 CFR Part 1604.11(a) (1985).

8. Catharine MacKinnon, introduction to "Comment on Sexual Harassment," *Capital University Law Review,* 10 (Spring 1981): i–viii; *Only Words* (Cambridge, Mass.: Harvard University Press, 1993), pp. 56–57, 61–62; also *Sexual Harassment of Working Women.*

9. In a 1990 policy statement, the EEOC said that, notwithstanding the guidelines' focus on sexual conduct or expression, sex-based harassment could also be accomplished through nonsexual conduct or expression. "EEOC Policy Guidance on Current Issues of Sexual Harassment," reprinted in *DLR* 60: E-5 (28 March 1990). Moreover, some federal courts have held that sexual harassment in violation of Title VII may consist of nonsexual behavior. See, e.g., *Andrews v. Philadelphia*, 895 F. 2d 1469, 1485 (3rd Cir. 1990). Nevertheless, the guidelines' focus on sexual conduct and expression no doubt is an important reason why so many campus and workplace definitions of sexual harassment replicate the same misplaced focus. That focus is certainly consistent with the views of Catherine MacKinnon, who has repeatedly asserted that her concern *is* sexual—and not sexist, but nonsexual—conduct or expression. See n. 8, supra.

10. *Harris v. Forklift Systems,* Inc., 114 S. Ct. 367 (1993).

11. Ibid.

12. *Robinson v. Jacksonville Shipyards, Inc.,* 760 F. Supp. 1486 (M.D. Fl. 1991).

13. Ibid., 1542.

14. David Moshman, "Banned at UN-L," *Academic Freedom Coalition of Nebraska Newsletter* 4 (2): 2.

15. Nat Hentoff, "Sexual Harassment by Francisco Goya," *Washington Post,* 27 December 1993.

16. Nancy C. Stumhofer, "Goya's 'Naked Maja' and the Classroom Climate," *Democratic Culture,* 3, no. 1 (1994): 18–22.

17. Liza Mundy, "The New Critics," *Lingua Franca,* September/October 1993, pp. 26–33, at p. 27.

18. Ibid., pp. 29–30.

19. Brief of Feminists for Free Expression, amicus curiae, *Johnson v. County of Los Angeles Fire Department,* p. 5.

20. *Stanley v. Georgia,* 394 U.S. 557 (1969).

21. *Johnson v. County of Los Angeles Fire Department,* U.S. District Court for the Central District of California, CV 93-7589 SVW (JGX), Findings of Fact, Conclusions of Law and Judgment, entered 10 June 1994 (holding that the policy was unconstitutional as applied to the quiet reading and possession of sexually oriented materials during a firefighter's personal time).

22. Brief of Feminists for Free Expression, amicus curiae, *Johnson v. County of Los Angeles Fire Department,* pp. 24–26.

23. Roiphe, *The Morning After,* pp. 100–101.

24. Sexual Harassment and Academic Freedom, Statement 3, National Association of Scholars, 1993.

25. Naomi Wolf, *Fire with Fire: The New Female Power and How It Will Change the 21st Century* (New York: Random House, 1993), p. 195.

26. Rudy Platiel, "Adult Magazine Complaint Enters New Phase," *Toronto Globe and Mail,* 4 January 1994; Reva Landau, "Bread, Milk, and Pornography," *Toronto Star,* 22 February 1993.

27. Tom Puleo, "Market Mores: Who Should Censor?" *Hartford Journal,* 13 January 1992.

28. Thomas McGeveran, "Bookstore Charged with Harassment: Complaint Says Pornography Magazines Violate Sexual Harassment Policy," *Carleton College Carletonian,* 29 May 1992; Chris Youngquist, "V.P. Decides R.A.P.

Case: Disputed Magazines Will Remain in Bookstore," *Carletonian,* 9 October 1992.

29. Laurence H. Tribe, *American Constitutional Law,* 2d. ed. (Mineola, N.Y.: The Foundation Press, 1988), pp. 920–28.

30. James R. Petersen, "The *Playboy* Read-in," *Playboy,* February 1992, pp. 37–39.

31. *Civil Rights Act of 1964* at 201, Pub. L. No. 88-352, 78 Stat. 243 (codified at 42 U.S.C. at 2000a [1982]) prohibiting discrimination and segregation in places of public accommodation.

32. Brief of Feminists for Free Expression, amicus curiae, *Johnson v. County of Los Angeles Fire Department,* pp. 6–7.

33. Mark Schapiro, "The Fine Art of Sexual Harassment: Aphrodite Gets Her Day in Court," *Harper's,* July 1994, pp. 62–63.

34. Editorial, "Hillary the Stupendous," *Washington Times,* 10 April 1993.

35. Quoted in Schapiro, "The Fine Art of Sexual Harassment," p. 63.

36. Cynthia Grant Bowman, "Street Harassment and the Informal Ghettoization of Women," *Harvard Law Review* 106 (1993): 517. The following three quotes appear on pages 575, 562, and 523, respectively.

37. Quoted in "A Move to Protect Women from 'Street Harassment,'" *New York Times,* 2 July 1993.

38. Marcia Pally, *Sex and Sensibility: Reflections on Forbidden Mirrors and the Will to Censor* (Hopewell, N.J.: Ecco Press, 1994), pp. 73, 75.

39. *In the Interest of Joseph T., a minor,* 430 S.E. 2d 523, 524 (1993).

40. Susan Fall telephone conversation with Thomas Hilbink, 25 July 1994.

41. *Bradwell v. Illinois,* 83 U.S. (16 Wall.) 130, 140 (1873) (concurring).

42. *Bailey v. State,* 219 S.W. 2d 424, 428 (Ark. 1949).

43. Kingsley R. Browne, "Title VII as Censorship: Hostile-Environment Harassment and the First Amendment," *Ohio State Law Journal* 52 (Spring 1991): 488.

44. *Muller v. Oregon,* 208 U.S. 412 (1908).

45. *Frontiero v. Richardson,* 411 U.S. 677, 684 (1973).

46. Sarah J. McCarthy, "Cultural Fascism," *Forbes,* 9 December 1991, p. 116.

## CHAPTER 7
*"Different Strokes for Different Folks": The Panoply of Pornographic Imagination*

1. Richard A. Posner, "Obsession," review of *Only Words* by Catharine A. MacKinnon, *New Republic,* 18 October 1993, pp. 31–36, p. 36.

2. Brief of the American Civil Liberties Union and the Indiana Civil Liberties Union, amici curiae, *American Booksellers Association v. Hudnut* (Filed in D. Ind. 1984), p. 1.

3. Carlin Meyer, "Sex, Censorship, and Women's Liberation" (unpublished), pp. 42-43. [A revised version of this manuscript was published in *Texas Law Review* 72 (1994): 1097–1201.]

4. Sallie Tisdale, "Talk Dirty to Me: A Woman's Taste for Pornography," *Harper's,* February 1992, pp. 37–46, p. 45.

5. Marjorie Heins, *Sex, Sin, and Blasphemy* (New York: The New Press, 1993), p. 142.

6. Tad Friend, "Yes: Feminist Women Who Like Sex," *Esquire,* February 1994, pp. 48–56.

7. Heins, *Sex, Sin, and Blasphemy,* p. 35; John R. Wilke, "Porn Broker: A Publicly Held Firm Turns X-Rated Videos into a Hot Business," *Wall Street Journal,* 11 July 1994.

8. Carin Rubinstein and Carol Tavris, "Survey Results," *Redbook,* September 1987, pp. 147–49, 214–25, at p. 214.

9. Marc Speigler, "Lust Be a Lady," *New City,* 12–18 May 1994, pp. 8-9.

10. Susan Sontag, "The Pornographic Imagination," in *Styles of Radical Will* (New York: Anchor Books, 1969), p. 36.

11. Tisdale, "Talk Dirty to Me," p. 45

12. Thelma McCormack, "If Pornography Is the Theory, Is Inequality the Practice?" (presented at public forum, *Refusing Censorship: Feminists and Activists Fight Back,* York, Canada, 12 November 1992), p. 32.

13. Pete Hamill, "Women on the Verge of a Legal Breakdown," *Playboy,* January 1993, p. 189.

14. McCormack, "If Pornography Is the Theory," p. 22.

15. Lisa Duggan, Nan D. Hunter, and Carole S. Vance, "False Promises: Feminist Anti-Pornography Legislation," in *Women against Censorship,* ed. Varda Burstyn (Vancouver: Douglas and McIntyre, 1985), pp. 130–151, at p. 140.

16. Carole S. Vance, epilogue to *Pleasure and Danger: Exploring Female Sexuality* (Boston: Routledge & Kegan Paul, 1984), p. 433.

17. Evelyn C. White, "Alice Walker Says Award Is No Treasure: State Presents Her with 'Decapitated' Art," *San Francisco Chronicle,* 16 April 1994.

18. Peter Hecht, "Hearings Set on Writings' Removal from Test," *San Diego Union-Tribune,* 8 March 1994; Carl Ingram, "Stories Deleted from Tests Reinstated," *Los Angeles Times,* 12 March 1994.

19. David Link, "In the Eye—or the Mind—of the Beholder; Art: Alice Walker's Criticism of the Robert Graham Art Echoes the Small-Mindedness of Her Own Critics," *Los Angeles Times,* 21 April 1994.

20. Caitlin Sullivan, "Bookstores Vandalized over 'Lesbian Porn' Issue," *Seattle Gay News,* 18 June 1993.

21. Ibid.

22. Christine Wenz, "In Our Heads," *Stranger,* 5-11 July 1993.

23. Ibid.

24. Heather Findlay, "Dyke Porn 101: How to Enjoy (and Defend) Your Porn," *On Our Backs,* November/December 1993, pp. 14–15, 42–43, at p. 14.

25. Wenz, "In Our Heads."

26. Suzanne "Zan" Scommodau and Tanya Turkovich, letter to the editor, *Seattle Gay News,* 25 June 1993.

27. Quoted in Jack Kammer, "Men and Women: Who's Got the Power?," *The Sun* (Baltimore), 21 December 1993.

28. Quoted ibid.

29. Veronica Vera, "Censored Artist, Activist Speaks Out," *Michigan Daily,* 30 November 1992.

30. Kammer, "Men and Women: Who's Got the Power?"

31. Quoted in Susan Brownmiller, *Against Our Will: Men, Women and Rape* (New York: Bantam, 1976), p. 363.

32. Sara Diamond, "Pornography: Image and Reality," in *Women against Censorship*, pp. 40–57, at p. 51.

33. Wendy McElroy, "Talking Sex, Not Gender," *Liberty* (in press).

34. Ibid.

35. Gary Day and Clive Bloom, eds., *Perspectives on Pornography: Sexuality in Film and Literature* (New York: St. Martin's Press, 1988), pp. 1–8, at p. 5.

36. Posner, "Obsession," p. 36.

37. Katie Roiphe, *The Morning After* (New York: Little, Brown, 1993), p. 151.

38. Hammill, "Women on the Verge," p. 188.

39. Heins, *Sex, Sin, and Blasphemy*, p. 145.

40. Shortly after this ad aired, President George Bush fired then-NEA chair John Frohnmayer. Heins, *Sex, Sin, and Blasphemy*, pp. 135, 167.

41. Edward de Grazia, *Girls Lean Back Everywhere: The Law of Obscenity and the Assault on Genius* (New York: Vintage Books, 1992), p. 589

42. Ibid., p. 588.

43. Susie Bright, telephone conversation with Thomas Hilbink, 21 July 1994.

44. Walter Kendrick, *The Secret Museum: Pornography in Modern Culture* (New York: Viking, 1987), p. 234.

45. Carole S. Vance, "More Danger, More Pleasure: A Decade after the Barnard Sexuality Conference," in *New York Law School Review Symposium: The Sex Panic* (forthcoming).

46. Catharine MacKinnon, *Only Words* (Cambridge, Mass.: Harvard University Press, 1993), p. 3.

47. Walter Berns, "Dirty Words," *Public Interest*, Winter 1994, pp. 119–125, at p. 121.

48. James Lindgren, "Defining Pornography," *University of Pennsylvania Law Review* 141 (April 1993): 1153-1275, at 1200.

49. Andrea Dworkin, *Ice and Fire* (New York: Weidenfeld and Nicholson, 1987), at, respectively, pp. 54, 64, 84–85, 101-102.

50. The two books by Dworkin that were seized were *Pornography: Men Possessing Women* and *Woman Hating*. Albert Nerenberg, "Fear Not, Brave Canadian: Customs Stands on Guard for Thee," *Montreal Gazette*, 22 January 1993.

51. *Ulrich's International Periodicals*, 32d ed. (New Providence, N.J.: R. R. Bowker, 1993).

52. John R. Wilke, "Porn Broker: A Publicly Held Firm Turns X-Rated Videos into a Hot Business," *Wall Street Journal*, 11 July 1994.

53. David Landis, "Regulating Porn: Does It Compute?" *USA Today*, 9 August 1994.

54. John Tierney, "Porn: The Low-Slung Engine of Progress," *New York Times*, 9 January 1994.

55. Catharine MacKinnon, "On Collaboration," in *Feminism Unmodified* (Cambridge, Mass.: Harvard University Press, 1987), pp. 198–205, at p. 199.

56. U.S. Department of Justice, *Beyond the Pornography Commission: The Federal Response* 6 (1988) (estimating the amount spent on sexually oriented magazines, films, telephone services, cable television, and videos).

57. Sontag, "Pornographic Imagination," p. 72.

58. *Cohen v. California*, 403 U.S. 15, 25 (1971).

## CHAPTER 8
### Positive Aspects of Pornographic Imagery

1. Quoted in Wendy Kaminer, "Exposing the New Authoritarians," *San Francisco Examiner,* 29 November 1992.
2. Sallie Tisdale, "Talk Dirty to Me: A Woman's Taste for Pornography," *Harper's,* February 1992, pp. 37–46, at p. 45.
3. Quoted in Kathleen Sullivan, book review of *Girls Lean Back Everywhere* by Edward de Grazia, *New Republic,* 28 September 1992, pp. 35-40, at p. 39.
4. Quoted in Edward de Grazia, *Girls Lean Back Everywhere: The Law of Obscenity and the Assault on Genius* (New York: Vintage Books, 1992), p. 613.
5. Tisdale, "Talk Dirty to Me," p. 45.
6. Quoted in Kathleen Currie and Art Levine, "Whip Me, Beat Me and While You're at It Cancel My NOW Membership: Feminists War against Each Other over Pornography," *Washington Monthly,* June 1987, p. 17.
7. Jack Kammer, "Men and Women: Who's Got the Power?" *The Sun* (Baltimore), 21 December 1993.
8. United States Department of Justice, *Attorney General's Commission on Pornography, Final Report,* (Washington, D.C.: U.S. Government Printing Office, 1986), p. 1028.
9. Patti Britton, letter to the Honorable Patrick A. Leahy, 10 February 1992.
10. Quoted in Hugh Hefner, "The Place of Pornography: A Symposium in *Harper's* on Pornography and the Media," *Playboy,* March 1985, p. 24.
11. Barbara Faye Waxman, quoted in interviews by Sally Chew, "Pornography: Does Women's Equality Depend on What We Do about It?" *Ms.,* January/February 1994, p. 45.
12. Paula Webster, "Pornography and Pleasure," in *Caught Looking: Feminism, Pornography, and Censorship,* ed. Kate Ellis et al. (East Haven, Conn.: Long River Books, 1986), pp. 30–35, at p. 35.
13. Judith Kegan Gardiner, "What I Didn't Get to Say about Pornography, Masculinity, and Repression," in *New York Law School Law Review Symposium: The Sex Panic* (forthcoming).
14. Quoted in John Strausbaugh, "Making Book," *New York Press,* 30 March–5 April 1994, pp. 12–13.
15. Lisa Palac, "How Dirty Pictures Changed My Life," *Playboy,* May 1994, pp. 80, 88.
16. Quoted in *On Our Backs,* November/December 1993.
17. Heather Findlay, "Dyke Porn 101: How to Enjoy (and Defend) Your Porn," *On Our Backs,* November/December 1993, p. 15.
18. Susie Bright, "Politics of Porn," *San Francisco Review of Books,* June/July 1994, pp. 12, 13.
19. Kathleen Sullivan, book review of *Girls Lean Back Everywhere* by Edward de Grazia, *New Republic,* 28 September 1992, pp. 35-40, p. 39.
20. Chris Bearchell, "Gay Porn Is Getting Skinned Alive," *Toronto Star,* 15 January 1993.
21. Pat Califia, "Among Us, Against Us," in *Caught Looking,* pp. 20–25, at p. 23.
22. Findlay, "Dyke Porn 101."
23. John Preston, "Whose Free Speech?" *Boston Phoenix,* 8 October 1993.

24. Quoted in Tim Kingston, "Canada's New Porn Wars: 'Little Sister' Gay/Lesbian Bookstore Battles Canadian Customs," *San Francisco Bay Times,* 4 November 1993.

25. Norma Ramos, in "Where do We Stand on Pornography?" (Roundtable), *Ms.,* January/February 1994, pp. 32–41.

26. Caitlin Sullivan, "Bookstores Vandalized over 'Lesbian Porn' Issue," *Seattle Gay News,* 9 July 1993.

27. Susan Estrich, *Real Rape* (Boston: Harvard University Press, 1987).

28. Catharine MacKinnon, *Only Words* (Cambridge, Mass.: Harvard University Press, 1993), p. 26.

29. Ibid., p. 58.

30. Kaminer, "Exposing the New Authoritarians."

31. Statute of Treasons, 25 Edward 3 St. 5, Chap. 2, (1350), in effect until 1694.

32. Quoted in Barry Brown, "Canada's New Pornography Laws Drawing Charges of Censorship," *Buffalo News,* 10 January 1994.

33. Catharine MacKinnon, "Turning Rape into Pornography: Postmodern Genocide," *Ms.,* July/August 1993, pp. 24–30.

34. MacKinnon, *Only Words,* p. 15.

35. Carlin Romano, "Between the Motion and the Act," *The Nation,* 15 November 1993, pp. 563–70.

36. Quoted in David Streitfeld, "Rape by the Written Word?" *Washington Post,* 4 January 1994.

37. Lindsay Waters, Harvard University Press (with cosigners Claire Silvers, Maria Eugenia Quintana, Paul Adams, Christopher Palma, Stephanie Gouse, Aida Donald), letter to the editor, *The Nation,* 27 December 1993, p. 786.

38. Jare Hester, "Critic Blasted for Rape Fantasy," *New York Daily News,* 22 November 1993.

39. Ibid.

40. Richard Lacayo, "Assault by Paragraph," *Time,* 17 January 1994, p. 62; Jeffrey Moussaieff Masson, letter to Carlin Romano, 28 November 1993.

41. Streitfeld, "Rape by the Written Word?"

42. Nancy Friday, *Women on Top* (New York: Simon & Schuster, 1991), pp. 4–5.

43. Jean MacKellar, in collaboration with Menacham Amir, *Rape: The Bait and the Trap: A Balanced, Humane, Up to Date Analysis of Its Causes and Control* (New York: Crown, 1975), p. 260.

44. Quoted in Digby Diehl, "Anne Rice: The *Playboy* Interview," *Playboy,* March 1993, pp. 53–64.

45. Ellen Willis, "Feminism, Moralism, and Pornography," in *Caught Looking,* pp. 54–59, p. 56.

46. Kathleen Sullivan, book review of *Girls Lean Back Everywhere,* p. 35.

47. Ann Snitow, Christine Stansell, and Sharon Thompson, eds., *Powers of Desire: The Politics of Sexuality* (New York: Monthly Review Press, 1983); Varda Burstyn, ed., *Women against Censorship* (Vancouver: Douglas and McIntyre, 1985); Carole S. Vance, ed., *Pleasure and Danger: Exploring Female Sexuality* (Boston: Routledge & Kegan Paul, 1984); Kate Ellis, Beth Jaker, Nan D. Hunter, Barbara O'Dair, and Abby Tallmer, eds., *Caught Looking: Feminism, Pornography, and Censorship* (East Haven, Conn.: Long River Books, 1986).

48. Ann Snitow, "Retrenchment versus Transformation: The Politics of the Antipornography Movement," in *Women against Censorship*, p. 107, pp. 115–16.

49. Myrna Kostash, "Second Thoughts," in *Women against Censorship*, pp. 32–38, p. 37.

50. Nan D. Hunter and Sylvia Law, Brief Amici Curiae of Feminist Anti-Censorship Taskforce, *University of Michigan Journal of Law Reform* 21 (1987–88): pp. 69–136, at p. 121.

51. Lisa Duggan, Nan D. Hunter, and Carole S. Vance, "False Promises: Feminist Anti-Pornography Legislation," in *Caught Looking*, pp. 72–85, at p. 82.

52. Sara Diamond, "Pornography: Image and Reality," in *Women Against Censorship*, pp. 40–57, at p. 57.

53. Ann Snitow, "Retrenchment vs. Transformation: The Politics of the Anti-Pornography Movement," in *Caught Looking*, pp. 10–17, at pp. 14–15.

54. Lynn Hunt, ed. *The Invention of Pornography: Obscenity and the Origins of Pornography, 1500–1800* (New York: Zone Books, 1993).

55. Walter Kendrick, *The Secret Museum: Pornography in Modern Culture* (New York: Viking, 1987), pp. 144–45.

56. Ibid., p. 219.

57. Ibid.

## CHAPTER 9
### Posing for Pornography: Coercion or Consent?

1. Karen, letter to *Ms.*, May/June 1994, p. 4.

2. See Nadine Strossen, "The Convergence of Feminist and Civil Liberties Principles in the Pornography Debate," review of *Women against Censorship*, ed. Varda Burstyn, *New York University Law Review* 62 (1987): 201–35, at 210 n. 42, citing legal authorities regarding these potential remedies.

3. Quoted in Pete Hamill, "Women on the Verge of a Legal Breakdown," *Playboy*, January 1993, p. 186.

4. Wendy McElroy, "The Unholy Alliance," *Liberty*, February 1993, p. 56.

5. Leora Tanenbaum, "The Politics of Porn: Forced Arguments," *In These Times*, 7 March 1994, pp. 17–20.

6. Andrea Dworkin quoted in "Where Do We Stand on Pornography?" (Roundtable), *Ms.*, January/February 1994, pp. 32–41, 37–38; Catharine MacKinnon quoted in Fred Strebeigh, "Defining Law on the Feminist Frontier," *New York Times Magazine*, 6 October 1991.

7. Quoted in Tanenbaum, "Politics of Porn," p. 19.

8. Quoted in Dan Greenberg and Thomas H. Tobiason, "The New Legal Puritanism of Catharine MacKinnon," *Ohio State Law Journal* 54 (Fall 1993): 1375-1424, at 1402-3

9. Ibid.

10. Tanenbaum, "Politics of Porn," p. 18.

11. Quoted ibid., p. 20.

12. Veronica Vera, testimony before the Senate Judiciary Committee, 30 October 1984.

13. Quoted in "The War against Pornography," *Newsweek,* 18 March 1985, pp. 58, 66.
14. Veronica Vera, testimony before the Senate Judiciary Committee, 30 October 1984.
15. Quoted in Tanenbaum, "Politics of Porn," p. 18.
16. Edward de Grazia, *Girls Lean Back Everywhere: The Law of Obscenity and the Assault on Genius* (New York: Vintage Books, 1992), p. 586.
17. Quoted in ibid., p. 593.
18. Quoted in ibid., pp. 594–95.
19. Karen De Crow, "Women Are Victims Again," *USA Today,* 5 October 1993.
20. Andrea Dworkin, *Intercourse* (New York: Free Press, 1987), p. 133.
21. *Butler v. the Queen,* 1 S. C. R. 452, 479 (1992, Canada).
22. Karen DeCrow, "Burger King and America's Real Family Values," *Penthouse,* May 1991, pp. 84–85.
23. Tanenbaum, "Politics of Porn," p. 19.
24. Quoted in ibid., pp. 19–20.
25. Susie Bright, "I Hate to Break This to You, Kitty, But . . . ," *San Diego Reader,* 18 November 1993, p. 36.
26. Richard Lacayo, "Accidents: A Death on the Shop Floor," *Time,* 16 September 1991, p. 28.
27. "About a Sixth of U.S. Crime Is at Job Sites," *New York Times,* 25 July 1994.
28. Richard A. Posner, "Obsession," review of *Only Words* by Catharine A. MacKinnon, *New Republic,* 18 October 1993, pp. 31–36, at p. 34.
29. Leonore Tiefer, "On Censorship and Women," *American Theatre,* January 1991, pp. 50–51.
30. Karen, letter to Nadine Strossen, 20 January 1993.
31. Cathy Young, untitled, in *New York Law School Law Review Symposium: The Sex Panic* (forthcoming).
32. Ibid.
33. Dworkin, *Intercourse,* pp. 222–23.
34. Catharine A. MacKinnon, "Privacy v. Equality: Beyond Roe v. Wade," in *Feminism Unmodified* (Cambridge, Mass.: Harvard University Press, 1987), p. 99.
35. Catharine A. MacKinnon, "Reflections on Sex Equality under Law," *Yale Law Journal* 100 (1991): 1281-1328, at 1300; *Toward a Feminist Theory of the State* (Cambridge, Mass.: Harvard University Press, 1989), p. 112, pp. 185-86; "Privacy v. Equality: Beyond Roe v. Wade," *Feminism Unmodified,* pp. 93-102, at pp. 94-96.
36. Jeanne Schroeder, untitled, in *New York Law School Law Review Symposium: The Sex Panic* (forthcoming).

## CHAPTER 10
*Would-Be Censors Subordinate Valuable Works to Their Agenda*

1. Betty Friedan, "Feminism," in *The Meese Commission Exposed: Proceedings of a National Coalition Against Censorship Public Information Briefing on the Attorney General's Commission on Pornography* (New York: National Coalition Against Censorship, 1987), pp. 24–25.

2. Ad Hoc Committee of Feminists for Free Expression, letter to the members of the Senate Judiciary Committee, 14 February 1992. Reprinted in Strossen, "A Feminist Critique of 'the' Feminist Critique of Pornography," *Virginia Law Review* 79 (August 1993): 1099-1190, at 1188-90.

3. Ann Lewis, "Speaking for Ourselves," in *New York Law School Law Review Symposium: The Sex Panic* (forthcoming).

4. Catharine MacKinnon, "Turning Rape into Pornography: Postmodern Genocide," *Ms.,* July/August 1993, pp. 24–30.

5. Brief of the American Civil Liberties Union and the Indiana Civil Liberties Union, amici curiae, *American Booksellers Association v. Hudnut* (filed in D. Ind. 1984), pp. 1a–7a.

6. *American Booksellers Association v. Hudnut,* 771 F. 2d 323, 332, 334 (7th Cir. 1986).

7. Robin Morgan, "Theory and Practice: Pornography and Rape," in *Take Back the Night,* ed. Laura Lederer (New York: William Morrow, 1980), pp. 134–47, at p. 137.

8. Robin Morgan, *Going Too Far: The Personal Chronicle of a Feminist* (New York: Random House, 1977), p. 169; Robin Morgan, letter to the editor, *The New York Times,* February 19, 1995, Section 7, page 38, column 1.

9. Brief of the American Civil Liberties Union and the Indiana Civil Liberties Union, amici curiae, *American Booksellers Association v. Hudnut* (filed in D. Ind. 1984), p. 8a.

10. Samuel Walker, *In Defense of American Liberties: A History of the ACLU* (New York: Oxford University Press, 1990), p. 351.

11. *American Booksellers Association v. Hudnut,* 771 F. 2d 323, 325–26 (7th Cir. 1985)(noting MacKinnon's statement that medical school textbooks meet her definition of pornography); Catharine MacKinnon, "The Palm Beach Hanging," *New York Times,* 15 December 1991 (referring to the rape prosecution against William Kennedy Smith, then a medical student, MacKinnon observed that "pornography [is] used in some medical schools to desensitize students").

12. James R. Petersen, "Catharine MacKinnon: Again," *Playboy,* August 1992, pp. 37–39. (Quotes MacKinnon as saying, "Women's sexual histories would be made into live oral pornography in court.")

13. Catharine MacKinnon, *Only Words* (Cambridge, Mass.: Harvard University Press, 1993), p. 66.

14. C. Edwin Baker, "Of Course, More Than Words," book review of *Only Words* by Catharine MacKinnon, *University of Chicago Law Review* 61 (1994): 1181–1182 n. 3 (quoting *Only Words* at pp. 65–66).

15. *NCAC Censorship News,* vol. 2, no. 53, 1994, p. 2.

16. Rebecca Chalker and Carol Downer, *A Woman's Book of Choices: Abortion, Menstrual Extraction, and R.U. 486* (New York: Four Walls Eight Windows, 1993).

17. Barbara Ehrenreich, foreword to *A Woman's Book of Choices* by Chalker and Downer, p. vii.

18. Barbara Seaman on *A Woman's Book of Choices,* back cover.

19. Chalker and Downer, *A Woman's Book of Choices,* p. 34.

20. Daniel Simon (co-publisher, Four Walls Eight Windows Press), letter to Andrea Dworkin, 18 September 1992.

21. Rebecca Chalker, letter to Erica Jong, president of The Authors Guild, 4 November 1992.

22. Clare McHugh, "In Feminist Abortion Book Squall, Bigfoot Dworkin Stops the Presses," *New York Observer,* 26 October 1992.

23. Ibid.

24. Marjorie Heins, "Why Boycotting Booksellers Is a Bad Idea," *On the Issues,* Fall 1991, pp. 22–23.

25. Chalker and Downer, *A Woman's Book of Choices,* p. 40.

26. Maureen Dezell, "Porn Wars: NOW's ongoing struggle with Censorship," *Boston Phoenix,* 2–8 July 1993.

27. Ibid.; Rebecca Chalker, telephone conversation with Thomas Hilbink, 7 July 1994. Chalker stated, "It wasn't just someone, it was a pro-Andrea faction within the New York State chapter."

28. Dan Simon letter to Andrea Dworkin, 18 September 1992.

29. ACLU Arts Censorship Project, "Anti-Censorship Feminists Condemn Suppression of Art Exhibit," news release, 16 November 1992; Marjorie Heins, "A Public University's Response to Students' Removal of an Art Exhibit," in *New York Law School Law Review Symposium: The Sex Panic* (forthcoming); Carol Jacobsen, "First Amendment Rights Need to Be Upheld," *Michigan Daily,* 6 November 1992; Reed Johnson, "Sex, Laws, and Videotape," *Detroit News,* 7 December 1992.

30. Tamar Lewin, "Furor on Exhibit at Law School Splits Feminists," *New York Times,* 13 November 1992.

31. Catharine MacKinnon letter to Ira Glasser, 12 August 1993.

32. Andrea Dworkin, "Pornography and Male Supremacy" and Catharine A. MacKinnon, "Pornography and Civil Rights," *Michigan Journal of Gender & Law* 1 (1993).

33. Lewin, "Furor on Exhibit."

34. Carol Jacobsen, "Anti-Porn Feminism vs. Feminist Art: Notes on the Censorship of 'Porn'im'age'ry: Picturing Prostitutes,'" in *New York Law School Law Review Symposium: The Sex Panic* (forthcoming).

35. Carol Jacobsen, "Anti-Porn Feminism"; Heins, "A Public University's Response"; Tamar Lewin, "Furor on Exhibit at Law School Splits Feminists," *New York Times,* 13 November 1992.

36. Liza Mundy, "The New Critics," *Lingua Franca,* September/October 1993, pp. 26–33, at p. 29; Laura Fraser, "Hear No Evil," *San Francisco Weekly,* 11 November 1992.

37. Veronica Vera, "Censored Artist, Activist Speaks Out," *Michigan Daily,* 30 November 1992.

38. Heins, in *New York Law School Law Review Symposium: The Sex Panic* (forthcoming).

39. Lewin, "Furor on Exhibit."

40. National Coalition Against Censorship, "NCAC Decries University of Michigan Censorship," press release, 16 November 1992.

41. See Lee Bollinger, "The Return of Porn'im'age'ry," *Law Quadrangle Notes,* Spring 1994, pp. 2–7.

42. Carole Vance, "Feminist Fundamentalism: Women against Images," *Art in America,* September 1993, pp. 35–39.

## CHAPTER 11
### Lessons from Enforcement: When the Powerful Get More Power

1. Ellen Willis, "An Unholy Alliance," *New York Newsday*, 25 February 1992.
2. Audre Lorde, "The Master's Tools Will Never Dismantle the Master's House," in *Sister Outsider Essays and Speeches* (San Francisco: Crossing Press, 1984), pp. 110–113.
3. George F. Will, "Pornography Scare," *Washington Post*, 28 October 1993.
4. Andrea Dworkin, *Our Blood: Prophecies and Discourses on Sexual Politics* (New York: Harper & Row, 1976), p. 20.
5. Wendy McElroy, "The Unholy Alliance," *Liberty*, February 1993, p. 53.
6. Pete Hamill, "Women on the Verge of a Legal Breakdown," *Playboy*, January 1993, p. 189.
7. Alan Dershowitz, "What Is Porn?" *ABA Journal*, 1 November 1986, p. 36.
8. Kenneth L. Karst, "Boundaries and Reasons: Freedom of Expression and the Subordination of Groups," *University of Illinois Law Review* 1990 (1990): 95–149, at 103–4.
9. See Laurence H. Tribe, *American Constitutional Law*, 2d ed. (Mineola, N.Y.: The Foundation Press), pp. 926–27.
10. *Beauharnais v. Illinois*, 343 U.S. 250, 275 (1952) (dissenting).
11. Eric Stein, "History against Free Speech: The New German Law against the 'Auschwitz'—and Other—'Lies,'" *Michigan Law Review* 85 (November 1986): 277–324, at 286.
12. Sandra Coliver, "Hate Speech Laws: Do They Work?" in *Striking a Balance: Hate Speech, Free Speech, and Non-Discrimination*, ed. Sandra Coliver. (Essex: Article 19, 1992), pp. 363–74, at pp. 373–74.
13. Aryeh Neier, *Defending My Enemy* (New York: E. P. Dutton, 1979), pp. 155–57.
14. Nadine Strossen, "Regulating Racist Speech: A Modest Proposal?" *Duke Law Journal* 1990 (1990): 484–583, at 554–55.
15. *Doe v. University of Michigan*, 721 F. Supp. 852 (E.D. Mich. 1989). The ACLU also successfully challenged a hate speech code at the University of Wisconsin. *UWM Post, Inc. v. Board of Regents of University of Wisconsin System*, 774 F. Supp. 1163 (E.D. Wis. 1991).
16. *Wu v. University of Conn.* (No. Civ. H89-649 PCD) (D. Conn. 1989).
17. NOW-New York State, "Canada Sounds Death-Knell for Free Speech," press release, 28 February 1992.
18. Quoted in Mary Kay Blakely, "Is One Woman's Sexuality Another Woman's Pornography?" *Ms.*, April 1985, pp. 37–38.
19. Anna Quindlen, "The Gag Rules," *New York Times*, 7 October 1992.
20. Quoted in Margaret A. Blanchard, "The American Urge to Censor: Freedom of Expression versus the Desire to Sanitize Society—From Anthony Comstock to 2 Live Crew," *William and Mary Law Review* 33 (1992): 741–851, at 766.
21. Ellen Chesler, *Woman of Valor: Margaret Sanger and the Birth Control Movement in America* (New York: Simon & Schuster, 1992), p. 70.
22. Ibid.
23. Cited in Blanchard, "The American Urge to Censor," 766.

24. *Mutual Film Corp. v. Industrial Commission,* 236 U.S. 230 (1915). This decision was reversed by *Winters v. New York,* 333 U.S. 507 (1948) and *Joseph Burstyn, Inc. v. Wilson,* 343 U.S. 495 (1952).

25. *Message Photo-Play Co. v. Bell,* 166 N.Y.S. 338 (1917).

26. Karst, "Boundaries and Reasons," 114, n. 79.

27. Mary Ware Dennett, *The Sex Side of Life: An Explanation for Young People* (New York: Published by Author, 1928).

28. *U.S. v. One Obscene Book Entitled "Married Love,"* 48 F. 2d 821 (S.D.N.Y. 1931); *U.S. v. One Book Entitled "Contraception,"* 51 F. 2d 525 (S.D.N.Y. 1931).

29. Tamar Lewin, "Guam's Abortion Law Tested by A.C.L.U. Lawyer's Speech," *New York Times,* 21 March 1990.

30. Quindlen, "The Gag Rules."

31. Quoted in Tim Kingston, "Canada's New Porn Wars: 'Little Sister' Gay/ Lesbian Bookstore Battles Canadian Customs," *San Francisco Bay Times,* 4 November 1993.

32. Quoted in Tamar Lewin, "Canada Court Says Porn Harms Women," *New York Times,* 28 February 1992.

33. Elaine Carol, in *Ideas—Feminism and Censorship,* transcript from the Canadian Broadcasting Company (Toronto: CBC Radio Works, 1993), p. 16.

34. Quoted in Rashida Dhooma, "Gay Demo Rakes Pornography Charges," *Toronto Sun,* n.d.

35. Quoted in Kingston, "Canada's New Porn Wars."

36. Ellen Flanders, in *Ideas—Feminism and Censorship,* p. 9.

37. Carl Wilson, "Northern Closure: Anti-Pornography Campaign in Canada," *The Nation,* 27 December 1993, p. 788.

38. "Canada Customs Hits Feminist Stores and Others," *Feminist Bookstore News,* March/April 1993, p. 21.

39. Karen Busby, "LEAF and Pornography: Litigating on Equality and Sexual Representations" (unpublished), p. 17.

40. Quoted in Camilla Gibb, "Project P Targets Lesbian Porn," *Quota,* May 1992, pp. 4–5, at p. 5.

41. Trish Thomas, in *Ideas—Feminism and Censorship,* p. 9.

42. *Her Majesty The Queen against John Bruce Scythes, Thomas Frank Ivison, and Ontario Corporation #620704 Operating as Glad Day Bookshop, Inc.,* Ontario Court of Justice (Provincial Division), 16 February 1993, C.H. Paris, j.

43. *Glad Day Bookshop v. Deputy Minister of National Revenue for Customs and Excise (DMVR),* Ontario Court of Justice (General Division), 14 July 1992.

44. Busby, "LEAF and Pornography," p. 17.

45. Chris Bearchell, "Gay Porn Is Getting Skinned Alive," *Toronto Star,* 15 January 1993.

46. Susan Ditta, in *Ideas—Feminism and Censorship,* p. 15.

47. Ibid.

48. Jacques Boivin, letter to Leanne Katz, 17 November 1993.

49. Brenda Cossman, *Ideas—Feminism and Censorship,* p. 16.

50. Editorial, "Reading between the Borderlines," *Toronto Globe and Mail,* 30 June 1992.

51. Pierre Berton, "How Otto Jelinek Guards Our Morals," *Toronto Star,* 29 May 1993.

52. Quoted in Bill Redden, "O for Christ's Sake Canada," *PDXS* (Portland), 30 August–12 September 1993.

53. Berton, "How Otto Jelinek Guards Our Morals."

54. "Canada Customs Hits Feminist Stores," *Feminist Bookstore News.*

55. Redden, "O for Christ's Sake Canada."

56. Diane DiMassa, *Hothead Paisan: Homicidal Lesbian Terrorist* (San Francisco: Cleis Press, 1993), pp. 120–21.

57. Sarah Scott, "Porn Police: Who Decides What to Ban at the Border," *Montreal Gazette,* 14 April 1993.

58. Mary Williams Walsh, "Chill Hits Canada's Pornography Law," *Los Angeles Times,* 6 September 1993.

59. Kingston, "Canada's New Porn Wars."

60. Leanne Katz, memo to Roz Udow, 23 September 1993. See also letter from Catharine A. MacKinnon to Leanne Katz, 11 November 1993 (expressing MacKinnon's disagreement with some aspects of Katz's description of the telephone call, but not the aspect described in the text).

61. Human Rights Watch Free Expression Project, *A Ruling Inspired by U.S. Anti-Pornography Activists Is Used to Restrict Lesbian and Gay Publications in Canada,* February 1994, pp. 8–9.

62. NCAC Working Group on Women, Censorship, and "Pornography," "MacKinnon/Dworkin 'Theories' Flunk Reality Test," press advisory, 10 November 1993; Mary Williams Walsh, "Chill Hits Canada's Porn Law," *Los Angeles Times,* 6 September 1993.

63. Act of June 30, 1987, ch. 24, 1987 Statute of Canada 633 (Can.) sec. 139.(2) Sexual Offenses: exception. 1994 Tremear's Criminal Code Section 163.1.

64. LEAF News Release, "Historic Gathering Condemns Targeting of Lesbian and Gay Materials and Sex Trade Workers," Toronto, 21 June 1993.

65. NCAC Working Group, "MacKinnon/Dworkin 'Theories' Flunk Reality Test."

66. Kathleen Mahoney, panel and group discussion at the 19th Annual Olin Conference, Washington University, St. Louis, Missouri, 20 October 1993.

67. Quoted in Kingston, "Canada's New Porn Wars."

68. Catharine MacKinnon, letter to *New York Times* opinion page editor Mitchel Levitas, 1 January 1994.

69. The three arguments were presented in the following: MacKinnon letter to Mitchel Levitas; MacKinnon answers to questions at National Press Club, 22 November 1993; Dworkin-MacKinnon press release, 26 August 1994; MacKinnon letter to Leanne Katz.

70. Attributed to William Ewart Gladstone, 1809–1898 in John Bartlett and Justin Kaplan, eds., *Bartlett's Familiar Quotations,* 16th ed. (Boston: Little, Brown, 1992), p. 446.

71. CENSORSTOP, "Canada Customs Evades Little Sister's Trial Action . . . Again," press release, 29 September 1993.

72. Human Rights Watch, *A Ruling Inspired by U.S. Anti-Pornography Activists,* p. 9.

73. Susan Faludi, *Backlash: The Undeclared War Against American Women* (New York: Crown, 1991), pp. 40–41.

74. Larry Baron and Murray A. Straus, "Sexual Stratification, Pornography, and Rape in the United States," in *Pornography and Sexual Aggression,* ed. Neil M. Malamuth and Edward Donnerstein (Orlando, Fla.: Academic Press, 1984), pp. 185, 205-6

75. Faludi, *Backlash,* p. xxi; Jeffrey Weeks, *Sexuality and Its Discontents* (New York: Routledge, Chapman and Hall, 1986) p. 233; Alan Soble, *Pornography: Marxism, Feminism, and the Future of Sexuality* (New Haven: Yale University Press, 1986), pp. 82, 84 ; Naomi Wolf, *The Beauty Myth: How the Images of Beauty Are Used against Women* (New York: William Morrow, 1991); Andrea Dworkin, "Why So-Called Radical Men Love and Need Pornography," in *Take Back the Night,* ed. Laura Lederer (New York: William Morrow, 1980), pp. 148, 153.

76. Catharine MacKinnon, *Only Words* (Cambridge, Mass.: Harvard University Press, 1993), p. 37.

## CHAPTER 12
### Why Censoring Pornography Would Not Reduce Discrimination or Violence against Women

1. Quoted in David Futrelle, "The Politics of Porn, Shameful Pleasures," *In These Times,* 7 March 1994, pp. 14-17.

2. *Butler v. the Queen* 1 SCR 452 (199), p. 505.

3. Marcia Pally, *Sex and Sensibility: Reflections on Forbidden Mirrors and the Will to Censor* (Hopewell, N.J.: Ecco Press, 1994).

4. Albert J. Reiss, Jr. and Jeffrey A. Roth, eds., *Understanding and Preventing Violence* (Washington, D.C.: National Academy Press, 1993), p. 111. (A project for the National Research Council.)

5. Judith Becker and Ellen Levine, paper presented to a meeting of the National Coalition Against Censorship, New York, N.Y., 17 June 1986.

6. Daniel Linz, Steven D. Penrod, and Edward Donnerstein, "The Attorney General's Commission on Pornography: The Gaps between 'Findings' and Facts," *American Bar Foundation Research Journal* 4 (Fall 1987): 713-36, at 723.

7. Edward Mulvey and Jeffrey Haugaard, *Surgeon General's Workshop on Pornography and Public Health* (Arlington, Virginia: U.S. Department of Health and Human Services, 1986).

8. Carol Krafka, "Sexually Explicit, Sexually Violent, and Violent Media: Effects of Multiple Naturalistic Exposures and Debriefing on Female Viewers" (Ph.D. dissertation, University of Wisconsin, 1985), p. 29.

9. Daniel Linz, Edward Donnerstein, and Steven Penrod, "The Effects of Long-Term Exposure to Violent and Sexually Degrading Depictions of Women," *Journal of Personality and Social Psychology* 55 (1988): 758-68.

10. Cynthia Gentry, "Pornography and Rape: An Empirical Analysis," *Deviant Behavior: An Interdisciplinary Journal* 12 (1991): 277–88, at 284.

11. Larry Baron and Murray Straus, "Four Theories of Rape: A Macrosociological Analysis," *Social Problems* 34, no. 5 (1987): 467-89.

12. Joseph Scott and Loretta Schwalm, "Pornography and Rape: An Exam-

ination of Adult Theater Rates and Rape Rates by State," in J. E. Scott and T. Hirchi (eds.), *Controversial Issues in Crime and Justice* (Beverly Hills: Sage, 1988).

13. Bureau of Justice Statistics, *Criminal Victimization in the United States* (Washington, D.C.: Government Printing Office, 1990); Pally, *Sex and Sensibility*, p. 22.

14. Richard J. Gelles and Murray Straus, *Intimate Violence: The Causes and Consequences of Abuse in the American Family* (New York: Touchstone, 1989), p. 112.

15. Pally, *Sex and Sensibility*, pp. 21, 23.

16. Baron and Straus, "Four Theories of Rape."

17. Pally, *Sex and Sensibility*, pp. 57-61.

18. Richard Posner, "Obsession," review of *Only Words* by Catharine Mac-Kinnon, *New Republic,* 18 October 1993, pp. 31–36, at p. 34.

19. Ellen Willis, "An Unholy Alliance," *New York Newsday,* 25 February 1992, p. 78.

20. *Memoirs v. Massachusetts,* 383 U.S. 413, 432 (1966) (concurring).

21. Williams Committee, *The British Inquiry into Obscenity and Film Censorship* (London, England: Home Office Research and Planning Unit, 1979).

22. Earl Finbar Murphy, "The Value of Pornography," *Wayne Law Review* 10 (1964): 655–80, at 668.

23. Pally, *Sex and Sensibility*, pp. 99–100.

24. Associated Press, "Atheist Loses Fight to Ban Bible at School," *Chicago Tribune,* 11 November 1992.

25. Pally, *Sex and Sensibility*, pp. 25-61.

26. Edward Donnerstein, "Erotica and Human Aggression," in *Aggression: Theoretical and Empirical Reviews,* ed. Richard Green and Edward Donnerstein (New York: Academic Press, 1983), pp. 127–28.

27. Quoted in Jane Brody, "Scientists Trace Aberrant Sexuality," *New York Times,* 23 January 1990.

28. Pally, *Sex and Sensibility*, p. 50.

29. Howard Barbaree and William Marshall, "The Role of Male Sexual Arousal in Rape: Six Models," *Journal of Consulting and Clinical Psychology* 59, no. 5 (1991): 621–30; Pally, *Sex and Sensibility*, pp. 44–45.

30. Susan Brownmiller, *Against Our Will: Men, Women, and Rape* (New York: Simon & Schuster, 1975); Susan Estrich, *Real Rape* (Boston: Harvard University Press, 1987).

31. Carlin Meyer, "Sex, Censorship, and Women's Liberation" (unpublished), pp. 42–43. [A revised version of this manuscript was published in *Texas Law Review* 72 (1994): 1097–1201.]

32. Thelma McCormack, "If Pornography Is the Theory, Is Inequality the Practice?" (presented at public forum, *Refusing Censorship: Feminists and Activists Fight Back,* York, Canada, 12 November 1992), p. 12.

33. Edward Donnerstein, Daniel Linz, and Steven Penrod, *The Question of Pornography: Research Findings and Policy Implications* (New York: Free Press, 1987), p. 107.

34. Catharine MacKinnon, "Not a Moral Issue," *Yale Law & Policy Review* 2 (1984): 321–45, at 325.

35. Percy H. Tannenbaum, "Emotional Arousal as a Mediator of Communi-

cation Effects," *Technical Report of the U.S. Commission on Obscenity and Pornography* 8 (1971), p. 353.

36. Timothy C. Brock, "Erotic Materials: A Commodity Theory Analysis of Availability and Desirability," *Technical Report of the U.S. Commission on Obscenity and Pornography* 6 (1971), pp. 131–37.

## CHAPTER 13
### *Toward Constructive Approaches to Reducing Discrimination and Violence against Women*

1. Betty Friedan, "Feminism," in *The Meese Commission Exposed: Proceedings of a National Coalition Against Censorship Public Information Briefing on the Attorney General's Commission on Pornography* (New York: National Coalition Against Censorship, 1987), pp. 24–25.

2. Molly Ivins, "Havin' Fun Fightin' for Freedom," in *New York Law School Law Review Symposium: The Sex Panic* (forthcoming).

3. Varda Burstyn, "Beyond Despair: Positive Strategies," in *Women against Censorship*, ed. Varda Burstyn (Vancouver: Douglas and McIntyre, 1985), pp. 152, 179.

4. Carlin Meyer, "Sex, Censorship, and Women's Liberation" (unpublished), p. 32. [A revised version of this manuscript was published in *Texas Law Review* 72 (1994): 1097–1201.]

5. Nan D. Hunter and Sylvia Law, Brief of Amici Curiae of Feminist Anti-Censorship Taskforce, *University of Michigan Journal of Law Reform* 21 (1987–88): pp. 69–136, at pp. 134–35.

6. Thelma McCormack, "If Pornography Is the Theory, Is Inequality the Practice?" (presented at public forum, *Refusing Censorship: Feminists and Activists Fight Back*, York, Canada, 7–8 November 1992), p. 26.

7. American Civil Liberties Union, *Restoring Civil Liberties: A Blueprint for Action for the Clinton Administration* (1992), p. 66.

8. Marcia Pally, *Sense and Censorship: The Vanity of the Bonfires* (New York: Americans for Constitutional Freedom and the Freedom to Read Foundation, 1991), p. 14.

9. "Policy No. 4: Censorship of Obscenity, Pornography and Indecency," *Policy Guide of the American Civil Liberties Union.* Adopted 1985.

10. S. Rep. No. 372, 102nd Congress, 2d sess. 34 (1992).

11. Nan D. Hunter, "S. 1521: A Rapist's Exculpation Act?" (unpublished), pp. 10–11.

12. Teller, "Movies Don't Cause Crime," *New York Times,* 17 January 1992.

13. *Schiro v. Clark,* 963 F. 2d 962, 972 (7th Cir., 1992).

14. Catharine MacKinnon, *Only Words* (Cambridge, Mass.: Harvard University Press, 1993), pp. 95–97.

15. Ibid., p. 96.

16. C. Edwin Baker, "Of Course, More Than Words," review of *Only Words* by Catharine MacKinnon, *University of Chicago Law Review* 61 (1994): 1181, 1207-8.

17. *Commonwealth v. Mignogna,* 585A.2d 1, 10 (Pennsylvania Superior Court, 1990).

18. Quoted in Tad Friend, "Yes: Feminist Women Who Like Sex," *Esquire,* February 1994, pp. 48–56, p. 54.
19. MacKinnon, *Only Words,* p. 12.
20. Neil Malamuth and Edward I. Donnerstein, "The Effects of Aggressive Pornographic Mass Media Stimuli," *Advances in Experimental Psychology* 15 (1982): 103, 129, 150–85.
21. Pally, *Sense and Censorship,* p. 34 (citing the report of the Surgeon General's Workshop on Pornography and Public Health, p. 50).
22. Edward I. Donnerstein and Daniel G. Linz, "Debate on Pornography," *Film Comment,* December 1984, pp. 34-35, at p. 35.
23. Dr. Judith Becker, professor of psychiatry and psychology, letter to Senator Hank Brown, 3 April 1992.
24. Shirley Feldman-Summers, "A Comment on the Meese Commission Report and the Dangers of Censorship," *Sexual Coercion and Assault* 1, no.6 (n.d.):179, 182.
25. Stephen Donaldson, "The Rape Crisis Behind Bars," *New York Times,* 29 December 1993.
26. Kathleen Maguire, Ann L. Pastore, Timothy J. Flanagan, eds. *Bureau of Justice Statistics Sourcebook of Criminal Justice Statistics—1992.* (Washington, D.C.: U.S. Department of Justice, 1993), p. 532, table 5.59.
27. Wendy Kaminer, "Feminists Against the First Amendment," *Atlantic Monthly,* November 1992, pp. 111–117, at p. 115.
28. Colleen Cobel, panel and group discussion at the 19th Annual Olin Conference, Washington University, St. Louis, Mo., 20 October 1993.
29. Edward de Grazia, *Girls Lean Back Everywhere: The Law of Obscenity and the Assault on Genius* (New York: Vintage Books, 1992), p. 586, citing Martin Morse Wooster, "Reagan's War on Porn," *Reason,* April 1986, pp. 29–33.
30. Pally, *Sense and Censorship,* p. 31.
31. Quoted in Digby Diehl, "Anne Rice: The *Playboy* Interview," *Playboy,* March 1993, pp. 53–64, at p. 56.
32. Pete Hamill, "Women on the Verge of a Legal Breakdown," *Playboy,* January 1993, pp. 138–40 and 184–90, at p. 188.
33. Lisa Steele, "A Capital Idea: Gendering in the Mass Media," in *Women against Censorship,* ed. Varda Burstyn, pp. 58–78, at p. 61.

# Index